Three Plays
of
Tennessee Williams

By Tennessee Williams

PLAYS

Baby Doll (a screenplay)
Cat on a Hot Tin Roof
The Eccentricities of a Nightingale *and*
   Summer and Smoke
The Glass Menagerie
The Milk Train Doesn't Stop Here Anymore
The Night of the Iguana
Orpheus Descending
Period of Adjustment
A Streetcar Named Desire
Suddenly Last Summer
Summer and Smoke
Three Plays
    The Rose Tattoo
    Camino Real
    Sweet Bird of Youth
27 Wagons Full of Cotton and Other Plays

POETRY

In the Winter of Cities

PROSE

The Roman Spring of Mrs. Stone
One Arm and Other Stories
Hard Candy and Other Stories
The Knightly Quest: A Novella and
   Four Short Stories

Three Plays
of
Tennessee Williams

The Rose Tattoo

Camino Real

Sweet Bird of Youth

A New Directions Book

Manufactured in the United States of America

New Directions Books are published for James Laughlin by
New Directions Publishing Corporation,
333 Sixth Avenue, New York 10014.

Contents

THE ROSE TATTOO

*O slinger! crack the nut of my eye! my heart
twittered with joy under the splendour of the
quicklime, the bird sings O Senectus! . . . the
streams are in their beds like the cries of
women and this world has more beauty than
a ram's skin painted red!*

St. John Perse: *Anabasis*
T. S. ELIOT TRANSLATION

To Frank in return for Sicily

THE TIMELESS WORLD OF A PLAY

Carson McCullers concludes one of her lyric poems with the line: "Time, the endless idiot, runs screaming 'round the world." It is this continual rush of time, so violent that it appears to be screaming, that deprives our actual lives of so much dignity and meaning, and it is, perhaps more than anything else, the *arrest of time* which has taken place in a completed work of art that gives to certain plays their feeling of depth and significance. In the London notices of *Death of a Salesman* a certain notoriously skeptical critic made the remark that Willy Loman was the sort of man that almost any member of the audience would have kicked out of an office had he applied for a job or detained one for conversation about his troubles. The remark itself possibly holds some truth. But the implication that Willy Loman is consequently a character with whom we have no reason to concern ourselves in drama, reveals a strikingly false conception of what plays are. Contemplation is something that exists outside of time, and so is the tragic sense. Even in the actual world of commerce, there exists in some persons a sensibility to the unfortunate situations of others, a capacity for concern and compassion, surviving from a more tender period of life outside the present whirling wire-cage of business activity. Facing Willy Loman across an office desk, meeting his nervous glance and hearing his querulous voice, we would be very likely to glance at our wrist watch and our schedule of other appointments. We would not kick him out of the office, no, but we would certainly *ease* him out with more expedition than Willy had feebly hoped for. But suppose there had been no wrist watch or office clock

3

and suppose there had *not* been the schedule of pressing appointments, and suppose that we were not actually facing Willy across a desk—and facing a person is *not* the best way to *see* him!—suppose, in other words, that the meeting with Willy Loman had somehow occurred in a world *outside* of time. Then I think we would receive him with concern and kindness and even with respect. If the world of a play did not offer us this occasion to view its characters under that special condition of a *world without time,* then, indeed, the characters and occurrences of drama would become equally pointless, equally trivial, as corresponding meetings and happenings in life.

The classic tragedies of Greece had tremendous nobility. The actors wore great masks, movements were formal, dance-like, and the speeches had an epic quality which doubtless were as removed from the normal conversation of their contemporary society as they seem today. Yet they did not seem false to the Greek audiences: the magnitude of the events and the passions aroused by them did not seem ridiculously out of proportion to common experience. And I wonder if this was not because the Greek audiences knew, instinctively or by training, that the created world of a play is removed from that element which makes people *little* and their emotions fairly inconsequential.

Great sculpture often follows the lines of the human body: yet the repose of great sculpture suddenly transmutes those human lines to something that has an absoluteness, a purity, a beauty, which would not be possible in a living mobile form.

A play may be violent, full of motion: yet it has that special kind of repose which allows contemplation and produces

4

the climate in which tragic importance is a possible thing, provided that certain modern conditions are met.

In actual existence the moments of love are succeeded by the moments of satiety and sleep. The sincere remark is followed by a cynical distrust. Truth is fragmentary, at best: we love and betray each other not in quite the same breath but in two breaths that occur in fairly close sequence. But the fact that passion occurred in *passing,* that it then declined into a more familiar sense of indifference, should not be regarded as proof of its inconsequence. And this is the very truth that drama wishes to bring us . . .

Whether or not we admit it to ourselves, we are all haunted by a truly awful sense of impermanence. I have always had a particularly keen sense of this at New York cocktail parties, and perhaps that is why I drink the martinis almost as fast as I can snatch them from the tray. This sense is the febrile thing that hangs in the air. Horror of insincerity, of *not meaning,* overhangs these affairs like the cloud of cigarette smoke and the hectic chatter. This horror is the only thing, almost, that is left unsaid at such functions. All social functions involving a group of people not intimately known to each other are always under this shadow. They are almost always (in an unconscious way) like that last dinner of the condemned: where steak or turkey, whatever the doomed man wants, is served in his cell as a mockingly cruel reminder of what the great-big-little-transitory world had to offer.

In a play, time is arrested in the sense of being confined. By a sort of legerdemain, events are made to remain *events,* rather than being reduced so quickly to mere *occurrences.* The audience can sit back in a comforting dusk to watch a world which is flooded with light and in which emotion and action have a dimension and dignity that they would likewise have in real existence, if only the shattering intrusion of time could be locked out.

About their lives people ought to remember that when they are finished, everything in them will be contained in a marvelous state of repose which is the same as that which they unconsciously admired in drama. The rush is temporary. The great and only possible dignity of man lies in his power deliberately to choose certain moral values by which to live as steadfastly as if he, too, like a character in a play, were immured against the corrupting rush of time. Snatching the eternal out of the desperately fleeting is the great magic trick of human existence. As far as we know, as far as there exists any kind of empiric evidence, there is no way to beat the game of *being* against *non-being,* in which non-being is the predestined victor on realistic levels.

Yet plays in the tragic tradition offer us a view of certain moral values in violent juxtaposition. Because we do not participate, except as spectators, we can view them clearly, within the limits of our emotional equipment. These people on the stage do not return our looks. We do not have to answer their questions nor make any sign of being in company with them, nor do we have to compete with their virtues nor resist their offenses. All at once, for this reason, we are able to *see* them! Our hearts are wrung by recognition and pity, so that the dusky shell of the auditorium where we are gathered anonymously together is flooded with an almost liquid warmth of unchecked human sympathies, relieved of self-consciousness, allowed to function . . .

Men pity and love each other more deeply than they permit themselves to know. The moment after the phone has

6

been hung up, the hand reaches for a scratch pad and scrawls a notation: "Funeral Tuesday at five, Church of the Holy Redeemer, don't forget flowers." And the same hand is only a little shakier than usual as it reaches, some minutes later, for a highball glass that will pour a stupefaction over the kindled nerves. Fear and evasion are the two little beasts that chase each other's tails in the revolving wire-cage of our nervous world. They distract us from feeling too much about things. Time rushes toward us with its hospital tray of infinitely varied narcotics, even while it is preparing us for its inevitably fatal operation . . .

So successfully have we disguised from ourselves the intensity of our own feelings, the sensibility of our own hearts, that plays in the tragic tradition have begun to seem untrue. For a couple of hours we may surrender ourselves to a world of fiercely illuminated values in conflict, but when the stage is covered and the auditorium lighted, almost immediately there is a recoil of disbelief. "Well, well!" we say as we shuffle back up the aisle, while the play dwindles behind us with the sudden perspective of an early Chirico painting. By the time we have arrived at Sardi's, if not as soon as we pass beneath the marquee, we have convinced ourselves once more that life has as little resemblance to the curiously stirring and meaningful occurrences on the stage as a jingle has to an elegy of Rilke.

This modern condition of his theater audience is something that an author must know in advance. The diminishing influence of life's destroyer, time, must be somehow worked into the context of his play. Perhaps it is a certain foolery, a certain distortion toward the grotesque, which will solve the problem for him. Perhaps it is only restraint, putting a mute on the strings that would like to break all bounds.

But almost surely, unless he contrives in some way to relate the dimensions of his tragedy to the dimensions of a world in which time is *included*—he will be left among his magnificent debris on a dark stage, muttering to himself: "Those fools . . ."

And if they could hear him above the clatter of tongues, glasses, chinaware and silver, they would give him this answer: "But you have shown us a world not ravaged by time. We admire your innocence. But we have seen our photographs, past and present. Yesterday evening we passed our first wife on the street. We smiled as we spoke but we didn't really see her! It's too bad, but we know what is true and not true, and at 3 A.M. your disgrace will be in print!"

—Tennessee Williams

SCENES

ACT ONE

SCENE 1 Evening
SCENE 2 Almost morning, the next day
SCENE 3 Noon of that day
SCENE 4 A late spring morning, three years later
SCENE 5 Immediately following
SCENE 6 Two hours later that day

ACT TWO

SCENE 1 Two hours later that day

ACT THREE

SCENE 1 Evening of the same day
SCENE 2 Just before dawn of the next day
SCENE 3 Morning

The Rose Tattoo was first produced by Cheryl Crawford at the Erlanger Theater in Chicago on December 29, 1950. It had its Broadway opening on February 3, 1951, at the Martin Beck Theater in New York City, with Daniel Mann as director, setting by Boris Aronson and music by David Diamond. Production Associate: Bea Lawrence. Assistant to Producer: Paul Bigelow.

Cast of the New York Production

SALVATORE	SALVATORE MINEO
VIVI	JUDY RATNER
BRUNO	SALVATORE TAORMINA
ASSUNTA	LUDMILLA TORETZKA
ROSA DELLE ROSE	PHYLLIS LOVE
SERAFINA DELLE ROSE	MAUREEN STAPLETON
ESTELLE HOHENGARTEN	SONIA SOREL
THE STREGA	DAISY BELMORE
GIUSEPPINA	ROSSANA SAN MARCO
PEPPINA	AUGUSTA MERIGHI
VIOLETTA	VIVIAN NATHAN
MARIELLA	PENNY SANTON
TERESA	NANCY FRANKLIN
FATHER DE LEO	ROBERT CARRICART
A DOCTOR	ANDREW DUGGAN
MISS YORKE	DORRIT KELTON
FLORA	JANE HOFFMAN
BESSIE	FLORENCE SUNDSTROM
JACK HUNTER	DON MURRAY
THE SALESMAN	EDDIE HYANS
ALVARO MANGIACAVALLO	ELI WALLACH
A MAN	DAVID STEWART
ANOTHER MAN	MARTIN BALSAM

AUTHOR'S PRODUCTION NOTES

The locale of the play is a village populated mostly by Sicilians somewhere along the Gulf Coast between New Orleans and Mobile. The time is the present.

As the curtain rises we hear a Sicilian folk-singer with a guitar. He is singing. At each major division of the play this song is resumed and it is completed at the final curtain.

The first lighting is extremely romantic. We see a frame cottage, in a rather poor state of repair, with a palm tree leaning dreamily over one end of it and a flimsy little entrance porch, with spindling pillars, sagging steps and broken rails, at the other end. The setting seems almost tropical, for, in addition to the palm trees, there are tall canes with feathery fronds and a fairly thick growth of pampas grass. These are growing on the slope of an embankment along which runs a highway, which is not visible, but the cars passing on it can occasionally be heard. The house has a rear door which cannot be seen. The facing wall of the cottage is either a transparency that lifts for the interior scenes, or is cut away to reveal the interior.

The romantic first lighting is that of late dusk, the sky a delicate blue with an opalescent shimmer more like water than air. Delicate points of light appear and disappear like lights reflected in a twilight harbor. The curtain rises well above the low tin roof of the cottage.

We see an interior that is as colorful as a booth at a carnival. There are many religious articles and pictures of ruby and gilt, the brass cage of a gaudy parrot, a large bowl of gold-

11

fish, cutglass decanters and vases, rose-patterned wallpaper and a rose-colored carpet; everything is exclamatory in its brightness like the projection of a woman's heart passionately in love. There is a small shrine against the wall between the rooms, consisting of a prie-dieu and a little statue of the Madonna in a starry blue robe and gold crown. Before this burns always a vigil light in its ruby glass cup. Our purpose is to show these gaudy, childlike mysteries with sentiment and humor in equal measure, without ridicule and with respect for the religious yearnings they symbolize.

An outdoor sign indicates that Serafina, whose home the cottage is, does "SEWING." The interior furnishings give evidence of this vocation. The most salient feature is a collection of dressmaker's dummies. There are at least seven of these life-size mannequins, in various shapes and attitudes. [They will have to be made especially for the play as their purpose is not realistic. They have pliable joints so that their positions can be changed. Their arms terminate at the wrist. In all their attitudes there is an air of drama, somewhat like the poses of declamatory actresses of the old school.] Principal among them are a widow and a bride who face each other in violent attitudes, as though having a shrill argument, in the parlor. The widow's costume is complete from black-veiled hat to black slippers. The bride's featureless head wears a chaplet of orange blossoms from which is depended a flowing veil of white marquisette, and her net gown is trimmed in white satin—lustrous, immaculate.

Most of the dummies and sewing equipment are confined to the dining room which is also Serafina's work room. In that room there is a tall cupboard on top of which are several dusty bottles of imported Sicilian Spumanti.

12

THE SETTING BY BORIS ARONSON FOR THE BROADWAY PRODUCTION

ACT ONE

It is the hour that the Italians call "prima sera," the beginning of dusk. Between the house and the palm tree burns the female star with an almost emerald lustre.

The mothers of the neighborhood are beginning to call their children home to supper, in voices near and distant, urgent and tender, like the variable notes of wind and water. There are three children: Bruno, Salvatore, and Vivi, ranged in front of the house, one with a red paper kite, one with a hoop, and the little girl with a doll dressed as a clown. They are in attitudes of momentary repose, all looking up at something—a bird or a plane passing over—as the mothers' voices call them.

BRUNO:
The white flags are flying at the Coast Guard station.

SALVATORE:
That means fair weather.

VIVI:
I love fair weather.

GIUSEPPINA:
Vivi! Vieni mangiare!

PEPPINA:
Salvatore! Come home!

VIOLETTA:
Bruno! Come home to supper!

[*The calls are repeated tenderly, musically.*

[*The interior of the house begins to be visible. Serafina delle Rose is seen on the parlor sofa, waiting for her hus-*

band Rosario's return. Between the curtains is a table set
lovingly for supper; there is wine in a silver ice-bucket
and a great bowl of roses.

[Serafina looks like a plump little Italian opera singer in
the role of Madame Butterfly. Her black hair is done in
a high pompadour that glitters like wet coal. A rose is
held in place by glittering jet hairpins. Her voluptuous
figure is sheathed in pale rose silk. On her feet are dainty
slippers with glittering buckles and French heels. It is
apparent from the way she sits, with such plump dignity,
that she is wearing a tight girdle. She sits very erect, in
an attitude of forced composure, her ankles daintily
crossed and her plump little hands holding a yellow paper
fan on which is painted a rose. Jewels gleam on her
fingers, her wrists and her ears and about her throat.
Expectancy shines in her eyes. For a few moments she
seems to be posing for a picture.

[Rosa delle Rose appears at the side of the house, near
the palm tree. Rosa, the daughter of the house, is a young
girl of twelve. She is pretty and vivacious, and has about
her a particular intensity in every gesture.]

SERAFINA:
Rosa, where are you?

ROSA:
Here, Mama.

SERAFINA:
What are you doing, cara?

ROSA:
I've caught twelve lightning bugs.

[The cracked voice of Assunta is heard, approaching.]

SERAFINA:

I hear Assunta! Assunta!

[*Assunta appears and goes into the house, Rosa follow-ing her in. Assunta is an old woman in a gray shawl, bear-ing a basket of herbs, for she is a fattuchiere, a woman who practises a simple sort of medicine. As she enters the children scatter.*]

ASSUNTA:

Vengo, vengo. Buona sera. Buona sera. There is something wild in the air, no wind but everything's moving.

SERAFINA:

I don't see nothing moving and neither do you.

ASSUNTA:

Nothing is moving so you can see it moving, but everything is moving, and I can hear the star-noises. Hear them? Hear the star-noises?

SERAFINA:

Naw, them ain't the star-noises. They're termites, eating the house up. What are you peddling, old woman, in those lit-tle white bags?

ASSUNTA:

Powder, wonderful powder. You drop a pinch of it in your husband's coffee.

SERAFINA:

What is it good for?

ASSUNTA:

What is a husband good for! I make it out of the dry blood of a goat.

SERAFINA:

Davero!

ASSUNTA:

Wonderful stuff! But be sure you put it in his coffee at supper, not in his breakfast coffee.

SERAFINA:

My husband don't need no powder!

ASSUNTA:

Excuse me, Baronessa. Maybe he needs the opposite kind of a powder, I got that, too.

SERAFINA:

Naw, naw, *no* kind of powder at all, old woman. [*She lifts her head with a proud smile.*]

[*Outside the sound of a truck is heard approaching up on the highway.*]

ROSA [*joyfully*]:

Papa's truck!

[*They stand listening for a moment, but the truck goes by without stopping.*]

SERAFINA [*to Assunta*]:

That wasn't him. It wasn't no 10-ton truck. It didn't rattle the shutters! Assunta, Assunta, undo a couple of hooks, the dress is tight on me!

ASSUNTA:

Is it true what I told you?

SERAFINA:

Yes, it is true, but nobody needed to tell me. Assunta, I'll tell you something which maybe you won't believe.

ASSUNTA:

It is impossible to tell me anything that I don't believe.

16

SERAFINA:

Va bene! Senti, Assunta!—I knew that I had conceived on the very night of conception! [*There is a phrase of music as she says this.*]

ASSUNTA:

Ahhhh?

SERAFINA:

Senti! That night I woke up with a burning pain on me, here, on my left breast! A pain like a needle, quick, quick, hot little stitches. I turned on the light, I uncovered my breast!—On it I saw the rose tattoo of my husband!

ASSUNTA:

Rosario's tattoo?

SERAFINA:

On me, on my breast, his tattoo! And when I saw it I knew that I had conceived . . .

[*Serafina throws her head back, smiling proudly, and opens her paper fan. Assunta stares at her gravely, then rises and hands her basket to Serafina.*]

ASSUNTA:

Ecco! *You* sell the powders! [*She starts toward the door.*]

SERAFINA:

You don't believe that I saw it?

ASSUNTA [*stopping*]:

Did Rosario see it?

SERAFINA:

I screamed. But when he woke up, it was gone. It only lasted a moment. But I *did* see it, and I *did* know, when I seen it, that I had conceived, that in my body another rose was growing!

17

ASSUNTA:

Did he believe that you saw it?

SERAFINA:

No. He laughed.—He laughed and I cried . . .

ASSUNTA:

And he took you into his arms, and you stopped crying!

SERAFINA:

Si!

ASSUNTA:

Serafina, for you everything has got to be different. A sign, a miracle, a wonder of some kind. You speak to Our Lady. You say that She answers your questions. She nods or shakes Her head at you. Look, Serafina, underneath Our Lady you have a candle. The wind through the shutters makes the candle flicker. The shadows move. Our Lady seems to be nodding!

SERAFINA:

She gives me signs.

ASSUNTA:

Only to you? Because you are more important? The wife of a barone? Serafina! In Sicily they called his uncle a baron, but in Sicily everybody's a baron that owns a piece of the land and a separate house for the goats!

SERAFINA:

They said to his uncle "Voscenza!" and they kissed their hands to him! [*She kisses the back of her hand repeatedly, with vehemence.*]

ASSUNTA:

His uncle in Sicily!—Si—But *here* what's he do? Drives a truck of bananas?

SERAFINA [*blurting out*]:
No! *Not* bananas!

ASSUNTA:
Not bananas?

SERAFINA:
Stai zitta! [*She makes a warning gesture.*]—No—Vieni
qui, Assunta! [*She beckons her mysteriously. Assunta approaches.*]

ASSUNTA:
Cosa dici?

SERAFINA:
On top of the truck is bananas! But underneath—something
else!

ASSUNTA:
Che altre cose?

SERAFINA:
Whatever it is that the Brothers Romano want hauled out
of the state, he hauls it for them, underneath the bananas!
[*She nods her head importantly.*] And money, he gets so
much it spills from his pockets! Soon I don't have to make
dresses!

ASSUNTA [*turning away*]:
Soon I think you will have to make a black veil!

SERAFINA:
Tonight is the last time he does it! Tomorrow he quits
hauling stuff for the Brothers Romano! He pays for the 10-
ton truck and works for himself. We live with dignity in
America, then! Own truck! Own house! And in the house
will be everything electric! Stove—deep-freeze—*tutto!*—
But tonight, stay with me . . . I can't swallow my heart!—

Not till I hear the truck stop in front of the house and his
key in the lock of the door!—When I call him, and him
shouting back, *"Si, sono qui!"* In his hair, Assunta, he has
—oil of roses. And when I wake up at night—the air, the
dark room's—full of—roses . . . Each time is the first time
with him. Time doesn't pass . . .

[*Assunta picks up a small clock on the cupboard and
holds it to her ear.*]

ASSUNTA:
Tick, tick, tick, tick.—You say the clock is a liar.

SERAFINA:
No, the clock is a fool. I don't listen to it. My clock is my
heart and my heart don't say tick-tick, it says love-love!
And now I have two hearts in me, both of them saying
love-love!

[*A truck is heard approaching, then passes. Serafina
drops her fan. Assunta opens a bottle of spumanti with a
loud pop. Serafina cries out.*]

ASSUNTA:
Stai tranquilla! Calmati! [*She pours her a glass of wine.*]
Drink this wine and before the glass is empty he'll be in
your arms!

SERAFINA:
I can't—swallow my heart!

ASSUNTA:
A woman must not have a heart that is too big to swallow!
[*She crosses to the door.*]

SERAFINA:
Stay with me!

ASSUNTA:

I have to visit a woman who drank rat poison because of a
heart too big for her to swallow.

[*Assunta leaves. Serafina returns indolently to the sofa.
She lifts her hands to her great swelling breasts and murmurs aloud:*]

SERAFINA:

Oh, it's so wonderful, having *two* lives in the body, not *one*
but two! [*Her hands slide down to her belly, luxuriously.*]
I am heavy with life, I am big, big, big with life! [*She
picks up a bowl of roses and goes into the back room.*]

[*Estelle Hohengarten appears in front of the house. She
is a thin blonde woman in a dress of Egyptian design,
and her blonde hair has an unnatural gloss in the clear,
greenish dusk. Rose appears from behind the house, calling out:*]

ROSA:

Twenty lightning bugs, Mama!

ESTELLE:

Little girl? Little girl?

ROSA [*resentfully*]:

Are you talking to me? [*There is a pause.*]

ESTELLE:

Come here. [*She looks Rosa over curiously.*] You're a twig
off the old rose-bush.—Is the lady that does the sewing in
the house?

ROSA:

Mama's at home.

ESTELLE:

I'd like to see her.

21

ROSA:

Mama?

SERAFINA:

Dimi?

ROSA:

There's a lady to see you.

SERAFINA:

Oh. Tell her to wait in the parlor. [*Estelle enters and stares curiously about. She picks up a small framed picture on the cupboard. She is looking at it as Serafina enters with a bowl of roses. Serafina speaks sharply.*] That is my husband's picture.

ESTELLA:

Oh!—I thought it was Valentino.—With a mustache.

SERAFINA [*putting the bowl down on the table*]:

You want something?

ESTELLE:

Yes. I heard you do sewing.

SERAFINA:

Yes, I do sewing.

ESTELLE:

How fast can you make a shirt for me?

SERAFINA:

That all depends. [*She takes the picture from Estelle and puts it back on the cupboard.*]

ESTELLE:

I got the piece of silk with me. I want it made into a shirt for a man I'm in love with. Tomorrow's the anniversary of the day we met . . . [*She unwraps a piece of rose-colored silk which she holds up like a banner.*]

22

SERAFINA [*involuntarily*]:
Che bella stoffa!—Oh, that would be wonderful stuff for a
lady's blouse or for a pair of pyjamas!

ESTELLE:
I want a man's shirt made with it.

SERAFINA:
Silk this color for a shirt for a *man?*

ESTELLE:
This man is wild like a Gypsy.

SERAFINA:
A woman should not encourage a man to be wild.

ESTELLE:
A man that's wild is hard for a woman to hold, huh? But
if he was tame—would the woman want to hold him? Huh?

SERAFINA:
I am a married woman in business. I don't know nothing
about wild men and wild women and I don't have much
time—so . . .

ESTELLE:
I'll pay you twice what you ask me.

[*Outside there is the sound of the goat bleating and the
jingle of its harness; then the crash of wood splintering.*]

ROSA [*suddenly appearing at the door*]:
Mama, the black goat is loose! [*She runs down the steps
and stands watching the goat. Serafina crosses to the door.*]

THE STREGA [*in the distance*]:
Hyeh, Billy, hyeh, hyeh, Billy!

ESTELLE:
I'll pay you three times the price that you ask me for it.

23

SERAFINA [*shouting*]:
Watch the goat! Don't let him get in our yard! [*to Estelle*]
—If I ask you five dollars?

ESTELLE:
I will pay you fifteen. Make it twenty; money is not the
object. But it's got to be ready tomorrow.

SERAFINA:
Tomorrow?

ESTELLE:
Twenty-five dollars! [*Serafina nods slowly with a stunned
look. Estelle smiles.*] I've got the measurements with me.

SERAFINA:
Pin the measurements and your name on the silk and the
shirt will be ready tomorrow.

ESTELLE:
My name is Estelle Hohengarten.

[*A little boy races excitedly into the yard.*]

THE BOY:
Rosa, Rosa, the black goat's in your yard!

ROSA [*calling*]:
Mama, the goat's in the yard!

SERAFINA [*furiously, forgetting her visitor*]:
Il becco della strega!—Scusi! [*She runs out onto the porch.*]
Catch him, catch him before he gets at the vines!

[*Rosa dances gleefully. The Strega runs into the yard.
She has a mop of wild grey hair and is holding her black
skirts up from her bare hairy legs. The sound of the goat's
bleating and the jingling of his harness is heard in the
windy blue dusk.*

24

[Serafina descends the porch steps. The high-heeled slippers, the tight silk skirt and the dignity of a baronessa make the descent a little gingerly. Arrived in the yard, she directs the goat-chase imperiously with her yellow paper fan, pointing this way and that, exclaiming in Italian.

[She fans herself rapidly and crosses back of the house. The goat evidently makes a sudden charge. Screaming, Serafina rushes back to the front of the house, all out of breath, the glittering pompadour beginning to tumble down over her forehead.]

SERAFINA:

Rosa! You go in the house! Don't look at the Strega!

[Alone in the parlor, Estelle takes the picture of Rosario. Impetuously, she thrusts it in her purse and runs from the house, just as Serafina returns to the front yard.]

ROSA *[refusing to move]*:
Why do you call her a witch?

[Serafina seizes her daughter's arm and propels her into the house.]

SERAFINA:

She has a white eye and every finger is crooked: *[She pulls Rosa's arm.]*

ROSA:

She has a cataract, Mama, and her fingers are crooked because, she has rheumatism!

SERAFINA:

Malocchio—the evil eye—*that's* what she's got! And her fingers are crooked because she shook hands with the devil.

25

Go in the house and wash your face with salt water and throw the salt water away! *Go in! Quick!* She's coming!

[*The boy utters a cry of triumph.*

[*Serafina crosses abruptly to the porch. At the same moment the boy runs triumphantly around the house leading the captured goat by its bell harness. It is a middle-sized black goat with great yellow eyes. The Strega runs behind with the broken rope. As the grotesque little procession runs before her—the Strega, the goat and the children—Serafina cries out shrilly. She crouches over and covers her face. The Strega looks back at her with a derisive cackle.*]

SERAFINA:

Malocchio! Malocchio!

[*Shielding her face with one hand, Serafina makes the sign of the horns with the other to ward off the evil eye. And the scene dims out.*]

SCENE TWO

It is just before dawn the next day. Father De Leo, a priest, and several black-shawled women, including Assunta, are standing outside the house. The interior of the house is very dim.

GIUSEPPINA:

There is a light in the house.

PEPPINA:

I hear the sewing machine!

VIOLETTA:

There's Serafina! She's working. She's holding up a piece of rose-colored silk.

ASSUNTA:

She hears our voices.

VIOLETTA:

She's dropped the silk to the floor and she's . . .

GIUSEPPINA:

Holding her throat! I think she . . .

PEPPINA:

Who's going to tell her?

VIOLETTA:

Father De Leo will tell her.

FATHER DE LEO:

I think a woman should tell her. I think Assunta must tell her that Rosario is dead.

ASSUNTA:

It will not be necessary to tell her. She will know when she sees us.

27

[*It grows lighter inside the house. Serafina is standing in a frozen attitude with her hand clutching her throat and her eyes staring fearfully toward the sound of voices.*]

ASSUNTA:
I think she already knows what we have come to tell her!

FATHER DE LEO:
Andiamo, Signore! We must go to the door.

[*They climb the porch steps. Assunta opens the door.*]

SERAFINA [*gasping*]:
Don't speak!

[*She retreats from the group, stumbling blindly backwards among the dressmaker's dummies. With a gasp she turns and runs out the back door. In a few moments we see her staggering about outside near the palm tree. She comes down in front of the house, and stares blindly off into the distance.*]

SERAFINA [*wildly*]:
Don't speak!

[*The voices of the women begin keening in the house. Assunta comes out and approaches Serafina with her arms extended. Serafina slumps to her knees, whispering hoarsely: "Don't speak!" Assunta envelopes her in the grey shawl of pity as the scene dims out.*]

SCENE THREE

It is noon of the same day. Assunta is removing a funeral wreath on the door of the house. A doctor and Father De Leo are on the porch.

THE DOCTOR:

She's lost the baby. [*Assunta utters a low moan of pity and crosses herself.*] Serafina's a very strong woman and that won't kill her. But she is trying not to breathe. She's got to be watched and not allowed out of the bed. [*He removes a hypodermic and a small package from his bag and hands them to Assunta.*]—This is morphia. In the arm with the needle if she screams or struggles to get up again.

ASSUNTA:

Capisco!

FATHER DE LEO:

One thing I want to make plain. The body of Rosario must not be burned.

THE DOCTOR:

Have you seen the "body of Rosario?"

FATHER DE LEO:

Yes, I have seen his body.

THE DOCTOR:

Wouldn't you say it was burned?

FATHER DE LEO:

Of course the body was burned. When he was shot at the wheel of the truck, it crashed and caught fire. But deliberate cremation is not the same thing. It's an abomination in the sight of God.

29

THE DOCTOR:

Abominations are something I don't know about.

FATHER DE LEO:

The Church has set down certain laws.

THE DOCTOR:

But the instructions of a widow have to be carried out.

FATHER DE LEO:

Don't you know why she wants the body cremated? So she can keep the ashes here in the house.

THE DOCTOR:

Well, why not, if that's any comfort to her?

FATHER DE LEO:

Pagan idolatry is what I call it!

THE DOCTOR:

Father De Leo, you love your people but you don't understand them. They find God in each other. And when they lose each other, they lose God and they're lost. And it's hard to help them.—Who is that woman?

[*Estelle Hohengarten has appeared before the house. She is black-veiled, and bearing a bouquet of roses.*]

ESTELLE:

I am Estelle Hohengarten.

[*Instantly there is a great hubbub in the house. The women mourners flock out to the porch, whispering and gesticulating excitedly.*]

FATHER DE LEO:

What have you come here for?

ESTELLE:

To say good-bye to the body.

FATHER DE LEO:

The casket is closed; the body cannot be seen. And you must never come here. The widow knows nothing about you. Nothing at all.

GIUSEPPINA:

We know about you!

PEPPINA:

Va via! Sporcacciona!

VIOLETTA:

Puttana!

MARIELLA:

Assassina!

TERESA:

You sent him to the Romanos.

FATHER DE LEO:

Shhh!

[*Suddenly the women swarm down the steps like a cloud of attacking birds, all crying out in Sicilian. Estelle crouches and bows her head defensively before their savage assault. The bouquet of roses is snatched from her black-gloved hands and she is flailed with them about the head and shoulders. The thorns catch her veil and tear it away from her head. She covers her white sobbing face with her hands.*]

FATHER DE LEO:

Ferme! Ferme! Signore, fermate vi nel nome di Dio!— Have a little respect!

[*The women fall back from Estelle, who huddles weeping on the walk.*]

31

ESTELLE:
See him, see him, just see him . . .

FATHER DE LEO:
The body is crushed and burned. Nobody can see it. Now go away and don't ever come here again, Estelle Hohengarten!

THE WOMEN [*in both languages, wildly*]:
Va via, va via, go way.

[*Rosa comes around the house. Estelle turns and retreats. One of the mourners spits and kicks at the tangled veil and roses. Father De Leo leaves. The others return inside, except Rosa.*

[*After a few moments the child goes over to the roses. She picks them up and carefully untangles the veil from the thorns.*

[*She sits on the sagging steps and puts the black veil over her head. Then for the first time she begins to weep, wildly, histrionically. The little boy appears and gazes at her, momentarily impressed by her performance. Then he picks up a rubber ball and begins to bounce it.*

[*Rosa is outraged. She jumps up, tears off the veil and runs to the little boy, giving him a sound smack and snatching the ball away from him.*]

ROSA:
Go home! My papa is dead!

[*The scene dims out, as the music is heard again.*]

SCENE FOUR

A June day, three years later. It is morning and the light is bright. A group of local mothers are storming Serafina's house, indignant over her delay in delivering the graduation dresses for their daughters. Most of the women are chattering continually in Sicilian, racing about the house and banging the doors and shutters. The scene moves swiftly and violently until the moment when Rosa finally comes out in her graduation dress.

GIUSEPPINA:
Serafina! Serafina delle Rose!

PEPPINA:
Maybe if you call her "Baronessa" she will answer the door. [*with a mocking laugh*] Call her "Baronessa" and kiss your hand to her when she opens the door.

GIUSEPPINA [*tauntingly*]:
Baronessa! [*She kisses her hand toward the door.*]

VIOLETTA:
When did she promise your dress?

PEPPINA:
All week she say, "Domani—domani—domani." But yestiddy I told her . . .

VIOLETTA:
Yeah?

PEPPINA:
Oh yeah. I says to her, "Serafina, domani's the high school graduation. I got to try the dress on my daughter *today*." "Domani," she says, "Sicuro! sicuro! sicuro!" So I start to

go away. Then I hear a voice call, "Signora! Signora!" So I turn round and I see Serafina's daughter at the window.

VIOLETTA:
Rosa?

PEPPINA:
Yeah, Rosa. An' you know how?

VIOLETTA:
How?

PEPPINA:
Naked! Nuda, nuda! [*She crosses herself and repeats a prayer.*] In nominis padri et figlio et spiritus sancti. Aaahh!

VIOLETTA:
What did she do?

PEPPINA:
Do? She say, "Signora! Please, you call this numero and ask for Jack and tell Jack my clothes are lock up so I can't get out from the house." Then Serafina come and she grab-a the girl by the hair and she pull her way from the window and she slam the shutters right in my face!

GIUSEPPINA:
Whatsa the matter the daughter?

VIOLETTA:
Who is this boy? Where did she meet him?

PEPPINA:
Boy! What boy? He's a sailor. [*At the word "sailor" the women say "Ahhh!"*] She met him at the high school dance and somebody tell Serafina. That's why she lock up the girl's clothes so she can't leave the house. She can't even go to the high school to take the examinations. Imagine!

34

VIOLETTA:

Peppina, this time *you* go to the door, yeah?

PEPPINA:

Oh yeah, I go. Now I'm getting nervous. [*The women all crowd to the door.*] Sera-feee-na!

VIOLETTA:

Louder, louder!

PEPPINA:

Apri la porta! Come on, come on!

THE WOMEN [*together*]:

Yeah, apri la porta! . . . Come on, hurry up! . . . Open up!

GIUSEPPINA:

I go get-a police.

VIOLETTA:

Whatsa matta? You want more trouble?

GIUSEPPINA:

Listen, I pay in advance five dollars and get no dress. Now what she wear, my daughter, to graduate in? A couple of towels and a rose in the hair? [*There is a noise inside: a shout and running footsteps.*]

THE WOMEN:

Something is going on in the house! I hear someone! Don't I? Don't you?

[*A scream and running footsteps are heard. The front door opens and Serafina staggers out onto the porch. She is wearing a soiled pink slip and her hair is wild.*]

SERAFINA:

Aiuto! Aiuto! [*She plunges back into the house.*]

[*Miss Yorke, a spinsterish high school teacher, walks quickly up to the house. The Sicilian women, now all chattering at once like a cloud of birds, sweep about her as she approaches.*]

MISS YORKE:

You ladies know I don't understand Italian! So, please . . .

[*She goes directly into the house. There are more outcries inside. The Strega comes and stands at the edge of the yard, cackling derisively.*]

THE STREGA [*calling back to someone*]:

The Wops are at it again!—She got the daughter lock up naked in there all week. Ho, ho, ho! She lock up all week —naked—shouting out the window tell people to call a number and give a message to Jack. Ho, ho, ho! I guess she's in trouble already, and only fifteen!—They ain't civilized, these Sicilians. In the old country they live in caves in the hills and the country's run by bandits. Ho, ho, ho! More of them coming over on the boats all the time. [*The door is thrown open again and Serafina reappears on the porch. She is acting wildly, as if demented.*]

SERAFINA [*gasping in a hoarse whisper*]:

She cut her wrist, my daughter, she cut her wrist! [*She runs out into the yard.*] Aiiii-eeee! Aiutatemi, aiutatemi! Call the dottore! [*Assunta rushes up to Serafina and supports her as she is about to fall to her knees in the yard.*] Get the knife away from her! Get the knife, please! Get the knife away from—she cut her wrist with—Madonna! Madonna mia . . .

ASSUNTA:

Smettila, smettila, Serafina.

36

MISS YORKE [*coming out of the back room*]:
Mrs. Delle Rose, your daughter has not cut her wrist. Now come back into the house.

SERAFINA [*panting*]:
Che dice, che dice? Che cosa? Che cosa dice?

MISS YORKE:
Your daughter's all right. Come back into the house. And you ladies please go away!

ASSUNTA:
Vieni, Serafina. Andiamo a casa. [*She supports the heavy, sagging bulk of Serafina to the steps. As they climb the steps one of the Sicilian mothers advances from the whispering group.*]

GIUSEPPINA [*boldly*]:
Serafina, we don't go away until we get our dresses.

PEPPINA:
The graduation begins and the girls ain't dressed.

[*Serafina's reply to this ill-timed request is a long, animal howl of misery as she is supported into the house. Miss Yorke follows and firmly closes the door upon the women, who then go around back of the house. The interior of the house is lighted up.*]

MISS YORKE [*to Serafina*]:
No, no, no, she's not bleeding. Rosa? Rosa, come here and show your mother that you are not bleeding to death.

[*Rosa appears silently and sullenly between the curtains that separate the two rooms. She has a small white handkerchief tied around one wrist. Serafina points at the wrist and cries out: "Aiieee!"*]

MISS YORKE [*severely*]:
Now *stop* that, Mrs. Delle Rose!

[*Serafina rushes to Rosa, who thrusts her roughly away.*]

ROSA:
Lasciami stare, Mama!—I'm so ashamed I could die. This is the way she goes around all the time. She hasn't put on clothes since my father was killed. For three years she sits at the sewing machine and never puts a dress on or goes out of the house, and now she has locked my clothes up so *I* can't go out. She wants me to be like her, a freak of the neighborhood, the way she is! Next time, next time, I won't cut my wrist but my throat! I don't want to live locked up with a bottle of ashes! [*She points to the shrine.*]

ASSUNTA:
Figlia, figlia, figlia, non devi parlare cosí!

MISS YORKE:
Mrs. Delle Rose, please give me the key to the closet so that your daughter can dress for the graduation!

SERAFINA [*surrendering the key*]:
Ecco la—chiave . . . [*Rosa snatches the key and runs back through the curtains.*]

MISS YORKE:
Now why did you lock her clothes up, Mrs. Delle Rose?

SERAFINA:
The wrist is still bleeding!

MISS YORKE:
No, the wrist is not bleeding. It's just a skin cut, a scratch. But the child is exhausted from all this excitement and hasn't eaten a thing in two or three days.

ROSA [*running into the dining room*]:
Four days! I only asked her one favor. Not to let me go out but to let Jack come to the house so she could meet him!— Then she locked my clothes up!

MISS YORKE:
Your daughter missed her final examinations at the high school, but her grades have been so good that she will be allowed to graduate with her class and take the examinations later.—You understand me, Mrs. Delle Rose!

[*Rosa goes into the back of the house.*]

SERAFINA [*standing at the curtains*]:
See the way she looks at me? I've got a wild thing in the house, and her wrist is still bleeding!

MISS YORKE:
Let's not have any more outbursts of emotion!

SERAFINA:
Outbursts of—you make me sick! Sick! Sick at my stomach you make me! Your school, you make all this trouble! You give-a this dance where she gets mixed up with a sailor.

MISS YORKE:
You are talking about the Hunter girl's brother, a sailor named Jack, who attended the dance with his sister?

SERAFINA:
"Attended with sister!"—Attended with *sister!*—My daughter, she's nobody's sister!

[*Rosa comes out of the back room. She is radiantly beautiful in her graduation gown.*]

ROSA:
Don't listen to her, don't pay any attention to her, Miss Yorke.—I'm ready to go to the high school.

SERAFINA [*stunned by her daughter's beauty, and speaking with a wheedling tone and gestures, as she crouches a little.*]

O tesoro, tesoro! Vieni qua, Rosa, cara!—Come here and kiss Mama one minute!—Don't go like that, now!

ROSA:
Lasciami stare!

[*She rushes out on the porch. Serafina gazes after her with arms slowly drooping from their imploring gesture and jaw dropping open in a look of almost comic desolation.*]

SERAFINA:
Ho solo te, solo te—in questo mondo!

MISS YORKE:
Now, now, Mrs. Delle Rose, no more excitement, please!

SERAFINA [*suddenly plunging after them in a burst of fury*]:
Senti, senti, per favore!

ROSA:
Don't you dare come out on the street like that!—*Mama!*

(*She crouches and covers her face in shame, as Serafina heedlessly plunges out into the front yard in her shocking deshabille, making wild gestures.*]

SERAFINA:
You give this dance where she gets mixed up with a sailor. What do you think you want to do at this high school? [*In weeping despair, Rosa runs to the porch.*] How high is this high school? Listen, how high is this high school? Look, look, look, I will show you! It's high as that horse's

dirt out there in the street! [*Serafina points violently out in front of the house.*] Si! 'Sta fetentissima scuola! Scuola maledetta!

[*Rosa cries out and rushes over to the palm tree, leaning against it, with tears of mortification.*]

MISS YORKE:

Mrs. Delle Rose, you are talking and behaving extremely badly. I don't understand how a woman that acts like you could have such a sweet and refined young girl for a daughter!—You don't deserve it!—Really . . . [*She crosses to the palm tree.*]

SERAFINA:

Oh, you want me to talk refined to you, do you? Then do me one thing! Stop ruining the girls at the high school! [*As Serafina paces about, she swings her hips in the exaggeratedly belligerent style of a parading matador.*]

ASSUNTA:

Piantala, Serafina! Andiamo a casa!

SERAFINA:

No, no, I ain't through talking to this here teacher!

ASSUNTA:

Serafina, look at yourself, you're not dressed!

SERAFINA:

I'm dressed okay; I'm not naked! [*She glares savagely at the teacher by the palm tree. The Sicilian mothers return to the front yard.*]

ASSUNTA:

Serafina, cara? Andiamo a casa, adesso!—Basta! Basta!

41

SERAFINA:

Aspetta!

ROSA:

I'm so ashamed I could die, I'm so ashamed. Oh, you don't know, Miss Yorke, the way that we live. She never puts on a dress; she stays all the time in that dirty old pink slip!— And talks to my father's ashes like he was living.

SERAFINA:

Teacher! Teacher, senti! What do you think you want to do at this high school? Sentite! per favore! You give this a dance! What kind of a spring dance is it? Answer this question, please, for me! What kind of a spring dance is it? She meet this boy there who don't even go to no high school. What kind of a boy? Guardate! *A sailor that wears a gold earring!* That kind of a boy is the kind of boy she meets there!—That's why I lock her clothes up so she can't go back to the high school! [*suddenly to Assunta*] She cut her wrist! It's still bleeding! [*She strikes her forehead three times with her fist.*]

ROSA:

Mama, you look disgusting! [*She rushes away.*]

[*Miss Yorke rushes after her. Serafina shades her eyes with one hand to watch them departing down the street in the brilliant spring light.*]

SERAFINA:

Did you hear what my daughter said to me?—"You look— disgusting."—She calls me . . .

ASSUNTA:

Now, Serafina, we must go in the house. [*She leads her gently to the porch of the little house.*]

SERAFINA [*proudly*]:
How pretty she look, my daughter, in the white dress, like
a bride! [*to all*] Excuse me! Excuse me, please! Go away!
Get out of my yard!

GIUSEPPINA [*taking the bull by the horns*]:
No, we ain't going to go without the dresses!

ASSUNTA:
Give the ladies the dresses so the girls can get dressed for
the graduation.

SERAFINA:
That one there, she only paid for the goods. I charge for the
work.

GIUSEPPINA:
Ecco! I got the money!

THE WOMEN:
We *got* the money!

SERAFINA:
The names are pinned on the dresses. Go in and get them.
[*She turns to Assunta.*] Did you hear what my daughter
called me? She called me "disgusting!"

[*Serafina enters the house, slamming the door. After a
moment the mothers come out, cradling the white voile
dresses tenderly in their arms, murmuring "carino!" and
"bellissimo!"*]

[*As they disappear the inside light is brought up and we
see Serafina standing before a glazed mirror, looking at
herself and repeating the daughter's word.*]

SERAFINA:
Disgusting!

[*The music is briefly resumed to mark a division.*]

43

Immediately following. Serafina's movements gather momentum. She snatches a long-neglected girdle out of a bureau drawer and holds it experimentally about her waist. She shakes her head doubtfully, drops the girdle and suddenly snatches the $8.98 hat off the millinery dummy and plants it on her head. She turns around distractedly, not remembering where the mirror is. She gasps with astonishment when she catches sight of herself, snatches the hat off and hastily restores it to the blank head of the dummy. She makes another confused revolution or two, then gasps with fresh inspiration and snatches a girlish frock off a dummy —an Alice blue gown with daisies crocheted on it. The dress sticks on the dummy. Serafina mutters savagely in Sicilian. She finally overcomes this difficulty but in her exasperation she knocks the dummy over. She throws off the robe and steps hopefully into the gown. But she discovers it won't fit over her hips. She seizes the girdle again; then hurls it angrily away. The parrot calls to her; she yells angrily back at the parrot: "Zitto!"

In the distance the high school band starts playing. Serafina gets panicky that she will miss the graduation ceremonies, and hammers her forehead with her fist, sobbing a little. She wriggles despairingly out of the blue dress and runs out back in her rayon slip just as Flora and Bessie appear outside the house. Flora and Bessie are two female clowns of middle years and juvenile temperament. Flora is tall and angular; Bessie is rather stubby. They are dressed for a gala. Flora runs up the steps and bangs at the cottage door.

BESSIE:

I fail to understand why it's so important to pick up a polka-dot blouse when it's likely to make us miss the twelve o'clock train.

FLORA:

Serafina! Serafina!

BESSIE:

We only got fifteen minutes to get to the depot and I'll get faint on the train if I don't have m' coffee . . .

FLORA:

Git a coke on th' train, Bessie.

BESSIE:

Git nothing on the train if we don't git the train!

[*Serafina runs back out of the bedroom, quite breathless, in a purple silk dress. As she passes the millinery dummy she snatches the hat off again and plants it back on her head.*]

SERAFINA:

Wrist-watch! Wrist-watch! Where'd I put th' wrist-watch? [*She hears Flora shouting and banging and rushes to the door.*]

BESSIE:

Try the door if it ain't open.

FLORA [*pushing in*]:

Just tell me, is it ready or not?

SERAFINA:

Oh! You. Don't bother me. I'm late for the graduation of my daughter and now I can't find her graduation present.

FLORA:

You got plenty of time.

45

SERAFINA:
Don't you hear the band playing?

FLORA:
They're just warming up. Now, Serafina, where is my blouse?

SERAFINA:
Blouse? Not ready! I had to make fourteen graduation dresses!

FLORA:
A promise is a promise and an excuse is just an excuse!

SERAFINA:
I got to get to the high school!

FLORA:
I got to get to the depot in that blouse!

BESSIE:
We're going to the American Legion parade in New Orleans.

FLORA:
There, there, there, there it is! [*She grabs the blouse from the machine.*] Get started, woman, stitch them bandanas together! If you don't do it, I'm a-gonna report you to the Chamber of Commerce and git your license revoked!

SERAFINA [*anxiously*]:
What license you talking about? I got no license!

FLORA:
You hear that, Bessie? *She hasn't got no license!*

BESSIE:
She ain't even got a license?

SERAFINA [*crossing quickly to the machine*]:
I—I'll stitch them together! But if you make me late to my daughter's graduation, I'll make you sorry some way . . .

[*She works with furious rapidity. A train whistle is heard.*]

BESSIE [*wildly and striking at Flora with her purse*]:
Train's pullin' out! Oh, God, you made us miss it!

FLORA:
Bessie, you know there's another at 12:45!

BESSIE:
It's the selfish—principle of it that makes me sick! [*She walks rapidly up and down.*]

FLORA:
Set down, Bessie. Don't wear out your feet before we git to th' city . . .

BESSIE:
Molly tole me the town was full of excitement. They're dropping paper sacks full of water out of hotel windows.

FLORA:
Which hotel are they dropping paper sacks out of?

BESSIE:
What a fool question! The Monteleone Hotel.

FLORA:
That's an old-fashioned hotel.

BESSIE:
It might be old-fashioned but you'd be surprised at some of the modern, up-to-date things that go on there.

FLORA:
I heard, I heard that the Legionnaires caught a girl on Canal Street! They tore the clothes off her and sent her home in a taxi!

BESSIE:
I double dog dare anybody to try that on me!

47

FLORA:

You?! Huh! You never need any assistance gittin' undressed!

SERAFINA [*ominously*]:

You two ladies watch how you talk in there. This here is a Catholic house. You are sitting in the same room with Our Lady and with the blessed ashes of my husband!

FLORA [*acidly*]:

Well, ex-cuse *me!* [*She whispers maliciously to Bessie.*] It sure is a pleasant surprise to see you wearing a dress, Serafina, but the surprise would be twice as pleasant if it was more the right size. [*to Bessie, loudly*] She used to have a sweet figure, a little bit plump but attractive, but setting there at that sewing machine for three years in a kimona and not stepping out of the house has naturally given her hips!

SERAFINA:

If I didn't have hips I would be a very uncomfortable woman when I set down.

[*The parrot squawks. Serafina imitates its squawk.*]

FLORA:

Polly want a cracker?

SERAFINA:

No. He don't want a cracker! What is she doing over there at that window?

BESSIE:

Some Legionnaires are on the highway!

FLORA:

A Legionnaire? No kidding?

[*She springs up and joins her girl friend at the window. They both laugh fatuously, bobbing their heads out the window.*]

BESSIE:
He's looking this way; yell something!

FLORA [*leaning out the window*]:
Mademoiselle from Armentieres, parley-voo!

BESSIE [*chiming in rapturously*]:
Mademoiselle from Armentieres, parley-voo!

A VOICE OUTSIDE [*gallantly returning the salute*]:
Mademoiselle from Armentieres, hadn't been kissed for forty years!

BOTH GIRLS [*together; very gaily*]:
Hinky-dinky parley-voooo!

[*They laugh and applaud at the window. The Legionnaires are heard laughing. A car horn is heard as the Legionnaires drive away. Serafina springs up and rushes over to the window, jerks them away from it and slams the shutters in their faces.*]

SERAFINA [*furiously*]:
I told you wimmen that you was not in a honky-tonk! Now take your blouse and git out! Get out on the streets where you kind a wimmen belong.—This is the house of Rosario delle Rose and those are his ashes in that marble urn and I won't have—unproper things going on here or dirty talk, neither!

FLORA:
Who's talking dirty?

BESSIE:
What a helluva nerve.

49

FLORA:

I want you to listen!

SERAFINA:

You are, you are, dirty talk, all the time men, men, men!
You men-crazy things, you!

FLORA:

Sour grapes—sour grapes is your trouble! You're wild with
envy!

BESSIE:

Isn't she green with jealousy? Huh!

SERAFINA [*suddenly and religiously*]:

When I think of men I think about my husband. My husband was a Sicilian. We had love together every night of
the week, we never skipped one, from the night we was
married till the night he was killed in his fruit truck on
that road there! [*She catches her breath in a sob.*] And
maybe that is the reason I'm not man-crazy and don't like
hearing the talk of women that are. But I am interested,
now, in the happiness of my daughter who's graduating
this morning out of high school. And now I'm going to be
late, the band is playing! And I have lost her wrist watch!
—her graduation present! [*She whirls about distractedly.*]

BESSIE:

Flora, let's go!—The hell with that goddam blouse!

FLORA:

Oh, no, just wait a minute! I don't accept insults from no
one!

SERAFINA:

Go on, go on to New Orleans, you two man-crazy things,
you! And pick up a man on Canal Street but not in my
house, at my window, in front of my dead husband's ashes!

[*The high school band is playing a martial air in the distance. Serafina's chest is heaving violently; she touches her heart and momentarily seems to forget that she must go.*] I am not at all interested, I am not interested in men getting fat and bald in soldier-boy play suits, tearing the clothes off girls on Canal Street and dropping paper sacks out of hotel windows. I'm just not interested in that sort of mancrazy business. I remember my husband with a body like a young boy and hair on his head as thick and black as mine is and skin on him smooth and sweet as a yellow rose petal.

FLORA:

Oh, a *rose,* was he?

SERAFINA:

Yes, yes, a rose, a rose!

FLORA:

Yes, a rose of a Wop!—of a gangster!—shot smuggling dope under a load of bananas!

BESSIE:

Flora, Flora, let's go!

SERAFINA:

My folks was peasants, contadini, but he—he come from *land*-owners! *Signorile,* my husband!—At night I sit here and I'm satisfied to remember, because I had the best.—Not the third best and not the second best, but the *first* best, the *only* best!—So now I stay here and am satisfied now to remember, . . .

BESSIE:

Come on, come out! To the depot!

FLORA:

Just wait, I wanta hear this, it's too good to miss!

51

SERAFINA:

I count up the nights I held him all night in my arms, and I can tell you how many. Each night for twelve years. Four thousand—three hundred—and eighty. The number of nights I held him all night in my arms. Sometimes I didn't sleep, just held him all night in my arms. And I am satisfied with it. I grieve for him. Yes, my pillow at night's never dry—but I'm satisfied to remember. And I would feel cheap and degraded and not fit to live with my daughter or under the roof with the urn of his blessed ashes, those —ashes of a rose—if after that memory, after knowing that man, I went to some other, some middle-aged man, not young, not full of young passion, but getting a pot belly on him and losing his hair and smelling of sweat and liquor— and trying to fool myself that *that* was love-making! I *know* what love-making was. And I'm satisfied just to remember . . . [*She is panting as though she had run upstairs.*] Go on, you do it, you go on the streets and let them drop their sacks of dirty water on you!—I'm satisfied to remember the love of a man that was mine—*only mine!* Never touched by the hand of *nobody! Nobody* but *me!*— Just me! [*She gasps and runs out to the porch. The sun floods her figure. It seems to astonish her. She finds herself sobbing. She digs in her purse for her handkerchief.*]

FLORA [*crossing to the open door*]:
Never touched by nobody?

SERAFINA [*with fierce pride*]:
Never nobody but me!

FLORA:
I know somebody that could a tale unfold! And not so far from here neither. Not no further than the Square Roof is, that place on Esplanade!

BESSIE:

Estelle Hohengarten!

FLORA:

Estelle Hohengarten!—the blackjack dealer from Texas!

BESSIE:

Get into your blouse and let's go!

FLORA:

Everybody's known it but Serafina. I'm just telling the facts that come out at the inquest while she was in bed with her eyes shut tight and the sheet pulled over her head like a female ostrich! Tie this damn thing on me! It was a romance, not just a fly-by-night thing, but a steady affair that went on for more than a year.

[*Serafina has been standing on the porch with the door open behind her. She is in the full glare of the sun. She appears to have been struck senseless by the words shouted inside. She turns slowly about. We see that her dress is unfastened down the back, the pink slip showing. She reaches out gropingly with one hand and finds the porch column which she clings to while the terrible words strike constantly deeper. The high school band continues as a merciless counterpoint.*]

BESSIE:

Leave her in ignorance. Ignorance is bliss.

FLORA:

He had a rose tattoo on his chest, the stuck-up thing, and Estelle was so gone on him she went down to Bourbon Street and had one put on her. [*Serafina comes onto the porch and Flora turns to her, viciously.*] Yeah, a rose tattoo on her chest same as the Wop's!

SERAFINA [*very softly*]:

Liar . . . [*She comes inside; the word seems to give her strength.*]

BESSIE [*nervously*]:
Flora, let's go, let's go!

SERAFINA [*in a terrible voice*]:
Liar!—*Lie*-arrrrr!

[*She slams the wooden door shut with a violence that shakes the walls.*]

BESSIE [*shocked into terror*]:
Let's get outa here, Flora!

FLORA:
Let her howl her head off. I don't care.

[*Serafina has snatched up a broom.*]

BESSIE:
What's she up to?

FLORA:
I don't care what she's up to!

BESSIE:
I'm a-scared of these Wops.

FLORA:
I'm not afraid of nobody!

BESSIE:
She's gonna hit you.

FLORA:
She'd better not hit me!

[*But both of the clowns are in retreat to the door. Serafina suddenly rushes at them with the broom. She flails Flora about the hips and shoulders. Bessie gets out. But Flora is trapped in a corner. A table is turned over. Bessie, outside, screams for the police and cries: "Murder! Murder!" The high school band is playing* The Stars and

Stripes Forever. *Flora breaks wildly past the flailing broom and escapes out of the house. She also takes up the cry for help. Serafina follows them out. She is flailing the brilliant noon air with the broom. The two women run off, screaming.*]

FLORA [*calling back*]:
I'm going to have her arrested! Police, police! I'm going to have you arrested!

SERAFINA:
Have me arrested, *have* me, you dirt, you devil, you *liar!* Li-i-arrrr!

[*She comes back inside the house and leans on the work table for a moment, panting heavily. Then she rushes back to the door, slams it and bolts it. Then she rushes to the windows, slams the shutters and fastens them. The house is now dark except for the vigil light in the ruby glass cup before the Madonna, and the delicate beams admitted through the shutter slats.*]

SERAFINA [*in a crazed manner*]:
Have me—have me—arrested—dirty slut—bitch—liar! [*She moves about helplessly, not knowing what to do with her big, stricken body. Panting for breath, she repeats the word "liar" monotonously and helplessly as she thrashes about. It is necessary for her, vitally necessary for her, to believe that the woman's story is a malicious invention. But the words of it stick in her mind and she mumbles them aloud as she thrashes crazily around the small confines of the parlor.*] Woman—Estelle—[*The sound of band music is heard.*] Band, band, already—started.—Going to miss—graduation. Oh! [*She retreats toward the Madonna.*] Estelle, Estelle Hohengarten?—"A shirt for a man I'm in love with! This

55

man—is—wild like a gypsy."—Oh, oh, Lady—The—rose-colored—silk. [*She starts toward the dining room, then draws back in terror.*] No, no, no, no, no! I don't remember! It wasn't that name, I don't remember the name! [*The band music grows louder.*] High school—graduation—late! I'll be—late for it.—Oh, Lady, give me a—*sign!* [*She cocks her head toward the statue in a fearful listening attitude.*] Che? Che dice, Signora? *Oh, Lady! Give me a sign!*

[*The scene dims out.*]

56

It is two hours later. The interior of the house is in complete darkness except for the vigil light. With the shutters closed, the interior is so dark that we do not know Serafina is present. All that we see clearly is the starry blue robe of Our Lady above the flickering candle of the ruby glass cup. After a few moments we hear Serafina's voice, very softly, in the weak, breathless tone of a person near death.

SERAFINA [*very softly*]:
Oh, Lady, give me a sign . . .

[*Gay, laughing voices are heard outside the house. Rosa and Jack appear, bearing roses and gifts. They are shouting back to others in a car.*]

JACK:
Where do we go for the picnic?

A GIRL'S VOICE [*from the highway*]:
We're going in three sailboats to Diamond Key.

A MAN'S VOICE:
Be at Municipal Pier in half an hour.

ROSA:
Pick us up here! [*She races up the steps.*] Oh, the door's locked! Mama's gone *out!* There's a key in that bird bath.

[*Jack opens the door. The parlor lights up faintly as they enter.*]

JACK:
It's dark in here.

ROSA:
Yes, Mama's gone out!

JACK:
How do you know she's out?

ROSA:
The door was locked and all the shutters are closed! Put down those roses.

JACK:
Where shall I . . .

ROSA:
Somewhere, anywhere!—Come here! [*He approaches her rather diffidently.*] I want to teach you a little Dago word. The word is "bacio."

JACK:
What does this word mean?

ROSA:
This and this and this! [*She rains kisses upon him till he forcibly removes her face from his.*] Just think. A week ago Friday—I didn't know boys existed!—Did you know girls existed before the dance?

JACK:
Yes, I knew they existed . . .

ROSA [*holding him*]:
Do you remember what you said to me on the dance floor? "Honey, you're dancing too close?"

JACK:
Well, it was—hot in the Gym and the—floor was crowded.

ROSA:
When my girl friend was teaching me how to dance, I asked her, "How do you know which way the boy's going to move?" And she said, "You've got to feel how he's going to move with your body!" I said, "How do you feel with your body?" And she said, "By pressing up close!"—That's

58

why I pressed up close! I didn't realize that I was—Ha, ha! Now you're blushing! Don't go *away!*—And a few minutes later you said to me, "Gee, you're beautiful!" I said, "Excuse me," and ran to the ladies' room. Do you know why? To look at myself in the mirror! And I saw that I was! For the first time in my life I was beautiful! You'd made me beautiful when you *said* that I was!

JACK [*humbly*]:
You *are* beautiful, Rosa! So much, I . . .

ROSA:
You've changed, *too.* You've stopped laughing and joking. Why have you gotten so old and serious, Jack?

JACK:
Well, honey, you're sort of . . .

ROSA:
What am I "sort of?"

JACK [*finding the exact word*]:
Wild! [*She laughs. He seizes the bandaged wrist.*] I didn't know nothing like this was going to happen.

ROSA:
Oh, that, that's nothing! I'll take the handkerchief off and you can forget it.

JACK:
How could you do a thing like that over me? I'm—nothing!

ROSA:
Everybody is nothing until you love them!

JACK:
Give me that handkerchief. I want to show it to my shipmates. I'll say, "This is the blood of a beautiful girl who cut her wrist with a knife because she loved me!"

ROSA:

Don't be so pleased with yourself. It's mostly Mercurochrome!

SERAFINA [*violently, from the dark room adjoining*]:
Stai zitta!—Cretina!

[*Rosa and Jack draw abruptly apart.*]

JACK [*fearfully*]:
I knew somebody was here!

ROSA [*sweetly and delicately*]:
Mama? Are you in there, Mama?

SERAFINA:

No, no, no, I'm not, I'm dead and buried!

ROSA:

Yes, Mama's in there!

JACK:

Well, I—better go and—wait outside for a—while . . .

ROSA:

You stay right here!—Mama?—Jack is with me.—Are you dressed up nicely? [*There is no response.*] Why's it so dark in here?—Jack, open the shutters!—I want to introduce you to my mother . . .

JACK:

Hadn't I better go and . . .

ROSA:

No. Open the shutters!

[*The shutters are opened and Rosa draws apart the curtains between the two rooms. Sunlight floods the scene. Serafina is revealed slumped in a chair at her work table in the dining room near the Singer sewing machine. She*

60

is grotesquely surrounded by the dummies, as though she had been holding a silent conference with them. Her appearance, in slovenly deshabille, is both comic and shocking.]

ROSA [*terribly embarrassed*]:
Mama, Mama, you said you were dressed up pretty! Jack, stay out for a minute! What's happened, Mama?

[Jack remains in the parlor. Rosa pulls the curtains, snatches a robe and flings it over Serafina. She brushes Serafina's hair back from her sweat-gleaming face, rubs her face with a handkerchief and dusts it with powder. Serafina submits to this cosmetic enterprise with a dazed look.]

ROSA [*gesturing vertically*]:
Su, su, su, su, su, su, su, su, su!

[Serafina sits up slightly in her chair, but she is still looking stupefied. Rosa returns to the parlor and opens the curtains again.]

ROSA:
Come in, Jack! Mama is ready to meet you!

[Rosa trembles with eagerness as Jack advances nervously from the parlor. But before he enters Serafina collapses again into her slumped position, with a low moan.]

ROSA [*violently*]:
Mama, Mama, su, Mama! [*Serafina sits half erect.*] She didn't sleep good last night.—Mama, this is Jack Hunter!

JACK:
Hello, Mrs. Delle Rose. It sure is a pleasure to meet you.

61

[*There is a pause. Serafina stares indifferently at the boy.*]

ROSA:

Mama, Mama, say something!

JACK:

Maybe your Mama wants me to . . . [*He makes an awkward gesture toward the door.*]

ROSA:

No, no, Mama's just tired. Mama makes dresses; she made a whole lot of dresses for the graduation! How many, Mama, how many graduation dresses did you have to make?

SERAFINA [*dully*]:
Fa niente . . .

JACK:

I was hoping to see you at the graduation, Mrs. Delle Rose.

ROSA:

I guess that Mama was too worn out to go.

SERAFINA:

Rosa, shut the front door, shut it and lock it. There was a—policeman . . . [*There is a pause.*] What?—What?

JACK:

My sister was graduating. My mother was there and my aunt was there—a whole bunch of cousins—I was hoping that you could—all—get together . . .

ROSA:

Jack brought you some flowers.

JACK:

I hope you are partial to roses as much as I am. [*He hands her the bouquet. She takes them absently.*]

ROSA:

Mama, say something, say something simple like "Thanks."

SERAFINA:

Thanks.

ROSA:

Jack, tell Mama about the graduation; describe it to her.

JACK:

My mother said it was just like fairyland.

ROSA:

Tell her what the boys wore!

JACK:

What did—what did they wear?

ROSA:

Oh, you know what they wore. They wore blue coats and white pants and each one had a carnation! And there were three couples that did an old-fashioned dance, a minuet, Mother, to Mendelssohn's *Spring Song!* Wasn't it lovely, Jack? But one girl slipped; she wasn't used to long dresses! She slipped and fell on her—ho, ho! Wasn't it funny, Jack, wasn't it, wasn't it, Jack?

JACK [*worriedly*]:

I think that your Mama . . .

ROSA:

Oh, my prize, my prize, I have forgotten my prize!

JACK:

Where is it?

ROSA:

You set them down by the sewing sign when you looked for the key.

JACK:
Aw, excuse me, I'll get them. [*He goes out through the parlor. Rosa runs to her mother and kneels by her chair.*]

ROSA [*in a terrified whisper*]:
Mama, something has happened! What has happened, Mama? Can't you tell me, Mama? Is it because of this morning? Look. I took the bandage off, it was only a scratch! So, Mama, forget it! Think it was just a bad dream that never happened! Oh, Mama! [*She gives her several quick kisses on the forehead. Jack returns with two big books tied in white satin ribbon.*]

JACK:
Here they are.

ROSA:
Look what I got, Mama.

SERAFINA [*dully*]:
What?

ROSA:
The Digest of Knowledge!

JACK:
Everything's in them, from Abracadabra to Zoo! My sister was jealous. She just got a diploma!

SERAFINA [*rousing a bit*]:
Diploma, where is it? Didn't you get no diploma?

ROSA:
Si, si, Mama! Eccolo! Guarda, guarda! [*She holds up the diploma tied in ribbon.*]

SERAFINA:
Va bene.—Put it in the drawer with your father's clothes.

64

JACK:

Mrs. Delle Rose, you should be very, very proud of your daughter. She stood in front of the crowd and recited a poem.

ROSA:

Yes, I did. Oh, I was so excited!

JACK:

And Mrs. Delle Rose, your daughter, Rosa, was so pretty when she walked on the stage—that people went "Oooooooooo!" —like that! Y'know what I mean? They all went— "Ooooooooo!" Like a—like a—*wind* had—blown over! Because your daughter, Rosa, was so—*lovely* looking! [*He has crouched over to Serafina to deliver this description close to her face. Now he straightens up and smiles proudly at Rosa.*] How does it feel to be the mother of the prettiest girl in the world?

ROSA [*suddenly bursting into pure delight*]:
Ha, ha, ha, ha, ha, ha! [*She throws her head back in rapture.*]

SERAFINA [*rousing*]:
Hush!

ROSA:

Ha, ha, ha, ha, ha, ha, ha, ha, ha, ha! [*She cannot control her ecstatic laughter. She presses her hand to her mouth but the laughter still bubbles out.*]

SERAFINA [*suddenly rising in anger*]:
Pazza, pazza, pazza! Finiscila! Basta, via! [*Rosa whirls around to hide her convulsions of joy. To Jack:*] Put the prize books in the parlor, and shut the front door; there was a policeman come here because of—some trouble . . . [*Jack takes the books.*]

65

ROSA:

Mama, I've never seen you like this! What will Jack think, Mama?

SERAFINA:

Why do I care what Jack thinks?—You wild, wild crazy thing, you—with the eyes of your—father . . .

JACK [*returning*]:

Yes, ma'am, Mrs. Delle Rose, you certainly got a right to be very proud of your daughter.

SERAFINA [*after a pause*]:

I am proud of the—memory of her—father.—He was a baron . . . [*Rosa takes Jack's arm.*] And who are *you*? What are you?—per piacere!

ROSA:

Mama, I just introduced him; his name is Jack Hunter.

SERAFINA:

Hunt-er?

JACK:

Yes, ma'am, Hunter. Jack Hunter.

SERAFINA:

What are you hunting?—Jack?

ROSA:

Mama!

SERAFINA:

What all of 'em are hunting? To have a good time, and the Devil cares who pays for it? I'm sick of men, I'm almost as sick of men as I am of wimmen.—Rosa, get out while I talk to this boy!

ROSA:

I didn't bring Jack here to be insulted!

JACK:

Go on, honey, and let your Mama talk to me. I think your Mama has just got a slight wrong—impression . . .

SERAFINA [*ominously*]:
Yes, I got an impression!

ROSA:

I'll get dressed! Oh, Mama, don't spoil it for me!—the happiest day of my life! [*She goes into the back of the house.*]

JACK [*after an awkward pause*]:
Mrs. Delle Rose . . .

SERAFINA [*correcting his pronunciation*]:
Delle Rose!

JACK:

Mrs. Delle Rose, I'm sorry about all this. Believe me, Mrs. Delle Rose, the last thing I had in mind was getting mixed up in a family situation. I come home after three months to sea, I docked at New Orleans, and come here to see my folks. My sister was going to a high school dance. She took me with her, and there I met your daughter.

SERAFINA:

What did you do?

JACK:

At the high school dance? We danced! My sister had told me that Rose had a very strict mother and wasn't allowed to go on dates with boys so when it was over, I said, "I'm sorry you're not allowed to go out." And she said, "Oh! What gave you the idea I *wasn't!*" So then I thought my sister had made a mistake and I made a date with her for the next night.

SERAFINA:

What did you do the next night?

67

JACK:

The next night we went to the movies.

SERAFINA:

And what did you do—that night?

JACK:

At the movies? We ate a bag of popcorn and watched the movie!

SERAFINA:

She come home at midnight and said she had been with a girl-friend studying "civics."

JACK:

Whatever story she told you, it ain't my fault!

SERAFINA:

And the night after that?

JACK:

Last Tuesday? We went roller skating!

SERAFINA:

And afterwards?

JACK:

After the skating? We went to a drug store and had an ice cream soda!

SERAFINA:

Alone?

JACK:

At the drug store? No. It was crowded. And the skating rink was full of people skating!

SERAFINA:

You mean that you haven't been alone with my Rosa?

JACK:

Alone or not alone, what's the point of that question? I still don't see the point of it.

SERAFINA:

We are Sicilians. We don't leave the girls with the boys they're not engaged to!

JACK:

Mrs. Delle Rose, this is the United States.

SERAFINA:

But we are Sicilians, and we are not cold-blooded.—My girl is a *virgin!* She *is*—or she *was*—I would like to know—*which!*

JACK:

Mrs. Delle Rose! I got to tell you something. You might not believe it. It is a hard thing to say. But I am—*also a*—*virgin* . . .

SERAFINA:

What? No. I do not believe it.

JACK:

Well, it's true, though. This is the first time—I . . .

SERAFINA:

First time you *what?*

JACK:

The first time I really wanted to . . .

SERAFINA:

Wanted to what?

JACK:

Make—love . . .

SERAFINA:

You? A sailor?

JACK [*sighing deeply*]:
Yes, ma'am. I had opportunities to!—But I—always thought of my mother . . . I always asked myself, would she or would she not—think—this or that person was—decent!

SERAFINA:
But with my daughter, my Rosa, your mother tells you *okay?*—go ahead, son!

JACK:
Mrs. Delle Rose! [*with embarrassment*]—Mrs. Delle Rose, I . . .

SERAFINA:
Two weeks ago I was slapping her hands for scratching mosquito bites. She rode a bicycle to school. Now all at once—I've got a wild thing in the house. She says she's in love. And you? Do you say *you're* in love?

JACK [*solemnly*]:
Yes, ma'am, I do, I'm in love!—very much . . .

SERAFINA:
Bambini, tutti due, bambini!

[*Rosa comes out, dressed for the picnic.*]

ROSA:
I'm ready for Diamond Key!

SERAFINA:
Go out on the porch. Diamond Key!

ROSA [*with a sarcastic curtsy*]:
Yes, Mama!

SERAFINA:
What are you? Catholic?

JACK:
Me? Yes, ma'am, Catholic.

SERAFINA:
You don't look Catholic to me!

ROSA [*shouting, from the door*]:
Oh, God, Mama, how do Catholics look? How do they look different from anyone else?

SERAFINA:
Stay out till I call you! [*Rosa crosses to the bird bath and prays. Serafina turns to Jack.*] Turn around, will you?

JACK:
Do what, ma'am?

SERAFINA:
I said, *turn around!* [*Jack awkwardly turns around.*] Why do they make them Navy pants so tight?

ROSA [*listening in the yard*]:
Oh, my God . . .

JACK [*flushing*]:
That's a question you'll have to ask the Navy, Mrs. Delle Rose.

SERAFINA:
And that gold earring, what's the gold earring for?

ROSA [*yelling from the door*]:
For crossing the equator, Mama; he crossed it three times. He was initiated into the court of Neptune and gets to wear a gold earring! He's a shellback!

[*Serafina springs up and crosses to slam the porch door. Rosa runs despairingly around the side of the house and leans, exhausted with closed eyes, against the trunk of a palm tree. The Strega creeps into the yard, listening.*]

71

SERAFINA:

You see what I got. A wild thing in the house!

JACK:

Mrs. Delle Rose, I guess that Sicilians are very emotional people . . .

SERAFINA:

I want nobody to take advantage of that!

JACK:

You got the wrong idea about me, Mrs. Delle Rose.

SERAFINA:

I know what men want—not to eat popcorn with girls or to slide on ice! And boys are the same, only younger.— Come here. Come here!

[*Rosa hears her mother's passionate voice. She rushes from the palm tree to the back door and pounds on it with both fists.*]

ROSA:

Mama! Mama! Let me in the door, Jack!

JACK:

Mrs. Delle Rose, your daughter is calling you.

SERAFINA:

Let her call!—Come here. [*She crosses to the shrine of Our Lady.*] *Come here!*

[*Despairing of the back door, Rosa rushes around to the front. A few moments later she pushes open the shutters of the window in the wall and climbs half in. Jack crosses apprehensively to Serafina before the Madonna.*]

SERAFINA:

You said you're Catholic, ain't you?

JACK:

Yes, ma'am.

SERAFINA:

Then kneel down in front of Our Lady!

JACK:

Do—do what, did you say?

SERAFINA:

I said to get down on your knees in front of Our Lady!

[*Rosa groans despairingly in the window. Jack kneels awkwardly upon the hassock.*]

ROSA:

Mama, Mama, *now* what?!

[*Serafina rushes to the window, pushes Rosa out and slams the shutters.*]

SERAFINA [*returning to Jack*]:

Now say after me what I say!

JACK:

Yes, ma'am.

[*Rosa pushes the shutters open again.*]

SERAFINA:

I promise the Holy Mother that I will respect the innocence of the daughter of . . .

ROSA [*in anguish*]:

Ma-*maaa!*

SERAFINA:

Get back out of that window!—Well? Are you gonna say it?

JACK:

Yes, ma'am. What was it, again?

SERAFINA:
I promise the Holy Mother . . .

JACK:
I promise the Holy Mother . . .

SERAFINA:
As I hope to be saved by the Blessed Blood of Jesus . . .

JACK:
As I hope to be saved by the . . .

SERAFINA:
Blessed Blood of . . .

JACK:
Jesus . . .

SERAFINA:
That I will respect the innocence of the daughter, Rosa, of Rosario delle Rose.

JACK:
That I will respect the innocence—of—Rosa . . .

SERAFINA:
Cross yourself! [*He crosses himself.*] Now get up, get up, get up! I am satisfied now . . .

[*Rosa jumps through the window and rushes to Serafina with arms outflung and wild cries of joy.*]

SERAFINA:
Let me go, let me breathe! [*Outside the Strega cackles derisively.*]

ROSA:
Oh, wonderful Mama, don't breathe! Oh, Jack! *Kiss* Mama! *Kiss Mama!* Mama, please kiss Jack!

SERAFINA:

Kiss? Me? No, no, no, no!—Kiss my *hand* . . .

[*She offers her hand, shyly, and Jack kisses it with a loud smack. Rosa seizes the wine bottle.*]

ROSA:

Mama, get some wine glasses!

[*Serafina goes for the glasses, and Rosa suddenly turns to Jack. Out of her mother's sight, she passionately grabs hold of his hand and presses it, first to her throat, then to her lips and finally to her breast. Jack snatches her hand away as Serafina returns with the glasses. Voices are heard calling from the highway.*]

VOICES OUTSIDE:

Ro-osa!—Ro-osa!—Ro-osa!

[*A car horn is heard blowing.*]

SERAFINA:

Oh, I forgot the graduation present.

[*She crouches down before the bureau and removes a fancily wrapped package from its bottom drawer. The car horn is honking, and the voices are calling.*]

ROSA:

They're calling for us! *Coming!* Jack! [*She flies out the door, calling back to her mother.*] G'bye, Mama!

JACK [*following Rosa*]:

Good-bye, Mrs. Delle Rose!

SERAFINA [*vaguely*]:

It's a Bulova wrist watch with seventeen jewels in it . . . [*She realizes that she is alone.*] Rosa! [*She goes to the*

*door, still holding out the present. Outside the car motor
roars, and the voices shout as the car goes off. Serafina stumbles outside, shielding her eyes with one hand, extending
the gift with the other.*] Rosa, Rosa, your present! Regalo,
regalo—tesoro!

[*But the car has started off, with a medley of voices
shouting farewells, which fade quickly out of hearing.
Serafina turns about vaguely in the confusing sunlight
and gropes for the door. There is a derisive cackle from
the witch next door. Serafina absently opens the package
and removes the little gold watch. She winds it and then
holds it against her ear. She shakes it and holds it again
to her ear. Then she holds it away from her and glares at
it fiercely.*]

SERAFINA [*pounding her chest three times*]:
Tick—tick—tick! [*She goes to the Madonna and faces it.*]
Speak to me, Lady! Oh, Lady, give me a sign!

[*The scene dims out.*]

ACT TWO

It is two hours later the same day.

Serafina comes out onto the porch, barefooted, wearing a rayon slip. Great shadows have appeared beneath her eyes; her face and throat gleam with sweat. There are dark stains of wine on the rayon slip. It is difficult for her to stand, yet she cannot sit still. She makes a sick moaning sound in her throat almost continually.

A hot wind rattles the cane-brake. Vivi, the little girl, comes up to the porch to stare at Serafina as at a strange beast in a cage. Vivi is chewing a licorice stick which stains her mouth and her fingers. She stands chewing and staring. Serafina evades her stare. She wearily drags a broken grey wicker chair down off the porch, all the way out in front of the house, and sags heavily into it. It sits awry on a broken leg.

Vivi sneaks toward her. Serafina lurches about to face her angrily. The child giggles and scampers back to the porch.

SERAFINA [*sinking back into the chair*]:
Oh, Lady, Lady, Lady, give me a—sign . . . [*She looks up at the white glare of the sky.*]

[*Father De Leo approaches the house. Serafina crouches low in the chair to escape his attention. He knocks at the door. Receiving no answer, he looks out into the yard, sees her, and approaches her chair. He comes close to address her with a gentle severity.*]

FATHER DE LEO:
Buon giorno, Serafina.

SERAFINA [*faintly, with a sort of disgust*]:
Giorno . . .

FATHER DE LEO:
I'm surprised to see you sitting outdoors like this. What is
that thing you're wearing?—I think it's an undergarment!
—It's hanging off one shoulder, and your head, Serafina,
looks as if you had stuck it in a bucket of oil. Oh, I see now
why the other ladies of the neighborhood aren't taking
their afternoon naps! They find it more entertaining to sit
on the porches and watch the spectacle you are putting on
for them!—Are you listening to me?—I must tell you that
the change in your appearance and behavior since Rosario's
death is shocking—shocking! A woman can be dignified in
her grief but when it's carried too far it becomes a sort of
self-indulgence. Oh, I knew this was going to happen when
you broke the Church law and had your husband cremated!
[*Serafina lurches up from the chair and shuffles back to the
porch. Father De Leo follows her.*]—Set up a little idola-
trous shrine in your house and give worship to a bottle of
ashes. [*She sinks down upon the steps.*]—Are you listening
to me?

[*Two women have appeared on the embankment and
descend toward the house. Serafina lurches heavily up to
meet them, like a weary bull turning to face another attack.*]

SERAFINA:
You ladies, what you want? I don't do sewing! Look, I quit
doing sewing. [*She pulls down the* "SEWING" *sign and
hurls it away.*] Now you got places to go, you ladies, go
places! Don't hang around front of my house!

FATHER DE LEO:
The ladies want to be friendly.

SERAFINA:
Naw, they don't come to be friendly. They think they know something that Serafina don't know; they think I got *these* on my head! [*She holds her fingers like horns at either side of her forehead.*] Well, I ain't got them! [*She goes padding back out in front of the house. Father De Leo follows.*]

FATHER DE LEO:
You called me this morning in distress over something.

SERAFINA:
I called you this morning but now it is afternoon.

FATHER DE LEO:
I had to christen the grandson of the Mayor.

SERAFINA:
The Mayor's important people, not Serafina!

FATHER DE LEO:
You don't come to confession.

SERAFINA [*starting back toward the porch*]:
No, I don't come, I don't go, I—Ohhh! [*She pulls up one foot and hops on the other.*]

FATHER DE LEO:
You stepped on something?

SERAFINA [*dropping down on the steps*]:
No, no, no, no, no, I don't step on—noth'n . . .

FATHER DE LEO:
Come in the house. We'll wash it with antiseptic. [*She lurches up and limps back toward the house.*] Walking barefooted you will get it infected.

SERAFINA:

Fa niente . . .

[*At the top of the embankment a little boy runs out with a red kite and flourishes it in the air with rigid gestures, as though he were giving a distant signal. Serafina shades her eyes with a palm to watch the kite, and then, as though its motions conveyed a shocking message, she utters a startled soft cry and staggers back to the porch. She leans against a pillar, running her hand rapidly and repeatedly through her hair. Father De Leo approaches her again, somewhat timidly.*]

FATHER DE LEO:

Serafina?

SERAFINA:

Che, che, che cosa vuole?

FATHER DE LEO:

I am thirsty. Will you go in the house and get me some water?

SERAFINA:

Go in. Get you some water. The faucet is working.—I can't go in the house.

FATHER DE LEO:

Why can't you go in the house?

SERAFINA:

The house has a tin roof on it. I got to breathe.

FATHER DE LEO:

You can breathe in the house.

SERAFINA:

No, I can't breathe in the house. The house has a tin roof on it and I . . .

[*The Strega has been creeping through the cane-brake pretending to search for a chicken.*]

THE STREGA:

Chick, chick, chick, chick, chick? [*She crouches to peer under the house.*]

SERAFINA:

What's that? Is that the . . . ? Yes, the Strega! [*She picks up a flower pot containing a dead plant and crosses the yard.*] Strega! Strega! [*The Strega looks up, retreating a little.*] Yes, you, I mean you! You ain't look for no chick! Getta hell out of my yard! [*The Strega retreats, viciously muttering, back into the cane-brake. Serafina makes the protective sign of the horns with her fingers. The goat bleats.*]

FATHER DE LEO:

You have no friends, Serafina.

SERAFINA:

I don't want friends.

FATHER DE LEO:

You are still a young woman. Eligible for—loving and— bearing again! I remember you dressed in pale blue silk at Mass one Easter morning, yes, like a lady wearing a—piece of the—weather! Oh, how proudly you walked, *too* proudly! —But now you crouch and shuffle about barefooted; you live like a convict, dressed in the rags of a convict. You have no companions; women you don't mix with. You . . .

SERAFINA:

No, I don't mix with them women. [*glaring at the women on the embankment*] The dummies I got in my house, I mix with them better because they don't make up no lies!— What kind of women are them? [*mimicking fiercely*]

"Eee, Papa, eeee, baby, eee, me, me, me! At thirty years old they got no more use for the letto matrimoniale, no. The big bed goes to the basement! They get little beds from Sears Roebuck and sleep on their bellies!

FATHER DE LEO:

Attenzione!

SERAFINA:

They make the life without glory. Instead of the heart they got the deep-freeze in the house. The men, they don't feel no glory, not in the house with them women; they go to the bars, fight in them, get drunk, get fat, put horns on the women because the women don't give them the love which is glory.—I did, I give him the glory. To me the big bed was beautiful like a religion. Now I lie on it with dreams, with memories only! But it is still beautiful to me and I don't believe that the man in my heart gave me horns! [*The women whisper.*] What, what are they saying? Does ev'rybody know something that I don't know?—No, all I want is a sign, a sign from Our Lady, to tell me the lie is a lie! And then I . . . [*The women laugh on the embankment. Serafina starts fiercely toward them. They scatter.*] Squeak, squeak, squawk, squawk! Hens—like water thrown on them! [*There is the sound of mocking laughter.*]

FATHER DE LEO:

People are laughing at you on all the porches.

SERAFINA:

I'm laughing, too. Listen to me, I'm laughing! [*She breaks into loud, false laughter, first from the porch, then from the foot of the embankment, then crossing in front of the house.*]

Ha, ha, ha, ha, ha, ha, ha! Now ev'rybody is laughing. Ha, ha, ha, ha, ha, ha!

FATHER DE LEO:

Zitta ora!—Think of your daughter.

SERAFINA [*understanding the word "daughter"*]:
You, *you* think of my daughter! Today you give out the diplomas, today at the high school you give out the prizes, diplomas! You give to my daughter a set of books call the Digest of Knowledge! What does she know? How to be cheap already?—Oh, yes, that is what to learn, how to be cheap and to cheat!—You know what they do at this high school? They ruin the girls there! They give the spring dance because the girls are man-crazy. And there at that dance my daughter goes with a sailor that has in his ear a gold ring! And pants so tight that a woman ought not to look at him! This morning, this morning she cuts with a knife her wrist if I don't let her go!—Now all of them gone to some island, they call it a picnic, all of them, gone in a—boat!

FATHER DE LEO:

There *was* a school picnic, chaperoned by the teachers.

SERAFINA:

Oh, lo so, lo so! The man-crazy old-maid teachers!—They all run wild on the island!

FATHER DE LEO:

Serafina delle Rose! [*He picks up the chair by the back and hauls it to the porch when she starts to resume her seat.*]—I *command* you to go in the house.

SERAFINA:

Go in the house? I will. I will go in the house if you will answer one question.—Will you answer one question?

83

FATHER DE LEO:
I will if I know the answer.

SERAFINA:
Aw, you know the answer!—You used to hear the confessions of my husband. [*She turns to face the priest.*]

FATHER DE LEO:
Yes, I heard his confessions . . .

SERAFINA [*with difficulty*]:
Did he ever speak to you of a *woman*?

[*A child cries out and races across in front of the house. Father De Leo picks up his panama hat. Serafina paces slowly toward him. He starts away from the house.*]

SERAFINA [*rushing after him*]:
Aspettate! Aspettate un momento!

FATHER DE LEO [*fearfully, not looking at her*]:
Che volete?

SERAFINA:
Rispondetemi! [*She strikes her breast.*] Did he speak of a woman to you?

FATHER DE LEO:
You know better than to ask me such a question. I don't break the Church laws. The secrets of the confessional are sacred to me. [*He walks away.*]

SERAFINA [*pursuing and clutching his arm*]:
I got to know. You could tell me.

FATHER DE LEO:
Let go of me, Serafina!

SERAFINA:
Not till you tell me, Father. Father, you tell me, please tell me! Or I will go mad! [*in a fierce whisper*] I will go back

84

in the house and smash the urn with the ashes—if you don't tell me! I will go mad with the doubt in my heart and I will smash the urn and scatter the ashes—of my husband's body!

FATHER DE LEO:

What could I tell you? If you would not believe the known facts about him . . .

SERAFINA:

Known facts, who knows the known facts?

[*The neighbor women have heard the argument and begin to crowd around, muttering in shocked whispers at Serafina's lack of respect.*]

FATHER DE LEO [*frightened*]:

Lasciatemi, lasciatemi stare!—Oh, Serafina, I am too old for this—please!—Everybody is . . .

SERAFINA [*in a fierce, hissing whisper*]:

Nobody knew my rose of the world but me and now they can lie because the rose ain't living. They want the marble urn broken; they want me to smash it. They want the rose ashes scattered because I had too much glory. They don't want glory like *that* in nobody's heart. They want—mouse-squeaking!—known facts.—Who knows the known facts? You—padres—wear black because of the fact that the facts are known by nobody!

FATHER DE LEO:

Oh, Serafina! There are people watching!

SERAFINA:

Let them watch something. That will be a change for them. —It's been a long time I wanted to break out like this and now I . . .

FATHER DE LEO:

I am too old a man; I am not strong enough. I am sixty-seven years old! Must I call for help, now?

SERAFINA:

Yes, call! Call for help, but I won't let you go till you tell me!

FATHER DE LEO:

You're not a respectable woman.

SERAFINA:

No, I'm not a respectable; I'm a woman.

FATHER DE LEO:

No, you are not a woman. You are an animal!

SERAFINA:

Si, si, animale! Sono animale! Animale. Tell them all, shout it all to them, up and down the whole block! The widow Delle Rose is not respectable, she is not even a woman, she is an animal! She is attacking the priest! She will tear the black suit off him unless he tells her the whores in this town are lying to her!

[*The neighbor women have been drawing closer as the argument progresses, and now they come to Father De Leo's rescue and assist him to get away from Serafina, who is on the point of attacking him bodily. He cries out, "Officer! Officer!" but the women drag Serafina from him and lead him away with comforting murmurs.*]

SERAFINA [*striking her wrists together*]:

Yes, it's me, it's me!! Lock me up, lock me, lock me up! Or I will—*smash!*—the marble . . . [*She throws her head far back and presses her fists to her eyes. Then she rushes crazily to the steps and falls across them.*]

ASSUNTA:

Serafina! Figlia! Figlia! Andiamo a casa!

SERAFINA:

Leave me alone, old woman.

[*She returns slowly to the porch steps and sinks down on them, sitting like a tired man, her knees spread apart and her head cupped in her hands. The children steal back around the house. A little boy shoots a bean-shooter at her. She starts up with a cry. The children scatter, shrieking. She sinks back down on the steps, then leans back, staring up at the sky, her body rocking.*]

SERAFINA:

Oh, Lady, Lady, Lady, give me a sign!

[*As if in mocking answer, a novelty salesman appears and approaches the porch. He is a fat man in a seersucker suit and a straw hat with a yellow, red and purple band. His face is beet-red and great moons of sweat have soaked through the armpits of his jacket. His shirt is lavender, and his tie, pale blue with great yellow polka dots, is a butterfly bow. His entrance is accompanied by a brief, satiric strain of music.*]

THE SALESMAN:

Good afternoon, lady. [*She looks up slowly. The salesman talks sweetly, as if reciting a prayer.*] I got a little novelty here which I am offering to just a few lucky people at what we call an introductory price. Know what I mean? Not a regular price but a price which is less than what it costs to manufacture the article, a price we are making for the sake of introducing the product in the Gulf Coast territory. Lady, this thing here that I'm droppin' right in youah lap is bigger than television; it's going to revolutionize the domestic life of America.—Now I don't do house to house canvassing. I sell directly to merchants but when I stopped over there to have my car serviced, I seen you taking the air on the steps and I thought I would just drop over and . . .

[*There is the sound of a big truck stopping on the highway, and a man's voice, Alvaro's, is heard, shouting.*]

ALVARO:
Hey! Hey, you road hog!

THE SALESMAN [*taking a sample out of his bag*]:
Now, lady, this little article has a deceptive appearance. First of all, I want you to notice how *compact* it is. It takes up no more space than . . .

[*Alvaro comes down from the embankment. He is about twenty-five years old, dark and very goodlooking. He is one of those Mediterranean types that resemble glossy young bulls. He is short in stature, has a massively sculptural torso and bluish-black curls. His face and manner are clownish; he has a charming awkwardness. There is a startling, improvised air about him; he frequently seems surprised at his own speeches and actions, as though he had not at all anticipated them. At the moment when we first hear his voice the sound of a timpani begins, at first very pianissimo, but building up as he approaches, till it reaches a vibrant climax with his appearance to Serafina beside the house.*]

ALVARO:
Hey.

THE SALESMAN [*without glancing at him*]:
Hay is for horses!—Now, madam, you see what happens when I press this button?

[*The article explodes in Serafina's face. She slaps it away with an angry cry. At the same time Alvaro advances, trembling with rage, to the porch steps. He is sweating and stammering with pent-up fury at a world of frustrations which are temporarily localized in the gross figure of this salesman.*]

ALVARO:
Hey, you! Come here! What the hell's the idea, back there at that curve? You make me drive off the highway!

THE SALESMAN [*to Serafina*]:
Excuse me for just one minute. [*He wheels menacingly about to face Alvaro.*] Is something giving you gas pains, Maccaroni?

ALVARO:
My name is not Maccaroni.

THE SALESMAN:
All right. Spaghetti.

ALVARO [*almost sobbing with passion*]:
I am not maccaroni. I am not spaghetti. I am a human being that drives a truck of bananas. I drive a truck of bananas for the Southern Fruit Company for a living, not to play cowboys and Indians on no highway with no rotten road hog. You got a 4-lane highway between Pass Christian and here. I give you the sign to pass me. You tail me and give me the horn. You yell "Wop" at me and "Dago." "Move over, Wop, move over, Dago." Then at the goddam curve, you go pass me and make me drive off the highway and yell back "Son of a bitch of a Dago!" I don't like that, no, no! And I am glad you stop here. Take the cigar from your mouth, take out the cigar!

89

THE SALESMAN:
Take it out for me, greaseball.

ALVARO:
If I take it out I will push it down your throat. I got three dependents! If I fight, I get fired, but I will fight and get fired. Take out the cigar!

[*Spectators begin to gather at the edge of the scene. Serafina stares at the truck driver, her eyes like a somnambule's. All at once she utters a low cry and seems about to fall.*]

ALVARO:
Take out the cigar, take out, take out the cigar!

[*He snatches the cigar from the salesman's mouth and the salesman brings his knee up violently into Alvaro's groin. Bending double and retching with pain, Alvaro staggers over to the porch.*]

THE SALESMAN [*shouting, as he goes off*]:
I got your license number, Maccaroni! I know your boss!

ALVARO [*howling*]:
Drop dead! [*He suddenly staggers up the steps.*] Lady, lady, I got to go in the house!

[*As soon as he enters, he bursts into rending sobs, leaning against a wall and shaking convulsively. The spectators outside laugh as they scatter. Serafina slowly enters the house. The screen door rasps loudly on its rusty springs as she lets it swing gradually shut behind her, her eyes remaining fixed with a look of stupefied wonder upon the sobbing figure of the truck driver. We must understand her profound unconscious response to this sudden contact with distress as acute as her own. There is a*]

*long pause as the screen door makes its whining, catlike
noise swinging shut by degrees.*]

SERAFINA:

Somebody's—in my house? [*finally, in a hoarse, tremulous
whisper*] What are you—doing in here? Why have you—
come in my house?

ALVARO:

Oh, lady—leave me alone!—Please—now!

SERAFINA:

You—got no business—in here . . .

ALVARO:

I got to cry after a fight. I'm sorry, lady. I . . .
[*The sobs still shake him. He leans on a dummy.*]

SERAFINA:

Don't lean on my dummy. Sit down if you can't stand up.
—What is the matter with you?

ALVARO:

I always cry after a fight. But I don't want people to see
me. It's not like a man. [*There is a long pause; Serafina's
attitude seems to warm toward the man.*]

SERAFINA:

A man is not no different from no one else . . . [*All at once
her face puckers up, and for the first time in the play Serafina begins to weep, at first soundlessly, then audibly. Soon
she is sobbing as loudly as Alvaro. She speaks between sobs.*]
—I always cry—when somebody else is crying . . .

ALVARO:

No, no, lady, *don't* cry! Why should *you* cry? I will stop. I
will stop in a minute. This is not like a man. I am ashame
of myself. I will stop now; please, lady . . .

91

[*Still crouching a little with pain, a hand clasped to his abdomen, Alvaro turns away from the wall. He blows his nose between two fingers. Serafina picks up a scrap of white voile and gives it to him to wipe his fingers.*]

SERAFINA:
Your jacket is torn.

ALVARO [*sobbing*]:
My company jacket is torn?

SERAFINA:
Yes . . .

ALVARO:
Where is it torn?

SERAFINA [*sobbing*]:
Down the—back.

ALVARO:
Oh, Dio!

SERAFINA:
Take it off. I will sew it up for you. I do—sewing.

ALVARO:
Oh, Dio! [*sobbing*] I got three dependents! [*He holds up three fingers and shakes them violently at Serafina.*]

SERAFINA:
Give me—give me your jacket.

ALVARO:
He took down my license number!

SERAFINA:
People are always taking down license numbers and telephone numbers and numbers that don't mean nothing—all them numbers . . .

ALVARO:

Three, three dependents! Not citizens, even! No relief checks, no nothing! [*Serafina sobs.*] He is going to complain to the boss.

SERAFINA:

I wanted to cry all day.

ALVARO:

He said he would fire me if I don't stop fighting!

SERAFINA:

Stop crying so I can stop crying.

ALVARO:

I am a sissy. Excuse me. I am ashame.

SERAFINA:

Don't be ashame of nothing, the world is too crazy for people to be ashame in it. I'm not ashame and I had two fights on the street and my daughter called me "disgusting." I got to sew this by hand; the machine is broke in a fight with two women.

ALVARO:

That's what—they call a cat fight . . . [*He blows his nose.*]

SERAFINA:

Open the shutters, please, for me. I can't see to work. [*She has crossed to her work table. He goes over to the window. As he opens the shutters, the light falls across his fine torso, the undershirt clinging wetly to his dark olive skin. Serafina is struck and murmurs: "Ohhh . . ." There is the sound of music.*]

ALVARO:

What, lady?

SERAFINA [*in a strange voice*]:
The light on the body was like a man that lived here . . .

ALVARO:
Che dice?

SERAFINA:
Niente.—Ma com'è strano!—Lei è Napoletano? [*She is threading a needle.*]

ALVARO:
Io sono Siciliano! [*Serafina sticks her finger with her needle and cries out.*] Che fa?

SERAFINA:
I—stuck myself with the—needle!—You had—better wash up . . .

ALVARO:
Dov'è il gabinetto?

SERAFINA [*almost inaudibly*]:
Dietro. [*She points vaguely back.*]

ALVARO:
Con permesso! [*He moves past her. As he does so, she picks up a pair of broken spectacles on the work table. Holding them up by the single remaining side piece, like a lorgnette, she inspects his passing figure with an air of stupefaction. As he goes out, he says:*] A kick like that can have serious consequences! [*He goes into the back of the house.*]

SERAFINA [*after a pause*]: Madonna Santa!—*My husband's body*, with the head of a *clown*! [*She crosses to the Madonna.*] O Lady, O Lady! [*She makes an imploring gesture.*] Speak to me!—What are you saying?—Please, Lady, I can't hear you! Is it a sign? Is it a sign of something?

What does it mean? Oh, *speak to me,* Lady!—Everything
is too strange!

[*She gives up the useless entreaty to the impassive statue.
Then she rushes to the cupboard, clambers up on a chair
and seizes a bottle of wine from the top shelf. But she
finds it impossible to descend from the chair. Clasping
the dusty bottle to her breast, she crouches there, helplessly whimpering like a child, as Alvaro comes back in.*]

ALVARO:
Ciao!

SERAFINA:
I can't get up.

ALVARO:
You mean you can't get down?

SERAFINA:
I mean I—can't get down . . .

ALVARO:
Con permesso, Signora! [*He lifts her down from the chair.*]

SERAFINA:
Grazie.

ALVARO:
I am ashame of what happen. Crying is not like a man.
Did anyone see me?

SERAFINA:
Nobody saw you but me. To me it don't matter.

ALVARO:
You are simpatica, molto!—It was not just the fight that
makes me break down. I was like this all today! [*He shakes
his clenched fists in the air.*]

SERAFINA:

You and—me, too!—What was the trouble today?

ALVARO:

My name is Mangiacavallo which means "Eat-a-horse."
It's a comical name, I know. Maybe two thousand and seventy years ago one of my grandfathers got so hungry that
he ate up a horse! That ain't my fault. Well, today at the
Southern Fruit Company I find on the pay envelope not
"Mangiacavallo" but "EAT A HORSE" in big print! Ha, ha,
ha, very funny!—I open the pay envelope! In it I find a
notice.—The wages have been *garnishee!* You know what
garnishee is? [*Serafina nods gravely.*] Garnishee!—Eat a
horse!—Road hog!—All in one day is too much! I go
crazy, I boil, I cry, and I am ashame but I am not able to
help it!—Even a Wop truck driver's a human being! And
human beings must cry . . .

SERAFINA:

Yes, they must cry. I couldn't cry all day but now I have
cried and I am feeling much better.—I will sew up the
jacket . . .

ALVARO [*licking his lips*]:

What is that in your hand? A bottle of vino?

SERAFINA:

This is Spumanti. It comes from the house of the family of
my husband. The Delle Rose! A very great family. I was a
peasant, but I married a baron!—No, I still don't believe it!
I married a baron when I didn't have shoes!

ALVARO:

Excuse me for asking—but where is the Baron, now? [*Serafina points gravely to the marble urn.*] Where did you say?

SERAFINA:

Them're his ashes in that marble urn.

ALVARO:

Ma! Scusatemi! Scusatemi! [*crossing himself*]—I hope he is resting in peace.

SERAFINA:

It's him you reminded me of—when you opened the shutters. Not the face but the body.—Please get me some ice from the icebox in the kitchen. I had a—very bad day . . .

ALVARO:

Oh, ice! Yes—ice—I'll get some . . . [*As he goes out, she looks again through the broken spectacles at him.*]

SERAFINA:

Non posso crederlo!—A clown of a face like that with my husband's body!

[*There is the sound of ice being chopped in the kitchen. She inserts a corkscrew in the bottle but her efforts to open it are clumsily unsuccessful. Alvaro returns with a little bowl of ice. He sets it down so hard on the table that a piece flies out. He scrambles after it, retrieves it and wipes it off on his sweaty undershirt.*]

SERAFINA:

I think the floor would be cleaner!

ALVARO:

Scusatemi!—I wash it again?

SERAFINA:

Fa niente!

ALVARO:

I am a—clean!—I . . .

SERAFINA:

Fa niente, niente!—The bottle should be in the ice but the next best thing is to pour the wine over the bottle.

ALVARO:
You mean over the ice?

SERAFINA:
I mean over the . . .

ALVARO:
Let me open the bottle. Your hands are not used to rough work. [*She surrenders the bottle to him and regards him through the broken spectacles again.*]

SERAFINA:
These little bits of white voile on the floor are not from a snowstorm. I been making voile dresses for high school graduation.—One for my daughter and for thirteen other girls.—All of the work I'm not sure didn't kill me!

ALVARO:
The wine will make you feel better.

[*There is a youthful cry from outside.*]

SERAFINA:
There is a wild bunch of boys and girls in this town. In Sicily the boys would dance with the boys because a girl and a boy could not dance together unless they was going to be married. But here they run wild on islands!—boys, girls, man-crazy teachers . . .

ALVARO:
Ecco! [*The cork comes off with a loud pop. Serafina cries out and staggers against the table. He laughs. She laughs with him, helplessly, unable to stop, unable to catch her breath.*]—I like a woman that laughs with all her heart.

SERAFINA:
And a woman that cries with her heart?

ALVARO:
I like everything that a woman does with her heart.

[*Both are suddenly embarrassed and their laughter dies
out. Serafina smooths down her rayon slip. He hands
her a glass of the sparkling wine with ice in it. She murmurs "Grazie."*]

[*Unconsciously the injured finger is lifted again to her
lip and she wanders away from the table with the glass
held shakily.*]

ALVARO [*continuing nervously*]:
I see you had a bad day.

SERAFINA:
Sono così—stanca . . .

ALVARO [*suddenly springing to the window and shouting*]:
Hey, you kids, git down off that truck! Keep your hands
off them bananas! [*At the words "truck" and "bananas"
Serafina gasps again and spills some wine on her slip.*]
Little buggers!—Scusatemi . . .

SERAFINA:
You haul—you haul bananas?

ALVARO:
Si, Signora.

SERAFINA:
Is it a 10-ton truck?

ALVARO:
An 8-ton truck.

SERAFINA:
My husband hauled bananas in a 10-ton truck.

ALVARO:
Well, he was a baron.

SERAFINA:
Do you haul just bananas?

ALVARO:
Just bananas. What else would I haul?

SERAFINA:
My husband hauled bananas, but underneath the bananas was something else. He was—wild like a—Gypsy.—"Wild —like a—Gypsy?" Who said that?—I hate to start to remember, and then not remember . . .

[*The dialogue between them is full of odd hesitations, broken sentences and tentative gestures. Both are nervously exhausted after their respective ordeals. Their fumbling communication has a curious intimacy and sweetness, like the meeting of two lonely children for the first time. It is oddly luxurious to them both, luxurious as the first cool wind of evening after a scorching day. Serafina idly picks up a little Sicilian souvenir cart from a table.*]

SERAFINA:
The priest was against it.

ALVARO:
What was the priest against?

SERAFINA:
Me keeping the ashes. It was against the Church law. But I had to have something and that was all I could have. [*She sets down the cart.*]

ALVARO:
I don't see nothing wrong with it.

SERAFINA:
You don't?

ALVARO:

No! Niente!—The body would've decayed, but ashes always stay clean.

SERAFINA [*eagerly*]:

Si, si, bodies decay, but ashes always stay clean! Come here. I show you this picture—my wedding. [*She removes a picture tenderly from the wall.*] Here's me a bride of fourteen, and this—this—*this!* [*drumming the picture with her finger and turning her face to Alvaro with great lustrous eyes*] My husband! [*There is a pause. He takes the picture from her hand and holds it first close to his eyes, then far back, then again close with suspirations of appropriate awe.*] Annnh?—Annnnh?—Che dice!

ALVARO [*slowly, with great emphasis*]:

Che bell' uomo! Che bell' uomo!

SERAFINA [*replacing the picture*]:

A rose of a man. On his chest he had the tattoo of a rose. [*then, quite suddenly*]—Do you believe strange things, or do you doubt them?

ALVARO:

If strange things didn't happen, I wouldn't be here. You wouldn't be here. We wouldn't be talking together.

SERAFINA:

Davvero! I'll tell you something about the tattoo of my husband. My husband, he had this rose tattoo on his chest. One night I woke up with a burning pain on me here. I turn on the light. I look at my naked breast and on it I see the rose tattoo of my husband, on me, on *my* breast, *his* tattoo.

ALVARO:

Strano!

101

SERAFINA:

And that was the night that—I got to speak frankly to tell you . . .

ALVARO:

Speak frankly! We're grown-up people.

SERAFINA:

That was the night I conceived my son—the little boy that was lost when I lost my husband . . .

ALVARO:

Che cosa—strana!—Would you be willing to show me the rose tattoo?

SERAFINA:

Oh, it's gone now, it only lasted a moment. But I did see it. I saw it clearly.—Do you believe me?

ALVARO:

Lo credo!

SERAFINA:

I don't know why I told you. But I like what you said. That bodies decay but ashes always stay clean—immacolate!—But, you know, there are some people that want to make everything dirty. Two of them kind of people come in the house today and told me a terrible lie in front of the ashes.—So awful a lie that if I thought it was true—I would smash the urn—and throw the ashes away! [*She hurls her glass suddenly to the floor.*] Smash it, *smash it like that!*

ALVARO:

Ma!—Baronessa!

[*Serafina seizes a broom and sweeps the fragments of glass away.*]

SERAFINA:

And take this broom and sweep them out the back door like so much trash!

ALVARO [*impressed by her violence and a little awed*]:
What lie did they tell you?

SERAFINA:

No, no, no! I don't want to talk about it! [*She throws down the broom.*] I just want to forget it; it wasn't true, it was false, false, false!—as the hearts of the bitches that told it . . .

ALVARO:

Yes. I would forget anything that makes you unhappy.

SERAFINA:

The memory of a love don't make you unhappy unless you believe a lie that makes it dirty. I don't believe in the lie. The ashes are clean. The memory of the rose in my heart is perfect!—Your glass is weeping . . .

ALVARO:

Your glass is weeping too.

[*While she fills his glass, he moves about the room, looking here and there. She follows him. Each time he picks up an article for inspection she gently takes it from him and examines it herself with fresh interest.*]

ALVARO:

Cozy little homelike place you got here.

SERAFINA:

Oh, it's—molto modesto.—You got a nice place too?

ALVARO:

I got a place with three dependents in it.

SERAFINA:
What—dependents?

ALVARO [*counting them on his fingers*]:
One old maid sister, one feeble-minded grandmother, one
lush of a pop that's not worth the powder it takes to blow
him to hell.—They got the parchesi habit. They play the
game of parchesi, morning, night, noon. Passing a bucket
of beer around the table . . .

SERAFINA:
They got the beer habit, too?

ALVARO:
Oh, yes. And the numbers habit. This spring the old maid
sister gets female trouble—mostly mental, I think—she turns
the housekeeping over to the feeble-minded grandmother,
a very sweet old lady who don't think it is necessary to pay
the grocery bill so long as there's money to play the numbers. She plays the numbers. She has a perfect system except it don't ever work. And the grocery bill goes up, up,
up, up, up!—so high you can't even see it!—Today the
Ideal Grocery Company garnishees my wages . . . There,
now! I've told you my life . . . [*The parrot squawks. He
goes over to the cage.*] Hello, Polly, how's tricks?

SERAFINA:
The name ain't Polly. It ain't a she; it's a he.

ALVARO:
How can you tell with all them tail feathers? [*He sticks
his finger in the cage, pokes at the parrot and gets bitten.*]
Owww!

SERAFINA [*vicariously*]:
Ouuu . . . [*Alvaro sticks his injured finger in his mouth.
Serafina puts her corresponding finger in her mouth. He*

104

crosses to the telephone.] I told you watch out.—What are you calling, a doctor?

ALVARO:

I am calling my boss in Biloxi to explain why I'm late.

SERAFINA:

The call to Biloxi is a ten-cent call.

ALVARO:

Don't worry about it.

SERAFINA:

I'm not worried about it. You will pay it.

ALVARO:

You got a sensible attitude toward life . . . Give me the Southern Fruit Company in Biloxi—seven-eight-seven!

SERAFINA:

You are a bachelor. With three dependents? [*She glances below his belt.*]

ALVARO:

I'll tell you my hopes and dreams!

SERAFINA:

Who? Me?

ALVARO:

I am hoping to meet some sensible older lady. Maybe a lady a little bit older than me.—I don't care if she's a little too plump or not such a stylish dresser! [*Serafina self-consciously pulls up a dangling strap.*] The important thing in a lady is understanding. Good sense. And I want her to have a well-furnished house and a profitable little business of some kind . . . [*He looks about him significantly.*]

SERAFINA:

And such a lady, with a well-furnished house and business, what does she want with a man with three dependents with the parchesi and the beer habit, playing the numbers!

ALVARO:

Love and affection!—in a world that is lonely—and cold!

SERAFINA:

It might be lonely but I would not say "cold" on this particular day!

ALVARO:

Love and affection is what I got to offer on hot or cold days in this lonely old world and is what I am looking for. I got nothing else. Mangiacavallo has nothing. In fact, he is the grandson of the village idiot of Ribera!

SERAFINA [*uneasily*]:
I see you like to make—jokes!

ALVARO:

No, no joke!—Davvero!—He chased my grandmother in a flooded rice field. She slip on a wet rock.—Ecco! Here I am.

SERAFINA:
You ought to be more respectful.

ALVARO:

What have I got to respect? The rock my grandmother slips on?

SERAFINA:
Yourself at least! Don't you work for a living?

ALVARO:

If I *don't* work for a living I would respect myself *more*. Baronessa, I am a healthy young man, existing without no love life. I look at the magazine pictures. Them girls in the advertisement—you know what I mean? A little bitty thing here? A little bitty thing there?

[*He touches two portions of his anatomy. The latter portion embarrasses Serafina, who quietly announces:*]

SERAFINA:
The call is ten cents for three minutes. Is the line busy?

ALVARO:
Not the line, but the boss.

SERAFINA:
And the charge for the call goes higher. That ain't the phone of a millionaire you're using!

ALVARO:
I think you talk a poor mouth. [*He picks up the piggy bank and shakes it.*] This pig sounds well-fed to me.

SERAFINA:
Dimes and quarters.

ALVARO:
Dimes and quarters're better than nickels and dimes. [*Serafina rises severely and removes the piggy bank from his grasp.*] Ha, ha, ha! You think I'm a bank robber?

SERAFINA:
I think you are maleducato! Just get your boss on the phone or hang the phone up.

ALVARO:
What, what! Mr. Siccardi? How tricks at the Southern Fruit Comp'ny this hot afternoon? Ha, ha, ha!—Mangia-cavallo!—What? You got the complaint already? Sentite, per favore! This road hog was—Mr. Siccardi? [*He jiggles the hook; then slowly hangs up.*] A man with three dependents!—out of a job . . . [*There is a pause.*]

SERAFINA:

Well, you better ask the operator the charges.

ALVARO:

Oofla! A man with three dependents—out of a job!

SERAFINA:

I can't see to work no more. I got a suggestion to make. Open the bottom drawer of that there bureau and you will find a shirt in white tissue paper and you can wear that one while I am fixing this. And call for it later. [*He crosses to the bureau.*]—It was made for somebody that never called for it. [*He removes the package.*] Is there a name pinned to it?

ALVARO:

Yes, it's . . .

SERAFINA [*fiercely, but with no physical movement*]:

Don't tell me the name! Throw it away, out the window!

ALVARO:

Perchè?

SERAFINA:

Throw it, throw it away!

ALVARO [*crumpling the paper and throwing it through the window*]:

Ecco fatto! [*There is a distant cry of children as he unwraps the package and holds up the rose silk shirt, exclaiming in Latin delight at the luxury of it.*] Colore di rose! Seta! Seta pura!—Oh, this shirt is too good for Mangiacavallo! Everything here is too good for Mangiacavallo!

SERAFINA:

Nothing's too good for a man if the man is good.

ALVARO:

The grandson of a village idiot is not that good.

SERAFINA:
No matter whose grandson you are, put it on; you are welcome to wear it.

ALVARO [*slipping voluptuously into the shirt*]:
Ssssssss!

SERAFINA:
How does it feel, the silk, on you?

ALVARO:
It feels like a girl's hands on me! [*There is a pause, while
he shows her the whiteness of his teeth.*]

SERAFINA [*holding up her broken spectacles*]:
It will make you less trouble.

ALVARO:
There is nothing more beautiful than a gift between people!
—Now you are smiling!—You like me a little bit better?

SERAFINA [*slowly and tenderly*]:
You know what they should of done when you was a
baby? They should of put tape on your ears to hold them
back so when you grow up they wouldn't stick out like the
wings of a little kewpie! [*She touches his ear, a very slight
touch, betraying too much of her heart. Both laugh a little
and she turns away, embarrassed.*]

[*Outside the goat bleats and there is the sound of splintering timber. One of the children races into the front
yard, crying out.*]

SALVATORE:
Mizz' Dell' Rose! The black goat's in your yard!

SERAFINA:
Il becco della strega!

109

[*Serafina dashes to the window, throws the shutters violently open and leans way out. This time, she almost feels relief in this distraction. The interlude of the goat chase has a quality of crazed exaltation. Outside is heard the wild bleating of the goat and the jingling of his harness.*]

SERAFINA:
Miei pomodori! Guarda i miei pomodori!

THE STREGA [*entering the front yard with a broken length of rope, calling out*]:
Heyeh, Billy! Heyeh. Heyeh, Billy!

SERAFINA [*making the sign of horns with her fingers*]:
There is the Strega! She lets the goat in my yard to eat my tomatoes! [*backing from the window*] She has the eye; she has the malocchio, and so does the goat! The goat has the evil eye, too. He got in my yard the night that I lost Rosario and my boy! Madonna, Madonna mia! Get that goat out of my yard! [*She retreats to the Madonna, making the sign of the horns with her fingers, while the goat chase continues outside.*]

ALVARO:
Now take it easy! I will catch the black goat and give him a kick that he will never forget!

[*Alvaro runs out the front door and joins in the chase. The little boy is clapping together a pair of tin pan lids which sound like cymbals. The effect is weird and beautiful with the wild cries of the children and the goat's bleating. Serafina remains anxiously half way between the shutters and the protecting Madonna. She gives a furious imitation of the bleating goat, contorting her face with loathing. It is the fury of woman at the desire she suffers. At last the goat is captured.*]

110

BRUNO:
Got him, got him, got him!

ALVARO:
Vieni presto, Diavolo!

[*Alvaro appears around the side of the house with a tight hold on the broken rope around the goat's neck. The boy follows behind, gleefully clapping the tin lids together, and further back follows the Strega, holding her broken length of rope, her grey hair hanging into her face and her black skirts caught up in one hand, revealing bare feet and hairy legs. Serafina comes out on the porch as the grotesque little procession passes before it, and she raises her hand with the fingers making horns as the goat and the Strega pass her. Alvaro turns the goat over to the Strega and comes panting back to the house.*]

ALVARO:
Niente paura!—I got to go now.—You have been troppo gentile, Mrs. . . .

SERAFINA:
I am the widow of the Baron Delle Rose.—Excuse the way I'm—not dressed . . . [*He keeps hold of her hand as he stands on the porch steps. She continues very shyly, panting a little.*] I am not always like this.—Sometimes I fix myself up!—When my husband was living, when my husband comes home, when he was living—I had a clean dress on! And sometimes even, I—put a rose in my hair . . .

ALVARO:
A rose in your hair would be pretty!

SERAFINA:
But for a widow—it ain't the time of roses . . .

111

[*The sound of music is heard, of a mandolin playing.*]

ALVARO:

Naw, you make a mistake! It's always for everybody the time of roses! The rose is the heart of the world like the heart is the—heart of the—body! But you, Baronessa—you know what I think you have done?

SERAFINA:

What—what have I—done?

ALVARO:

You have put your heart in the marble urn with the ashes. [*Now singing is heard along with the music, which continues to the end of the scene.*] And if in a storm sometime, or sometime when a 10-ton truck goes down the highway —the marble urn was to *break*! [*He suddenly points up at the sky.*] Look! Look, Baronessa!

SERAFINA [*startled*]:

Look? Look? I don't see!

ALVARO:

I was pointing at your heart, broken out of the urn and away from the ashes!—*Rondinella felice!* [*He makes an airy gesture toward the fading sky.*]

SERAFINA:

Oh! [*He whistles like a bird and makes graceful winglike motions with his hands.*] Buffone, buffone—piantatela! I take you serious—then you make it a joke . . . [*She smiles involuntarily at his antics.*]

ALVARO:

When can I bring the shirt back?

SERAFINA:

When do you pass by again?

ALVARO:

I will pass by tonight for supper. Volete?

SERAFINA:

Then look at the window tonight. If the shutters are open
and there is a light in the window, you can stop by for your
—jacket—but if the shutters are closed, you better not stop
because my Rosa will be home. Rosa's my daughter. She has
gone to a picnic—maybe—home early—but you know how
picnics are. They—wait for the moon to—start singing.—
Not that there's nothing wrong in two grown-up people
having a quiet conversation!—but Rosa's fifteen—I got to
be careful to set her a perfect example.

ALVARO:

I will look at the window.—I will look at the win-dooow!
[*He imitates a bird flying off with gay whistles.*]

SERAFINA:

Buffone!

ALVARO [*shouting from outside*]:

Hey, you little buggers, climb down off that truck! Lay
offa them bananas!

[*His truck is heard starting and pulling away. Serafina
stands motionless on the porch, searching the sky with
her eyes.*]

SERAFINA:

Rosario, forgive me! Forgive me for thinking the awful lie
could be true!

[*The light in the house dims out. A little boy races into
the yard holding triumphantly aloft a great golden bunch
of bananas. A little girl pursues him with shrill cries. He
eludes her. They dash around the house. The light fades
and the curtain falls.*]

113

ACT THREE

It is the evening of the same day. The neighborhood chil-
dren are playing games around the house. One of them is
counting by fives to a hundred, calling out the numbers, as
he leans against the palm tree.

Serafina is in the parlor, sitting on the sofa. She is seated
stiffly and formally, wearing a gown that she has not worn
since the death of her husband, and with a rose in her hair.
It becomes obvious from her movements that she is wear-
ing a girdle that constricts her unendurably.

[*There is the sound of a truck approaching up on the*
highway. Serafina rises to an odd, crouching position.
But the truck passes by without stopping. The girdle is
becoming quite intolerable to Serafina and she decides
to take it off, going behind the sofa to do so. With much
grunting, she has gotten it down as far as her knees,
when there is the sound outside of another truck ap-
proaching. This time the truck stops up on the highway,
with a sound of screeching brakes. She realizes that
Alvaro is coming, and her efforts to get out of the girdle,
which is now pinioning her legs, become frantic. She
hobbles from behind the sofa as Alvaro appears in front
of the house.]

ALVARO [*gaily*]:
Rondinella felice! I will look at win-dooooo! Signora delle
Rose!

[*Serafina's response to this salutation is a groan of an-*
guish. She hobbles and totters desperately to the curtains
between the rooms and reaches them just in time to hide

*herself as Alvaro comes into the parlor from the porch
through the screen door. He is carrying a package and a
candy box.*]

ALVARO:

C'è nessuno?

SERAFINA [*at first inaudibly*]:

Si, si, sono qui. [*then loudly and hoarsely, as she finally
gets the girdle off her legs*] Si, si, sono qui! [*To cover her
embarrassment, she busies herself with fixing wine glasses
on a tray.*]

ALVARO:

I hear the rattle of glasses! Let me help you! [*He goes
eagerly through the curtain but stops short, astonished.*]

SERAFINA:

Is—something the—matter?

ALVARO:

I didn't expect to see you looking so pretty! You are a
young little widow!

SERAFINA:

You are—fix yourself up . . .

ALVARO:

I been to The Ideal Barber's! I got the whole works!

SERAFINA [*faintly, retreating from him a little*]:

You got—rose oil—in your hair . . .

ALVARO:

Olio di rose! You like the smell of it? [*Outside there is a
wild, distant cry of children, and inside a pause. Serafina
shakes her head slowly with the infinite wound of a recollection.*]—You—*don't*—like—the smell of it? Oh, then I
wash the smell *out*, I go and . . . [*He starts toward the
back. She raises her hand to stop him.*]

116

SERAFINA:

No, no, no, fa—niente.—I—*like* the smell of it . . .

[*A little boy races into the yard, ducks some invisible missile, sticks out his tongue and yells: "Yahhhhh!" Then he dashes behind the house.*]

SERAFINA:

Shall we—set down in the parlor?

ALVARO:

I guess that's better than standing up in the dining room. [*He enters formally.*]—Shall we set down on the sofa?

SERAFINA:

You take the sofa. I will set down on this chair.

ALVARO [*disappointed*]:

You don't like to set on a sofa?

SERAFINA:

I lean back too far on that sofa. I like a straight back behind me . . .

ALVARO:

That chair looks not comfortable to me.

SERAFINA:

This chair is a comfortable chair.

ALVARO:

But it's more easy to talk with two on a sofa!

SERAFINA:

I talk just as good on a chair as I talk on a sofa . . . [*There is a pause. Alvaro nervously hitches his shoulder.*] Why do you hitch your shoulders like that?

ALVARO:

Oh, that!—That's a—nervous—habit . . .

117

SERAFINA:

I thought maybe the suit don't fit you good . . .

ALVARO:

I bought this suit to get married in four years ago.

SERAFINA:

But didn't get married?

ALVARO:

I give her, the girl, a zircon instead of a diamond. She had it examined. The door was slammed in my face.

SERAFINA:

I think that maybe I'd do the same thing myself.

ALVARO:

Buy the zircon?

SERAFINA:

No, slam the door.

ALVARO:

Her eyes were not sincere looking. You've got sincere looking eyes. Give me your hand so I can tell your fortune! [*She pushes her chair back from him.*] I see two men in your life. One very handsome. One not handsome. His ears are too big but not as big as his heart! He has three dependents.—In fact he has four dependents! Ha, ha, ha!

SERAFINA:

What is the fourth dependent?

ALVARO:

The one that every man's got, his biggest expense, worst troublemaker and chief liability! Ha, ha, ha!

SERAFINA:

I hope you are not talking vulgar. [*She rises and turns her back to him. Then she discovers the candy box.*] What's that fancy red box?

ALVARO:

A present I bought for a nervous but nice little lady!

SERAFINA:

Chocolates? Grazie! Grazie! But I'm too fat.

ALVARO:

You are not fat, you are just pleasing and plump. [*He reaches way over to pinch the creamy flesh of her upper arm.*]

SERAFINA:

No, please. Don't make me nervous. If I get nervous again I will start to cry . . .

ALVARO:

Let's talk about something to take your mind off your troubles. You say you got a young daughter?

SERAFINA [*in a choked voice*]:
Yes. I got a young daughter. Her name is Rosa.

ALVARO:

Rosa, Rosa! She's pretty?

SERAFINA:

She has the eyes of her father, and his wild, stubborn blood! Today was the day of her graduation from high school. She looked so pretty in a white voile dress with a great big bunch of—roses . . .

ALVARO:

Not no prettier than her Mama, I bet—with that rose in your hair!

SERAFINA:

She's only fifteen.

ALVARO:

Fifteen?

119

SERAFINA [*smoothing her blue silk lap with a hesitant hand*]:
Yes, only fifteen . . .

ALVARO:
But has a boyfriend, does she?

SERAFINA:
She met a sailor.

ALVARO:
Oh, Dio! No wonder you seem to be nervous.

SERAFINA:
I didn't want to let her go out with this sailor. He had a gold ring in his ear.

ALVARO:
Madonna Santa!

SERAFINA:
This morning she cut her wrist—not much but enough to bleed—with a kitchen knife!

ALVARO:
Tch, tch! A very wild girl!

SERAFINA:
I had to give in and let her bring him to see me. He said he was Catholic. I made him kneel down in front of Our Lady there and give Her his promise that he would respect the innocence of my Rosa!—But how do I know that he was a Catholic, *really*?

ALVARO [*taking her hand*]:
Poor little worried lady! But you got to face facts. Sooner or later the innocence of your daughter cannot be respected. —Did he—have a—tattoo?

120

SERAFINA [*startled*]:
Did who have—what?

ALVARO:
The sailor friend of your daughter, did he have a tattoo?

SERAFINA:
Why do you ask me that?

ALVARO:
Just because most sailors have a tattoo.

SERAFINA:
How do I know if he had a tattoo or not!

ALVARO:
I got a tattoo!

SERAFINA:
You got a tattoo?

ALVARO:
Si, si, veramente!

SERAFINA:
What kind of tattoo you got?

ALVARO:
What kind you think?

SERAFINA:
Oh, I think—you have got—a South Sea girl without clothes
on . . .

ALVARO:
No South Sea girl.

SERAFINA:
Well, maybe a big red heart with MAMA written across it.

ALVARO:
Wrong again, Baronessa.

121

[*He takes off his tie and slowly unbuttons his shirt, gazing at her with an intensely warm smile. He divides the unbuttoned shirt, turning toward her his bare chest. She utters a gasp and rises.*]

SERAFINA:

No, no, no!—*Not a rose!* [*She says it as if she were evading her feelings.*]

ALVARO:

Si, si, una rosa!

SERAFINA:

I—don't feel good! The air is . . .

ALVARO:

Che fate, che fate, che dite?

SERAFINA:

The house has a tin roof on it!—The air is—I got to go outside the house to breathe! Scu—scusatemi! [*She goes out onto the porch and clings to one of the spindling porch columns for support, breathing hoarsely with a hand to her throat. He comes out slowly.*]

ALVARO [*gently*]:

I didn't mean to surprise you!—Mi dispiace molto!

SERAFINA [*with enforced calm*]:

Don't—talk about it! Anybody could have a rose tattoo.—It don't mean nothing.—You know how a tin roof is. It catches the heat all day and it don't cool off until—midnight . . .

ALVARO:

No, no, not until midnight. [*She makes a faint laughing sound, is quite breathless and leans her forehead against the porch column. He places his fingers delicately against the*

122

small of her back.] It makes it hot in the bedroom—so that you got to sleep without nothing on you . . .

SERAFINA:
No, you—can't stand the covers . . .

ALVARO:
You can't even stand a—*nightgown!* [*His fingers press her back.*]

SERAFINA:
Please. There is a strega next door; she's always watching!

ALVARO:
It's been so long since I felt the soft touch of a woman! [*She gasps loudly and turns to the door.*] Where are you going?

SERAFINA:
I'm going back in the house! [*She enters the parlor again, still with forced calm.*]

ALVARO [*following her inside*]:
Now, now, what is the matter?

SERAFINA:
I got a feeling like I have—forgotten something.

ALVARO:
What?

SERAFINA:
I can't remember.

ALVARO:
It couldn't be nothing important if you can't remember. Let's open the chocolate box and have some candy.

SERAFINA [*eager for any distraction*]:
Yes! Yes, open the box!

123

[*Alvaro places a chocolate in her hand. She stares at it blankly.*]

ALVARO:
Eat it, eat the chocolate. If you don't eat it, it will melt in your hand and make your fingers all gooey!

SERAFINA:
Please, I . . .

ALVARO:
Eat it!

SERAFINA [*weakly and gagging*]:
I can't, I can't, I would choke! Here, you eat it.

ALVARO:
Put it in my mouth! [*She puts the chocolate in his mouth.*] Now, look. Your fingers are gooey!

SERAFINA:
Oh!—I better go wash them! [*She rises unsteadily. He seizes her hands and licks her fingers.*]

ALVARO:
Mmmm! Mmmmm! Good, very good!

SERAFINA:
Stop that, stop that, stop that! That—ain't—nice . . .

ALVARO:
I'll lick off the chocolate for you.

SERAFINA:
No, no, no!—I am the mother of a fifteen-year-old girl!

ALVARO:
You're as old as your arteries, Baronessa. Now set back down. The fingers are now white as snow!

124

SERAFINA:

You don't—understand—how I feel . . .

ALVARO:

You don't understand how *I* feel.

SERAFINA [*doubtfully*]:

How do you—feel? [*In answer, he stretches the palms of his hands out toward her as if she were a fireplace in a freezing-cold room.*]—What does—*that*—mean?

ALVARO:

The night is warm but I feel like my hands are—freezing!

SERAFINA:

Bad—circulation . . .

ALVARO:

No, too *much* circulation! [*Alvaro becomes tremulously pleading, shuffling forward a little, slightly crouched like a beggar.*] Across the room I feel the sweet warmth of a lady!

SERAFINA [*retreating, doubtfully*]:

Oh, you talk a sweet mouth. I think you talk a sweet mouth to fool a woman.

ALVARO:

No, no, I know—I know that's what warms the world, that is what makes it the summer! [*He seizes the hand she hold defensively before her and presses it to his own breast in a crushing grip.*] Without it, the rose—the rose would not grow on the bush; the fruit would not grow on the tree!

SERAFINA:

I know, and the truck—the truck would not haul the bananas! But, Mr. Mangiacavallo, that is my hand, not a sponge. I got bones in it. Bones break!

ALVARO:

Scusatemi, Baronessa! [*He returns her hand to her with a bow.*] For me it is winter, because I don't have in my life the sweet warmth of a lady. I live with my hands in my pockets! [*He stuffs his hands violently into his pants' pockets, then jerks them out again. A small cellophane-wrapped disk falls on the floor, escaping his notice, but not Serafina's.*]—You don't like the poetry!—How can a man talk to you?

SERAFINA [*ominously*]:

I like the poetry good. Is that a piece of the poetry that you dropped out of your pocket? [*He looks down.*]—No, no, right by your foot!

ALVARO [*aghast as he realizes what it is that she has seen*]:

Oh, that's—that's nothing! [*He kicks it under the sofa.*]

SERAFINA [*fiercely*]:

You talk a sweet mouth about women. Then drop such a thing from your pocket?—Va via, vigliacco! [*She marches grandly out of the room, pulling the curtains together behind her. He hangs his head despairingly between his hands. Then he approaches the curtains timidly.*]

ALVARO [*in a small voice*]:

Baronessa?

SERAFINA:

Pick up what you dropped on the floor and go to the Square Roof with it. Buona notte!

ALVARO:

Baronessa! [*He parts the curtains and peeks through them.*]

SERAFINA:

I told you good night. Here is no casa privata. Io, non sono puttana!

126

ALVARO:

Understanding is—very—necessary!

SERAFINA:

I understand plenty. You think you got a good thing, a thing that is cheap!

ALVARO:

You make a mistake, Baronessa! [*He comes in and drops to his knees beside her, pressing his cheek to her flank. He speaks rhapsodically.*] So soft is a lady! So, so, so, so, so *soft* —is a lady!

SERAFINA:

Andate via, sporcaccione, andate a casa! Lasciatemi! Lasciatemi stare!

[*She springs up and runs into the parlor. He pursues. The chase is grotesquely violent and comic. A floor lamp is overturned. She seizes the chocolate box and threatens to slam it into his face if he continues toward her. He drops to his knees, crouched way over, and pounds the floor with his fists, sobbing.*]

ALVARO:

Everything in my life turns out like this!

SERAFINA:

Git up, git up, git up!—you village idiot's grandson! There is people watching you through that window, the—strega next door . . . [*He rises slowly.*] And where is the shirt that I loaned you? [*He shuffles abjectly across the room, then hands her a neatly wrapped package.*]

ALVARO:

My sister wrapped it up for you.—My sister was very happy I met this *nice* lady!

127

SERAFINA:

Maybe she thinks I will pay the grocery bill while she plays the numbers!

ALVARO:

She don't think nothing like that. She is an old maid, my sister. She wants—nephews—nieces . . .

SERAFINA:

You tell her for me I don't give nephews and nieces!

[*Alvaro hitches his shoulders violently in his embarrassment and shuffles over to where he had left his hat. He blows the dust off it and rubs the crown on his sleeve. Serafina presses a knuckle to her lips as she watches his awkward gestures. She is a little abashed by his humility. She speaks next with the great dignity of a widow whose respectability has stood the test.*]

SERAFINA:

Now, Mr. Mangiacavallo, please tell me the truth about something. *When* did you get the tattoo put on your chest?

ALVARO [*shyly and sadly, looking down at his hat*]:
I got it tonight—after supper . . .

SERAFINA:

That's what I thought. You had it put on because I told you about my husband's tattoo.

ALVARO:

I wanted to be—close to you . . . to make you—happy . . .

SERAFINA:

Tell it to the marines! [*He puts on his hat with an apologetic gesture.*] You got the tattoo and the chocolate box after supper, and then you come here to fool me!

ALVARO:

I got the chocolate box a long time ago.

SERAFINA:

How long ago? If that is not too much a personal question!

ALVARO:

I got it the night the door was slammed in my face by the
girl that I give—the zircon . . .

SERAFINA:

Let that be a lesson. Don't try to fool women. You are not
smart enough!—Now take the shirt back. You can keep it.

ALVARO:

Huh?

SERAFINA:

Keep it. I don't want it back.

ALVARO:

You just now said that you did.

SERAFINA:

It's a man's shirt, ain't it?

ALVARO:

You just now accused me of trying to steal it off you.

SERAFINA:

Well, you been making me nervous!

ALVARO:

Is it my fault you been a widow too long?

SERAFINA:

You make a mistake!

ALVARO:

You make a mistake!

SERAFINA:

Both of us make a mistake!

[*There is a pause. They both sigh profoundly.*]

ALVARO:

We should of have been friends, but I think we meet the wrong day.—Suppose I go out and come in the door again and we start all over?

SERAFINA:

No, I think it's no use. The day was wrong to begin with, because of two women. Two women, they told me today that my husband had put on my head the nanny-goat's horns!

ALVARO:

How is it possible to put horns on a widow?

SERAFINA:

That was before, before! They told me my husband was having a steady affair with a woman at the Square Roof. What was the name on the shirt, on the slip of paper? Do you remember the name?

ALVARO:

You told me to . . .

SERAFINA:

Tell me! Do you remember?

ALVARO:

I remember the name because I know the woman. The name was Estelle Hohengarten.

SERAFINA:

Take me there! Take me to the Square Roof!—Wait, wait!

[*She plunges into the dining room, snatches a knife out of the sideboard drawer and thrusts it in her purse. Then she rushes back, with the blade of the knife protruding from the purse.*]

ALVARO [*noticing the knife*]:
They—got a cover charge there . . .

SERAFINA:
I will charge them a cover! Take me there now, this minute!

ALVARO:
The fun don't start till midnight.

SERAFINA:
I will start the fun sooner.

ALVARO:
The floor show commences at midnight.

SERAFINA:
I will commence it! [*She rushes to the phone.*] Yellow Cab, please, Yellow Cab. I want to go to the Square Roof out of my house! Yes, you come to my house and take me to the Square Roof right this minute! My number is—what is my number? Oh my God, what is my number?—64 is my number on Front Street! Subito, subito—quick!

[*The goat bleats outside.*]

ALVARO:
Baronessa, the knife's sticking out of your purse. [*He grabs the purse.*] What do you want with this weapon?

SERAFINA:
To cut the lying tongue out of a woman's mouth! Saying she has on her breast the tattoo of my husband because he had put on me the horns of a goat! I cut the heart out of that woman, she cut the heart out of me!

ALVARO:
Nobody's going to cut the heart out of nobody!

[*A car is heard outside, and Serafina rushes to the porch.*]

131

SERAFINA [*shouting*]:
Hey, Yellow Cab, Yellow Cab, Yellow—Cab . . . [*The car passes by without stopping. With a sick moan she wanders into the yard. He follows her with a glass of wine.*]—Something hurts—in my heart . . .

ALVARO [*leading her gently back to the house*]:
Baronessa, drink this wine on the porch and keep your eyes on that star. [*He leads her to a porch pillar and places the glass in her trembling hand. She is now submissive.*] You know the name of that star? That star is Venus. She is the only female star in the sky. Who put her up there? Mr. Siccardi, the transportation manager of the Southern Fruit Company? No. She was put there by God. [*He enters the house and removes the knife from her purse.*] And yet there's some people that don't believe in nothing. [*He picks up the telephone.*] Esplanade 9-7-0.

SERAFINA:
What are you doing?

ALVARO:
Drink that wine and I'll settle this whole problem for you. [*on the telephone*] I want to speak to the blackjack dealer, please, Miss Estelle Hohengarten . . .

SERAFINA:
Don't talk to that woman, she'll lie!

ALVARO:
Not Estelle Hohengarten. She deals a straight game of cards.—Estelle? This is Mangiacavallo. I got a question to ask you which is a personal question. It has to do with a very goodlooking truckdriver, not living now but once on a time thought to have been a very well-known character at the Square Roof. His name was . . . [*He turns ques-*

tioningly to the door where Serafina is standing.] What
was his name, Baronessa?

SERAFINA [*hardly breathing*]:
Rosario delle Rose!

ALVARO:
Rosario delle Rose was the name. [*There is a pause.*]—È
vero?—Mah! Che peccato ...

[*Serafina drops her glass and springs into the parlor with
a savage outcry. She snatches the phone from Alvaro and
screams into it.*]

SERAFINA [*wildly*]:
This is the wife that's speaking! What do you know of my
husband, what is the lie?

[*A strident voice sounds over the wire.*]

THE VOICE [*loud and clear*]:
Don't you remember? I brought you the rose-colored silk to
make him a shirt. You said, "For a man?" and I said, "Yes,
for a man that's wild like a Gypsy!" But if you think I'm a
liar, come here and let me show you his rose tattooed on
my chest!

[*Serafina holds the phone away from her as though it
had burst into flame. Then, with a terrible cry, she hurls
it to the floor. She staggers dizzily toward the Madonna.
Alvaro seizes her arm and pushes her gently onto the
sofa.*]

ALVARO:
Piano, piano, Baronessa! This will be gone, this will pass in
a moment. [*He puts a pillow behind her, then replaces the
telephone.*]

SERAFINA [*staggering up from the sofa*]:
The room's—going round . . .

ALVARO:
You ought to stay lying down a little while longer. I know,
I know what you need! A towel with some ice in it to put
on your forehead—Baronessa.—You stay right there while
I fix it! [*He goes into the kitchen, and calls back.*] Torno
subito, Baronessa!

[*The little boy runs into the yard. He leans against the
bending trunk of the palm, counting loudly.*]

THE LITTLE BOY:
Five, ten, fifteen, twenty, twenty-five, thirty . . .

[*There is the sound of ice being chopped in the kitchen.*]

SERAFINA:
Dove siete, dove siete?

ALVARO:
In cucina!—Ghiaccio . . .

SERAFINA:
Venite qui!

ALVARO:
Subito, subito . . .

SERAFINA [*turning to the shrine, with fists knotted*]:
Non voglio, non voglio farlo!

[*But she crosses slowly, compulsively toward the shrine,
with a trembling arm stretched out.*]

THE LITTLE BOY:
Seventy-five, eighty, eighty-five, ninety, ninety-five, one hundred! [*then, wildly*] *Ready or not you shall be caught!*

134

[*At this cry, Serafina seizes the marble urn and hurls it violently into the furthest corner of the room. Then, instantly, she covers her face. Outside the mothers are heard calling their children home. Their voices are tender as music, fading in and out. The children appear slowly at the side of the house, exhausted from their wild play.*]

GIUSEPPINA:
Vivi! Vi-vi!

PEPINA:
Salvatore!

VIOLETTA:
Bruno! Come home, come home!

[*The children scatter. Alvaro comes in with the ice-pick.*]

ALVARO:
I broke the point of the ice-pick.

SERAFINA [*removing her hands from her face*]:
I don't want ice . . . [*She looks about her, seeming to gather a fierce strength in her body. Her voice is hoarse, her body trembling with violence, eyes narrow and flashing, her fists clenched.*] Now I show you how wild and strong like a man a woman can be! [*She crosses to the screen door, opens it and shouts.*] Buona notte, Mr. Mangiacavallo!

ALVARO:
You—you make me go *home*, now?

SERAFINA:
No, no; senti, cretino! [*in a strident whisper*] You make out like you are going. You drive the truck out of sight where the witch can't see it. Then you come back and I leave the back door open for you to come in. Now, tell me good-bye so all the neighbors can hear you! [*She shouts.*] Arrivederci!

135

ALVARO:

Ha, ha! Capish! [*He shouts too.*] Arrivederci! [*He runs to the foot of the embankment steps.*]

SERAFINA [*still more loudly*]:
Buona notte!

ALVARO:
Buona notte, Baronessa!

SERAFINA [*in a choked voice*]:
Give them my love; give everybody—my love . . . Arrivederci!

ALVARO:
Ciao!

[*Alvaro scrambles on down the steps and goes off. Serafina comes down into the yard. The goat bleats. She mutters savagely to herself.*]

SERAFINA:
Sono una bestia, una bestia feroce!

[*She crosses quickly around to the back of the house. As she disappears, the truck is heard driving off; the lights sweep across the house. Serafina comes in through the back door. She is moving with great violence, gasping and panting. She rushes up to the Madonna and addresses her passionately with explosive gestures, leaning over so that her face is level with the statue's.*]

SERAFINA:
Ora, ascolta, Signora! You hold in the cup of your hand this little house and you smash it! You break this little house like the shell of a bird in your hand, because you have hate Serafina?—Serafina that *loved* you!—No, no, no, you don't speak! I don't believe in you, Lady! You're just

136

a poor little doll with the paint peeling off, and now I blow
out the light and I forget you the way you forget Serafina!
[*She blows out the vigil light.*] Ecco—fatto!

[*But now she is suddenly frightened; the vehemence
and boldness have run out. She gasps a little and backs
away from the shrine, her eyes rolling apprehensively this
way and that. The parrot squawks at her. The goat bleats.
The night is full of sinister noises, harsh bird cries, the
sudden flapping of wings in the cane-brake, a distant
shriek of Negro laughter. Serafina retreats to the window
and opens the shutters wider to admit the moonlight. She
stands panting by the window with a fist pressed to her
mouth. In the back of the house a door slams open. Serafina catches her breath and moves as though for protection behind the dummy of the bride. Alvaro enters
through the back door, calling out softly and hoarsely,
with great excitement.*]

ALVARO:
Dove? Dove sei, cara?

SERAFINA [*faintly*]:
Sono qui . . .

ALVARO:
You have turn out the light!

SERAFINA:
The moon is enough . . . [*He advances toward her. His
white teeth glitter as he grins. Serafina retreats a few steps
from him. She speaks tremulously, making an awkward
gesture toward the sofa.*] Now we can go on with our—
conversation . . . [*She catches her breath sharply.*]

[*The curtain comes down.*]

137

SCENE TWO

It is just before daybreak of the next day. Rosa and Jack appear at the top of the embankment steps.

ROSA:
I thought they would never leave. [*She comes down the steps and out in front of the house, then calls back to him.*] Let's go down there.

[*He obeys hesitatingly. Both are very grave. The scene is played as close as possible to the audience. She sits very straight. He stands behind her with his hands on her shoulders.*]

ROSA [*leaning her head back against him*]:
This was the happiest day of my life, and this is the saddest night . . . [*He crouches in front of her.*]

SERAFINA [*from inside the house*]:
Aaaaaahhhhhhhh!

JACK [*springing up, startled*]:
What's that?

ROSA [*resentfully*]:
Oh! That's Mama dreaming about my father.

JACK:
I—feel like a—*heel!* I feel like a rotten heel!

ROSA:
Why?

JACK:
That promise I made your mother.

ROSA:
I hate her for it.

JACK:
Honey—Rosa, she—wanted to protect you.

[*There is a long-drawn cry from the back of the house: "Ohhhh—Rosario!"*]

ROSA:
She wanted me not to have what she's dreaming about . . .

JACK:
Naw, naw, honey, she—wanted to—protect you . . .

[*The cry from within is repeated softly.*]

ROSA:
Listen to her making love in her sleep! Is that what she wants *me* to do, just—*dream* about it?

JACK [*humbly*]:
She knows that her Rosa *is* a rose. And she wants her rose to have someone—better than *me* . . .

ROSA:
Better than—*you!* [*She speaks as if the possibility were too preposterous to think of.*]

JACK:
You see me through—rose-colored—glasses . . .

ROSA:
I see you with love!

JACK:
Yes, but your Mama sees me with—common sense . . . [*Serafina cries out again.*] I got to be going! [*She keeps a tight hold on him. A rooster crows.*] Honey, it's so late the roosters are crowing!

139

ROSA:
They're fools, they're fools, it's early!

JACK:
Honey, on that island I almost forgot my promise. Almost, but not quite. Do you understand, honey?

ROSA:
Forget the promise!

JACK:
I made it on my knees in front of Our Lady. I've got to leave now, honey.

ROSA [*clasping him fiercely*]:
You'd have to break my arms to!

JACK:
Rosa, Rosa! You want to drive me crazy?

ROSA:
I want you not to remember.

JACK:
You're a very young girl! Fifteen—fifteen is too young!

ROSA:
Caro, caro, carissimo!

JACK:
You got to save some of those feelings for when you're grown up!

ROSA:
Carissimo!

JACK:
Hold some of it back until you're grown!

ROSA:
I have been grown for two years!

JACK:
No, no, that ain't what I . . .

ROSA:
Grown enough to be married, and have a—baby!

JACK [*springing up*]:
Oh, good—Lord! [*He circles around her, pounding his palm repeatedly with his fist and champing his teeth together with a grimace. Suddenly he speaks.*] I got to be going!

ROSA:
You want me to scream? [*He groans and turns away from her to resume his desperate circle. Rosa is blocking the way with her body.*]—I know, I know! You don't want me! [*Jack groans through his gritting teeth.*] No, no, you don't want me . . .

JACK:
Now you listen to me! You almost got into trouble today on that island! You almost did, but not quite!—But it didn't quite happen and no harm is done and you can just—forget it . . .

ROSA:
It is the only thing in my life that I want to remember!—When are you going back to New Orleans?

JACK:
Tomorrow.

ROSA:
When does your—ship sail?

JACK:
Tomorrow.

ROSA:
Where to?

JACK:
Guatemala.

SERAFINA [*from the house*]:
Aahh!

ROSA:
Is that a long trip?

JACK:
After Guatemala, Buenos Aires. After Buenos Aires, Rio.
Then around the Straits of Magellan and back up the west
coast of South America, putting in at three ports before we
dock at San Francisco.

ROSA:
I don't think I will—ever see you again . . .

JACK:
The ship won't sink!

ROSA [*faintly and forlornly*]:
No, but—I think it could just happen once, and if it don't
happen that time, it never can—later . . . [*A rooster crows.
They face each other sadly and quietly.*] You don't need
to be very old to understand how it works out. One time,
one time, only once, it could be—God!—to remember.—
Other times? Yes—they'd be something.—But only once,
God—to remember . . . [*With a little sigh she crosses to
pick up his white cap and hand it gravely to him.*]—I'm
sorry to you it didn't—mean—that much . . .

JACK [*taking the cap and hurling it to the ground*]:
Look! Look at my knuckles! You see them scabs on my
knuckles? You know how them scabs got there? They got

142

there because I banged my knuckles that hard on the deck of the sailboat!

ROSA:

Because it—didn't quite happen? [*Jack jerks his head up and down in grotesquely violent assent to her question. Rosa picks up his cap and returns it to him again.*]—Because of the promise to Mama! I'll never forgive her . . . [*There is a pause.*] What time in the afternoon must you be on the boat?

JACK:

Why?

ROSA:

Just tell me what time.

JACK:

Five!—Why?

ROSA:

What will you be doing till five?

JACK:

Well, I could be a goddam liar and tell you I was going to —pick me a hatful of daisies in—Audubon Park.—Is that what you want me to tell you?

ROSA:

No, tell me the truth.

JACK:

All right, I'll tell you the truth. I'm going to check in at some flea-bag hotel on North Rampart Street. Then I'm going to get loaded! And then I'm going to get . . . [*He doesn't complete the sentence but she understands him. She places the hat more becomingly on his blond head.*]

143

ROSA:

Do me a little favor. [*Her hand slides down to his cheek and then to his mouth.*] Before you get loaded and before you—before you—

JACK:

Huh?

ROSA:

Look in the waiting room at the Greyhound bus station, please. At twelve o'clock, noon!

JACK:

Why?

ROSA:

You might find me there, waiting for you . . .

JACK:

What—what good would that do?

ROSA:

I never been to a hotel but I know they have numbers on doors and sometimes—numbers are—lucky.—Aren't they? —Sometimes?—Lucky?

JACK:

You want to buy me a ten-year stretch in the brig?

ROSA:

I want you to give me that little gold ring on your ear to put on my finger.—I want to give you my heart to keep forever! And ever! And ever! [*Slowly and with a barely audible sigh she leans her face against him.*] Look for me! I will be there!

JACK [*breathlessly*]:

In all of my life, I never felt nothing so sweet as the feel of your little warm body in my arms . . .

[*He breaks away and runs toward the road. From the foot of the steps he glares fiercely back at her like a tiger through the bars of a cage. She clings to the two porch pillars, her body leaning way out.*]

ROSA:
Look for me! I will be there!

[*Jack runs away from the house. Rosa returns inside. Listlessly she removes her dress and falls on the couch in her slip, kicking off her shoes. Then she begins to cry, as one cries only once in a lifetime, and the scene dims out.*]

SCENE THREE

The time is three hours later.

We see first the exterior view of the small frame building against a night sky which is like the starry blue robe of Our Lady. It is growing slightly paler.

[*The faint light discloses Rosa asleep on the couch. The covers are thrown back for it has been a warm night, and on the concave surface of the white cloth, which is like the dimly lustrous hollow of a shell, is the body of the sleeping girl which is clad only in a sheer white slip.*

[*A cock crows. A gentle wind stirs the white curtains inward and the tendrils of vine at the windows, and the sky lightens enough to distinguish the purple trumpets of the morning glory against the very dim blue of the sky in which the planet Venus remains still undimmed.*

[*In the back of the cottage someone is heard coughing hoarsely and groaning in the way a man does who has drunk very heavily the night before. Bedsprings creak as a heavy figure rises. Light spills dimly through the curtains, now closed, between the two front rooms.*

[*There are heavy, padding footsteps and Alvaro comes stumbling rapidly into the dining room with the last bottle of Spumanti in the crook of an arm, his eyes barely open, legs rubbery, saying, "Wuh-wuh-wuh-wuh-wuh-wuh . . ." like the breathing of an old dog. The scene should be played with the pantomimic lightness, almost fantasy, of an early Chaplin comedy. He is wearing only his trousers and his chest is bare. As he enters he collides*

146

*with the widow dummy, staggers back, pats her inflated
bosom in a timid, apologetic way, remarking:*]

ALVARO:
Scusami, Signora, I am the grandson of the village idiot of
Ribera!

[*Alvaro backs into the table and is propelled by the im-
pact all the way to the curtained entrance to the parlor. He
draws the curtains apart and hangs onto them, peering
into the room. Seeing the sleeping girl, he blinks several
times, suddenly makes a snoring sound in his nostrils and
waves one hand violently in front of his eyes as if to dis-
pel a vision. Outside the goat utters a long "Baaaaaaa-
aaaa!" As if in response, Alvaro whispers, in the same
basso key, "Che bella!" The first vowel of "bella" is enor-
mously prolonged like the "baaa" of the goat. On his rubbery legs he shuffles forward a few steps and leans over to
peer more intently at the vision. The goat bleats again.
Alvaro whispers more loudly: "Che bel-la!" He drains
the Spumanti, then staggers to his knees, the empty bottle
rolling over the floor. He crawls on his knees to the foot
of the bed, then leans against it like a child peering into
a candy shop window, repeating: "Che bel-la, che
bel-la!" with antiphonal responses from the goat outside.
Slowly, with tremendous effort, as if it were the sheer side
of a precipice, he clambers upon the couch and crouches
over the sleeping girl in a leap-frog position, saying "Che
bel-la!" quite loudly, this time, in a tone of innocently
joyous surprise. All at once Rosa wakens. She screams,
even before she is quite awake, and springs from the couch
so violently that Alvaro topples over to the floor.*]

[*Serafina cries out almost instantly after Rosa. She lunges
through the dining room in her torn and disordered*

nightgown. At the sight of the man crouched by the couch a momentary stupefaction turns into a burst of savage fury. She flies at him like a great bird, tearing and clawing at his stupefied figure. With one arm Alvaro wards off her blows, plunging to the floor and crawling into the dining room. She seizes a broom with which she flails him about the head, buttocks and shoulders while he scrambles awkwardly away. The assault is nearly wordless. Each time she strikes at him she hisses: "Sporcaccione!" He continually groans: "Dough, dough, dough!" At last he catches hold of the widow dummy which he holds as a shield before him while he entreats the two women.]

ALVARO:

Senti, Baronessa! Signorina! I didn't know what I was doin', I was dreamin', I was just dreamin'! I got turn around in the house; I got all twisted! I thought that you was your Mama!—Sono ubriaco! Per favore!

ROSA [*seizing the broom*]:
That's enough, Mama!

SERAFINA [*rushing to the phone*]:
Police!

ROSA [*seizing the phone*]:
No, no, no, no, no, no!—You want everybody to know?

SERAFINA [*weakly*]:
Know?—Know *what,* cara?

ROSA:
Just give him his clothes, now, Mama, and let him get out! [*She is clutching a bedsheet about herself.*]

ALVARO:
Signorina—young lady! I swear I was *dreaming!*

148

SERAFINA:

Don't speak to my daughter! [*then, turning to Rosa*]— Who is this man? How did this man get here?

ROSA [*coldly*]:

Mama, don't say any more. Just give him his clothes in the bedroom so he can get out!

ALVARO [*still crouching*]:

I am so sorry, so sorry! I don't remember a thing but that I was dreaming!

SERAFINA [*shoving him toward the back of the room with her broom*]:

Go on, go get your clothes on, you—idiot's grandson, you! —Svelto, svelto, più svelto! [*Alvaro continues his apologetic mumbling in the back room.*] Don't talk to me, don't say nothing! Or I will kill you!

[*A few moments later Alvaro rushes around the side of the house, his clothes half buttoned and his shirt-tails out.*]

ALVARO:

But, Baronessa, I *love* you! [*A tea kettle sails over his head from behind the house. The Strega bursts into laughter. Despairingly Alvaro retreats, tucking his shirt-tails in and shaking his head.*] Baronessa, Baronessa, I love you!

[*As Alvaro runs off, the Strega is heard cackling:*]

THE STREGA'S VOICE:

The Wops are at it again. Had a truckdriver in the house all night!

[*Rosa is feverishly dressing. From the bureau she has snatched a shimmering white satin slip, disappearing for a moment behind a screen to put it on as Serafina comes*] *padding sheepishly back into the room, her nightgown now covered by a black rayon kimona sprinkled with poppies, her voice tremulous with fear, shame and apology.*]

ROSA [*behind the screen*]:
Has the man gone?

SERAFINA:
That—man?

ROSA:
Yes, "that man!"

SERAFINA [*inventing desperately*]:
I don't know how he got in. Maybe the back door was open.

ROSA:
Oh, yes, maybe it was!

SERAFINA:
Maybe he—climbed in a window . . .

ROSA:
Or fell down the chimney, maybe! [*She comes from behind the screen, wearing the white bridal slip.*]

SERAFINA:
Why you put on the white things I save for your wedding?

ROSA:
Because I want to. That's a good enough reason. [*She combs her hair savagely.*]

SERAFINA:
I want you to understand about that man. That was a man that—that was—that was a man that . . .

150

ROSA:

You can't think of a lie?

SERAFINA:

He was a—truckdriver, cara. He got in a fight, he was chase by—policemen!

ROSA:

They chased him into your bedroom?

SERAFINA:

I took pity on him, I give him first aid, I let him sleep on the floor. He give me his promise—he . . .

ROSA:

Did he kneel in front of Our Lady? Did he promise that he would respect your innocence?

SERAFINA:

Oh, cara, cara! [*abandoning all pretense*] He was Sicilian; he had rose oil in his hair and the rose tattoo of your father. In the dark room I couldn't see his clown face. I closed my eyes and dreamed that he was your father! I closed my eyes! I dreamed that he was your father . . .

ROSA:

Basta, basta, non voglio sentire più niente! The only thing worse than a liar is a liar that's also a hypocrite!

SERAFINA:

Senti, per favore! [*Rosa wheels about from the mirror and fixes her mother with a long and withering stare. Serafina cringes before it.*] Don't look at me like that with the eyes of your father! [*She shields her face as from a terrible glare.*]

151

ROSA:

Yes, I am looking at you with the eyes of my father. I see you the way *he* saw you. [*She runs to the table and seizes the piggy bank.*] Like this, this *pig!* [*Serafina utters a long, shuddering cry like a cry of childbirth.*] I need five dollars. I'll take it out of this! [*Rosa smashes the piggy bank to the floor and rakes some coins into her purse. Serafina stoops to the floor. There is the sound of a train whistle. Rosa is now fully dressed, but she hesitates, a little ashamed of her cruelty—but only a little. Serafina cannot meet her daughter's eyes. At last the girl speaks.*]

SERAFINA:

How beautiful—is my daughter! Go to the boy!

ROSA [*as if she might be about to apologize*]:
Mama? He didn't touch me—he just said—"Che bella!"

[*Serafina turns slowly, shamefully, to face her. She is like a peasant in the presence of a young princess. Rosa stares at her a moment longer, then suddenly catches her breath and runs out of the house. As the girl leaves, Serafina calls:*]

SERAFINA:

Rosa, Rosa, the—wrist watch! [*Serafina snatches up the little gift box and runs out onto the porch with it. She starts to call her daughter again, holding the gift out toward her, but her breath fails her.*] Rosa, Rosa, the—wrist watch . . . [*Her arms fall to her side. She turns, the gift still ungiven. Senselessly, absently, she holds the watch to her ear again. She shakes it a little, then utters a faint, startled laugh.*]

[*Assunta appears beside the house and walks directly in, as though Serafina had called her.*]

SERAFINA:

Assunta, the urn is broken. The ashes are spilt on the floor and I can't touch them.

[*Assunta stoops to pick up the pieces of the shattered urn. Serafina has crossed to the shrine and relights the candle before the Madonna.*]

ASSUNTA:

There are no ashes.

SERAFINA:

Where—where are they? Where have the ashes gone?

ASSUNTA [*crossing to the shrine*]:

The wind has blown them away.

[*Assunta places what remains of the broken urn in Serafina's hands. Serafina turns it tenderly in her hands and then replaces it on the top of the prie-dieu before the Madonna.*]

SERAFINA:

A man, when he burns, leaves only a handful of ashes. No woman can hold him. The wind must blow him away.

[*Alvaro's voice is heard, calling from the top of the highway embankment.*]

ALVARO'S VOICE:

Rondinella felice!

[*The neighborhood women hear Alvaro calling, and there is a burst of mocking laughter from some of them. Then they all converge on the house from different directions and gather before the porch.*]

PEPPINA:

Serafina delle Rose!

GIUSEPPINA:
Baronessa! Baronessa delle Rose!

PEPPINA:
There is a man on the road without the shirt!

GIUSEPPINA [*with delight*]:
Si, si! Senza camicia!

PEPPINA:
All he got on his chest is a rose tattoo! [*to the women*] She lock up his shirt so he can't go to the high school?

[*The women shriek with laughter. In the house Serafina snatches up the package containing the silk shirt, while Assunta closes the shutters of the parlor windows.*]

SERAFINA:
Un momento! [*She tears the paper off the shirt and rushes out onto the porch, holding the shirt above her head defiantly.*] Ecco la camicia!

[*With a soft cry, Serafina drops the shirt, which is immediately snatched up by Peppina. At this point the music begins again, with a crash of percussion, and continues to the end of the play. Peppina flourishes the shirt in the air like a banner and tosses it to Giuseppina, who is now on the embankment. Giuseppina tosses it on to Mariella, and she in her turn to Violetta, who is above her, so that the brilliantly colored shirt moves in a zig-zag course through the pampas grass to the very top of the embankment, like a streak of flame shooting up a dry hill. The women call out as they pass the shirt along:*]

PEPPINA:
Guardate questa camicia! Coloro di rose!

MARIELLA [*shouting up to Alvaro*]:
Corragio, signor!

GIUSEPPINA:
Avanti, avanti, signor!

VIOLETTA [*at the top of the embankment, giving the shirt a final flourish above her*]:
Corragio, corragio! The Baronessa is waiting!

[*Bursts of laughter are mingled with the cries of the women. Then they sweep away like a flock of screaming birds, and Serafina is left upon the porch, her eyes closed, a hand clasped to her breast. In the meanwhile, inside the house, Assunta has poured out a glass of wine. Now she comes to the porch, offering the wine to Serafina and murmuring:*]

ASSUNTA:
Stai tranquilla.

SERAFINA [*breathlessly*]:
Assunta, I'll tell you something that maybe you won't believe.

ASSUNTA [*with tender humor*]:
It is impossible to tell me anything that I don't believe.

SERAFINA:
Just now I felt on my breast the burning again of the rose. I know what it means. It means that I have conceived! [*She lifts the glass to her lips for a moment and then returns it to Assunta.*] Two lives again in the body! Two, two lives again, two!

ALVARO'S VOICE [*nearer now, and sweetly urgent*]:
Rondinella felice!

[*Alvaro is not visible on the embankment but Serafina begins to move slowly toward his voice.*]

ASSUNTA:
Dove vai, Serafina?

SERAFINA [*shouting now, to Alvaro*]:
Vengo, vengo, amore!

[*She starts up the embankment toward Alvaro and the curtain falls as the music rises with her in great glissandi of sound.*]

*CAMINO REAL**

"In the middle of the journey of our life
I came to myself in a dark wood where the
straight way was lost."

CANTO I, DANTE'S Inferno

*Use Anglicized pronunciation: *Cá*-mino *Ré*al

For Elia Kazan

FOREWORD*

It is amazing and frightening how completely one's whole being becomes absorbed in the making of a play. It is almost as if you were frantically constructing another world while the world that you live in dissolves beneath your feet, and that your survival depends on completing this construction at least one second before the old habitation collapses.

More than any other work that I have done, this play has seemed to me like the construction of another world, a separate existence. Of course, it is nothing more nor less than my conception of the time and world that I live in, and its people are mostly archetypes of certain basic attitudes and qualities with those mutations that would occur if they had continued along the road to this hypothetical terminal point in it.

A convention of the play is existence outside of time in a place of no specific locality. If you regard it that way, I suppose it becomes an elaborate allegory, but in New Haven we opened directly across the street from a movie theatre that was showing *Peter Pan* in Technicolor and it did not seem altogether inappropriate to me. Fairy tales nearly always have some simple moral lesson of good and evil, but that is not the secret of their fascination any more, I hope, than the philosophical import that might be distilled from the fantasies of *Camino Real* is the principal element of its appeal.

To me the appeal of this work is its unusual degree of freedom. When it began to get under way I felt a new sensation of release, as if I could "ride out" like a tenor sax taking the breaks in a Dixieland combo or a piano in a bop session. You may call it self-indulgence, but I was not doing it merely for

---

* Written prior to the Broadway premiere of *Camino Real* and published in the New York *Times* on Sunday, March 15, 1953.

159

myself. I could not have felt a purely private thrill of release unless I had hope of sharing this experience with lots and lots of audiences to come.

My desire was to give these audiences my own sense of something wild and unrestricted that ran like water in the mountains, or clouds changing shape in a gale, or the continually dissolving and transforming images of a dream. This sort of freedom is not chaos nor anarchy. On the contrary, it is the result of painstaking design, and in this work I have given more conscious attention to form and construction than I have in any work before. Freedom is not achieved simply by working freely.

Elia Kazan was attracted to this work mainly, I believe, for the same reason—its freedom and mobility of form. I know that we have kept saying the word "flight" to each other as if the play were merely an abstraction of the impulse to fly, and most of the work out of town, his in staging, mine in cutting and revising, has been with this impulse in mind: the achievement of a continual flow. Speech after speech and bit after bit that were nice in themselves have been remorselessly blasted out of the script and its staging wherever they seemed to obstruct or divert this flow.

There have been plenty of indications already that this play will exasperate and confuse a certain number of people which we hope is not so large as the number it is likely to please. At each performance a number of people have stamped out of the auditorium, with little regard for those whom they have had to crawl over, almost as if the building had caught on fire, and there have been sibilant noises on the way out and demands for money back if the cashier was foolish enough to remain in his box.

I am at a loss to explain this phenomenon, and if I am being facetious about one thing, I am being quite serious about another when I say that I had never for one minute supposed that the play would seem obscure and confusing to anyone who was willing to meet it even less than halfway. It was a costly production, and for this reason I had to read it aloud, together with a few of the actors on one occasion, before large groups of prospective backers, before the funds to produce it were in the till. It was only then that I came up against the disconcerting surprise that some people would think that the play needed clarification.

My attitude is intransigent. I still don't agree that it needs any explanation. Some poet has said that a poem should not mean but be. Of course, a play is not a poem, not even a poetic play has quite the same license as a poem. But to go to *Camino Real* with the inflexible demands of a logician is unfair to both parties.

In Philadelphia a young man from a literary periodical saw the play and then cross-examined me about all its dream-like images. He had made a list of them while he watched the play, and afterward at my hotel he brought out the list and asked me to explain the meaning of each one. I can't deny that I use a lot of those things called symbols but being a self-defensive creature, I say that symbols are nothing but the natural speech of drama.

We all have in our conscious and unconscious minds a great vocabulary of images, and I think all human communication is based on these images as are our dreams; and a symbol in a play has only one legitimate purpose which is to say a thing more directly and simply and beautifully than it could be said in words.

I hate writing that is a parade of images for the sake of images; I hate it so much that I close a book in disgust when

161

it keeps on saying one thing is like another; I even get disgusted with poems that make nothing but comparisons between one thing and another. But I repeat that symbols, when used respectfully, are the purest language of plays. Sometimes it would take page after tedious page of exposition to put across an idea that can be said with an object or a gesture on the lighted stage.

To take one case in point: the battered portmanteau of Jacques Casanova is hurled from the balcony of a luxury hotel when his remittance check fails to come through. While the portmanteau is still in the air, he shouts: "Careful, I have—" —and when it has crashed to the street he continues—"fragile—mementoes . . ." I suppose that is a symbol, at least it is an object used to express as directly and vividly as possible certain things which could be said in pages of dull talk.

As for those patrons who departed before the final scene, I offer myself this tentative bit of solace: that these theatregoers may be a little domesticated in their theatrical tastes. A cage represents security as well as confinement to a bird that has grown used to being in it; and when a theatrical work kicks over the traces with such apparent insouciance, security seems challenged and, instead of participating in its sense of freedom, one out of a certain number of playgoers will rush back out to the more accustomed implausibility of the street he lives on.

To modify this effect of complaisance I would like to admit to you quite frankly that I can't say with any personal conviction that I have written a good play, I only know that I have felt a release in this work which I wanted you to feel with me.

Tennessee Williams

162

AFTERWORD

Once in a while someone will say to me that he would rather wait for a play to come out as a book than see a live performance of it, where he would be distracted from its true values, if it has any, by so much that is mere spectacle and sensation and consequently must be meretricious and vulgar. There are plays meant for reading. I have read them. I have read the works of "thinking playwrights" as distinguished from us who are permitted only to feel, and probably read them earlier and appreciated them as much as those who invoke their names nowadays like the incantation of Aristophanes' frogs. But the incontinent blaze of a live theatre, a theatre meant for seeing and for feeling, has never been and never will be extinguished by a bucket brigade of critics, new or old, bearing vessels that range from cut-glass punch bowl to Haviland tea-cup. And in my dissident opinion, a play in a book is only the shadow of a play and not even a clear shadow of it. Those who did not like *Camino Real* on the stage will not be likely to form a higher opinion of it in print, for of all the works I have written, this one was meant most for the vulgarity of performance. The printed script of a play is hardly more than an architect's blueprint of a house not yet built or built and destroyed.

The color, the grace and levitation, the structural pattern in motion, the quick interplay of live beings, suspended like fitful lightning in a cloud, these things are the play, not words on paper, nor thoughts and ideas of an author, those shabby things snatched off basement counters at Gimbel's.

My own creed as a playwright is fairly close to that expressed by the painter in Shaw's play *The Doctor's Dilemma*: "I believe in Michelangelo, Velasquez and Rembrandt; in the might of design, the mystery of color, the redemption of all things by beauty everlasting and the message of art that has made these hands blessed. Amen."

How much art his hands were blessed with or how much mine are, I don't know, but that art is a blessing is certain and that it contains its message is also certain, and I feel, as the painter did, that the message lies in those abstract beauties of form and color and line, to which I would add light and motion.

In these following pages are only the formula by which a play could exist.

Dynamic is a word in disrepute at the moment, and so, I suppose, is the word *organic,* but those terms still define the dramatic values that I value most and which I value more as they are more deprecated by the ones self-appointed to save what they have never known.

Tennessee Williams
June 1, 1953

EDITOR'S NOTE

The version of *Camino Real* here published is considerably revised over the one presented on Broadway. Following the opening there, Mr. Williams went to his home at Key West and continued to work on this play. When he left six weeks later to direct Donald Windham's *Starless Night* in Houston, Texas, he took the playing version with him and reworked it whenever time allowed. It was with him when he drove in leisurely fashion back to New York. As delivered to the publisher, the manuscript of *Camino Real* was typed on three different typewriters and on stationery of hotels across the country.

Three characters, a prologue and several scenes that were not in the Broadway production have been added, or reinstated from earlier, preproduction versions, while other scenes have been deleted.

Camino Real is divided into a Prologue and Sixteen "Blocks," scenes with no perceptible time lapse between them for the most part. There are intermissions indicated after Block Six and Block Eleven.

The action takes place in an unspecified Latin-American country.

Camino Real was first produced by Cheryl Crawford and Ethel Reiner, in association with Walter P. Chrysler, Jr., and following tryouts in New Haven and Philadelphia, it had its Broadway premiere on March 19, 1953, at the Martin Beck Theatre. The production was directed by Elia Kazan, with the assistance of Anna Sokolow; the setting and costumes were designed by Lemuel Ayers; and incidental music was contributed by Bernardo Ségall. Production associate: Anderson Lawler. Tennessee Williams was represented by Liebling-Wood.

Cast of the Broadway Production

GUTMAN	FRANK SILVERA
SURVIVOR	GUY THOMAJAN
ROSITA	AZA BARD
FIRST OFFICER	HENRY SILVA
JACQUES CASANOVA	JOSEPH ANTHONY
LA MADRECITA DE LOS PERDIDOS	VIVIAN NATHAN
HER SON	ROLANDO VALDEZ
KILROY	ELI WALLACH
FIRST STREET CLEANER	NEHEMIAH PERSOFF
SECOND STREET CLEANER	FRED SADOFF
ABDULLAH	ERNESTO GONZALEZ
A BUM IN A WINDOW	MARTIN BALSAM
A. RATT	MIKE GAZZO
THE LOAN SHARK	SALEM LUDWIG
BARON DE CHARLUS	DAVID J. STEWART
LOBO	RONNE AUL
SECOND OFFICER	WILLIAM LENNARD
A GROTESQUE MUMMER	GLUCK SANDOR
MARGUERITE GAUTIER	JO VAN FLEET

166

LADY MULLIGAN	LUCILLE PATTON
WAITER	PAGE JOHNSON
LORD BYRON	HURD HATFIELD
NAVIGATOR OF THE FUGITIVO	ANTONY VORNO
PILOT OF THE FUGITIVO	MARTIN BALSAM
MARKET WOMAN	CHARLOTTE JONES
SECOND MARKET WOMAN	JOANNA VISCHER
STREET VENDOR	RUTH VOLNER
LORD MULLIGAN	PARKER WILSON
THE GYPSY	JENNIE GOLDSTEIN
HER DAUGHTER, ESMERALDA	BARBARA BAXLEY
NURSIE	SALEM LUDWIG
EVA	MARY GREY
THE INSTRUCTOR	DAVID J. STEWART
ASSISTANT INSTRUCTOR	PARKER WILSON
MEDICAL STUDENT	PAGE JOHNSON
DON QUIXOTE	HURD HATFIELD
SANCHO PANZA	(Not in production)
PRUDENCE DUVERNOY	(Not in production)
OLYMPE	(Not in production)

Street Vendors: AZA BARD, ERNESTO GONZALEZ, CHARLOTTE JONES, GLUCK SANDOR, JOANNA VISCHER, RUTH VOLNER, ANTONY VORNO.

Guests: MARTIN BALSAM, MARY GREY, LUCILLE PATTON, JOANNA VISCHER, PARKER WILSON.

Passengers: MIKE GAZZO, MARY GREY, PAGE JOHNSON, CHARLOTTE JONES, WILLIAM LENNARD, SALEM LUDWIG, JOANNA VISCHER, RUTH VOLNER.

At the Fiesta: RONNE AUL, MARTIN BALSAM, AZA BARD, MIKE GAZZO, ERNESTO GONZALEZ, MARY GREY, CHARLOTTE JONES, WILLIAM LENNARD, NEHEMIAH PERSOFF, FRED SADOFF, GLUCK SANDOR, JOANNA VISCHER, ANTONY VORNO, PARKER WILSON.

167

THE NEW YORK PRODUCTION SET BY LEMUEL AYERS

PROLOGUE

As the curtain rises, on an almost lightless stage, there is a loud singing of wind, accompanied by distant, measured reverberations like pounding surf or distant shellfire. Above the ancient wall that backs the set and the perimeter of mountains visible above the wall, are flickers of a white radiance as though daybreak were a white bird caught in a net and struggling to rise.

The plaza is seen fitfully by this light. It belongs to a tropical seaport that bears a confusing, but somehow harmonious, resemblance to such widely scattered ports as Tangiers, Havana, Vera Cruz, Casablanca, Shanghai, New Orleans.

On stage left is the luxury side of the street, containing the façade of the Siete Mares hotel and its low terrace on which are a number of glass-topped white iron tables and chairs. In the downstairs there is a great bay window in which are seen a pair of elegant "dummies," one seated, one standing behind, looking out into the plaza with painted smiles. Upstairs is a small balcony and behind it a large window exposing a wall on which is hung a phoenix painted on silk: this should be softly lighted now and then in the play, since resurrections are so much a part of its meaning.

Opposite the hotel is Skid Row which contains the Gypsy's gaudy stall, the Loan Shark's establishment with a window containing a variety of pawned articles, and the "Ritz Men Only" which is a flea-bag hotel or flophouse and which has a practical window above its downstairs entrance, in which a bum will appear from time to time to deliver appropriate or contrapuntal song titles.

Upstage is a great flight of stairs that mount the ancient wall to a sort of archway that leads out into "Terra Incognita,"

169

as it is called in the play, a wasteland between the walled town and the distant perimeter of snow-topped mountains.

Downstage right and left are a pair of arches which give entrance to dead-end streets.

Immediately after the curtain rises a shaft of blue light is thrown down a central aisle of the theatre, and in this light, advancing from the back of the house, appears Don Quixote de la Mancha, dressed like an old "desert rat." As he enters the aisle he shouts, "Hola!", in a cracked old voice which is still full of energy and is answered by another voice which is impatient and tired, that of his squire, Sancho Panza. Stumbling with a fatigue which is only physical, the old knight comes down the aisle, and Sancho follows a couple of yards behind him, loaded down with equipment that ranges from a medieval shield to a military canteen or Thermos bottle. Shouts are exchanged between them.

QUIXOTE [*ranting above the wind in a voice which is nearly as old*]:
Blue is the color of distance!

SANCHO [*wearily behind him*]:
Yes, distance is blue.

QUIXOTE:
Blue is also the color of nobility.

SANCHO:
Yes, nobility's blue.

QUIXOTE:
Blue is the color of distance and nobility, and that's why an old knight should always have somewhere about him a bit of blue ribbon . . .

[*He jostles the elbow of an aisle-sitter as he staggers with fatigue; he mumbles an apology.*]

SANCHO:
Yes, a bit of blue ribbon.

QUIXOTE:
A bit of faded blue ribbon, tucked away in whatever remains of his armor, or borne on the tip of his lance, his—unconquerable lance! It serves to remind an old knight of distance that he has gone and distance he has yet to go . . .

[*Sancho mutters the Spanish word for excrement as several pieces of rusty armor fall into the aisle.*

[*Quixote has now arrived at the foot of the steps onto the forestage. He pauses there as if wandering out of or into a dream. Sancho draws up clanking behind him.*

[*Mr. Gutman, a lordly fat man wearing a linen suit and a pith helmet, appears dimly on the balcony of the Siete Mares, a white cockatoo on his wrist. The bird cries out harshly.*]

GUTMAN:
Hush, Aurora.

QUIXOTE:
It also reminds an old knight of that green country he lived in which was the youth of his heart, before such singing words as *Truth!*

SANCHO [*panting*]:
—Truth.

QUIXOTE:
Valor!

171

SANCHO:
—Valor.

QUIXOTE [*elevating his lance*]:
Devoir!

SANCHO:
—Devoir ...

QUIXOTE:
—turned into the meaningless mumble of some old monk hunched over cold mutton at supper!

[*Gutman alerts a pair of Guards in the plaza, who cross with red lanterns to either side of the proscenium where they lower black and white striped barrier gates as if the proscenium marked a frontier. One of them, with a hand on his holster, advances toward the pair on the steps.*]

GUARD:
Vien aquí.

[*Sancho hangs back but Quixote stalks up to the barrier gate. The Guard turns a flashlight on his long and exceedingly grave red face, "frisks" him casually for concealed weapons, examines a rusty old knife and tosses it contemptuously away.*]

Sus papeles! Sus documentos!

[*Quixote fumblingly produces some tattered old papers from the lining of his hat.*]

GUTMAN [*impatiently*]:
Who is it?

GUARD:
An old desert rat named Quixote.

GUTMAN:
Oh!—Expected!—Let him in.

[*The Guards raise the barrier gate and one sits down to smoke on the terrace. Sancho hangs back still. A dispute takes place on the forestage and steps into the aisle.*]

QUIXOTE:
Forward!

SANCHO:
Aw, naw. I know this place. [*He produces a crumpled parchment.*] Here it is on the chart. Look, it says here: "Continue until you come to the square of a walled town which is the end of the *Camino Real* and the beginning of the *Camino Real*. Halt there," it says, "and turn back, Traveler, for the spring of humanity has gone dry in this place and—"

QUIXOTE [*He snatches the chart from him and reads the rest of the inscription.*]:
"—there are no birds in the country except wild birds that are tamed and kept in—" [*He holds the chart close to his nose.*]

—Cages!

SANCHO [*urgently*]:
Let's go back to La Mancha!

QUIXOTE:
Forward!

SANCHO:
The time has come for retreat!

QUIXOTE:
The time for retreat never comes!

SANCHO:

I'm going back to *La Mancha!*
[*He dumps the knightly equipment into the orchestra pit.*]

QUIXOTE:
Without me?

SANCHO [*bustling up the aisle*]:
With you or without you, old tireless and tiresome master!

QUIXOTE [*imploringly*]:
Saaaaaan-chooooooooo!

SANCHO [*near the top of the aisle*]:
I'm going back to La *Maaaaaaaaan-chaaaaaaa* . . .

[*He disappears as the blue light in the aisle dims out. The Guard puts out his cigarette and wanders out of the plaza. The wind moans and Gutman laughs softly as the Ancient Knight enters the plaza with such a desolate air.*]

QUIXOTE [*looking about the plaza*]:
—Lonely . . .

[*To his surprise the word is echoed softly by almost unseen figures huddled below the stairs and against the wall of the town. Quixote leans upon his lance and observes with a wry smile—*]

—When so many are lonely as seem to be lonely, it would be inexcusably selfish to be lonely alone.

[*He shakes out a dusty blanket. Shadowy arms extend toward him and voices murmur.*]

VOICE:
Sleep. Sleep. Sleep.

QUIXOTE [*arranging his blanket*]:
Yes, I'll sleep for a while, I'll sleep and dream for a while
against the wall of this town . . .

[*A mandolin or guitar plays "The Nightingale of France."*]

—And my dream will be a pageant, a masque in which old
meanings will be remembered and possibly new ones discovered, and when I wake from this sleep and this disturbing
pageant of a dream, I'll choose one among its shadows to take
along with me in the place of Sancho . . .

[*He blows his nose between his fingers and wipes them on
his shirttail.*]

—For new companions are not as familiar as old ones but all
the same—they're old ones with only slight differences of face
and figure, which may or may not be improvements, and it
would be selfish of me to be lonely alone . . .

[*He stumbles down the incline into the Pit below the stairs
where most of the Street People huddle beneath awnings of
open stalls.*

[*The white cockatoo squawks.*]

GUTMAN:
Hush, Aurora.

QUIXOTE:
And tomorrow at this same hour, which we call madrugada,
the loveliest of all words, except the word alba, and that word
also means daybreak—
—Yes, at daybreak tomorrow I will go on from here with a
new companion and this old bit of blue ribbon to keep me
in mind of distance that I have gone and distance I have yet
to go, and also to keep me in mind of—

175

[*The cockatoo cries wildly.*

[*Quixote nods as if in agreement with the outcry and folds himself into his blanket below the great stairs.*]

GUTMAN [*stroking the cockatoo's crest*]:
Be still, Aurora. I know it's morning, Aurora.

[*Daylight turns the plaza silver and slowly gold. Vendors rise beneath white awnings of stalls. The Gypsy's stall opens. A tall, courtly figure, in his late middle years (Jacques Casanova) crosses from the Siete Mares to the Loan Shark's, removing a silver snuff box from his pocket as Gutman speaks. His costume, like that of all the legendary characters in the play (except perhaps Quixote) is generally "modern" but with vestigial touches of the period to which he was actually related. The cane and the snuff box and perhaps a brocaded vest may be sufficient to give this historical suggestion in Casanova's case. He bears his hawklike head with a sort of anxious pride on most occasions, a pride maintained under a steadily mounting pressure.*]

—It's morning and after morning. It's afternoon, ha ha! And now I must go downstairs to announce the beginning of that old wanderer's dream . . .

[*He withdraws from the balcony as old Prudence Duvernoy stumbles out of the hotel, as if not yet quite awake from an afternoon siesta. Chattering with beads and bracelets, she wanders vaguely down into the plaza, raising a faded green silk parasol, damp henna-streaked hair slipping under a monstrous hat of faded silk roses; she is searching for a lost poodle.*]

PRUDENCE:
Trique? Trique?

[Jacques comes out of the Loan Shark's replacing his case angrily in his pocket.]

JACQUES:

Why, I'd rather give it to a street beggar! This case is a Boucheron, I won it at faro at the summer palace, at Tsarskoe Selo in the winter of—

[The Loan Shark slams the door. Jacques glares, then shrugs and starts across the plaza. Old Prudence is crouched over the filthy gray bundle of a dying mongrel by the fountain.]

PRUDENCE:

Trique, oh, Trique!

[The Gypsy's son, Abdullah, watches, giggling.]

JACQUES *[reproving]*:

It is a terrible thing for an old woman to outlive her dogs.

[He crosses to Prudence and gently disengages the animal from her grasp.]

Madam, that is not Trique.

PRUDENCE:

—When I woke up she wasn't in her basket . . .

JACQUES:

Sometimes we sleep too long in the afternoon and when we wake we find things changed, Signora.

PRUDENCE:

Oh, you're Italian!

JACQUES:

I am from Venice, Signora.

PRUDENCE:

Ah, Venice, city of pearls! I saw you last night on the terrace

177

dining with—Oh, I'm so worried about her! I'm an old friend of hers, perhaps she's mentioned me to you. Prudence Duvernoy? I was her best friend in the old days in Paris, but now she's forgotten so much . . .

I hope you have influence with her!

[*A waltz of Camille's time in Paris is heard.*]

I want you to give her a message from a certain wealthy old gentleman that she met at one of those watering places she used to go to for her health. She resembled his daughter who died of consumption and so he adored Camille, lavished everything on her! What did she do? Took a young lover who hadn't a couple of pennies to rub together, disinherited by his father because of *her!* Oh, you can't do that, not now, not any more, you've got to be realistic on the Camino Real!

[*Gutman has come out on the terrace: he announces quietly—*]

GUTMAN:
Block One on the Camino Real.

PRUDENCE [*continuing*]:

Yes, you've got to be practical on it! Well, give her this message, please, Sir. He wants her back on any terms whatsoever! [*Her speech gathers furious momentum.*] Her evenings will be free. He wants only her mornings, mornings are hard on old men because their hearts beat slowly, and he wants only her mornings! Well, that's how it should be! A sensible arrangement! Elderly gentlemen have to content themselves with a lady's spare time before supper! Isn't that so? Of course so! And so I told him! I told him, Camille isn't well! She requires delicate care! Has many debts, creditors storm her door! "How much does she owe?" he asked me, and, oh, did I do some lightning mathematics! Jewels in pawn, I told him, pearls, rings, necklaces, bracelets, diamond ear-drops are in pawn! Horses put up for sale at a public auction!

JACQUES [*appalled by this torrent*]:
Signora, Signora, all of these things are—

PRUDENCE:
—What?

JACQUES:
Dreams!

[*Gutman laughs. A woman sings at a distance.*]

PRUDENCE [*continuing with less assurance*]:
—You're not so young as I thought when I saw you last night on the terrace by candlelight on the—Oh, but—Ho ho!—I bet there is *one* old fountain in this plaza that hasn't gone dry!

[*She pokes him obscenely. He recoils. Gutman laughs. Jacques starts away but she seizes his arm again, and the torrent of speech continues.*]

179

PRUDENCE:
Wait, wait, listen! Her candle is burning low. But how can
you tell? She might have a lingering end, and charity hospi-
tals? Why, you might as well take a flying leap into the
Streetcleaners' barrel. Oh, I've told her and told her not to
live in a dream! A dream is nothing to live in, why, it's gone
like a—

Don't let her elegance fool you! That girl has done the
Camino in carriages but she has also done it on foot! She
knows every stone the Camino is paved with! So tell her this.
You tell her, she won't listen to me!—Times and conditions
have undergone certain changes since we were friends in
Paris, and now we dismiss young lovers with skins of silk
and eyes like a child's first prayer, we put them away as
lightly as we put away white gloves meant only for summer,
and pick up a pair of black ones, suitable for winter . . .

[*The singing voice rises: then subsides.*]

JACQUES:
Excuse me, Madam.

[*He tears himself from her grasp and rushes into the Siete
Mares.*]

PRUDENCE [*dazed, to Gutman*]:
—What block is this?

GUTMAN:
Block One.

PRUDENCE:
I didn't hear the announcement . . .

GUTMAN [*coldly*]:
Well, now you do.

[*Olympe comes out of the lobby with a pale orange silk parasol like a floating moon.*]

OLYMPE:

Oh, there you are, I've looked for you high and low!—mostly low . . .

[*They float vaguely out into the dazzling plaza as though a capricious wind took them, finally drifting through the Moorish arch downstage right.*

[*The song dies out.*]

GUTMAN [*lighting a thin cigar*]:

Block Two on the Camino Real.

After Gutman's announcement, a hoarse cry is heard. A figure in rags, skin blackened by the sun, tumbles crazily down the steep alley to the plaza. He turns about blindly, murmuring: "A donde la fuente?" He stumbles against the hideous old prostitute Rosita who grins horribly and whispers something to him, hitching up her ragged, filthy skirt. Then she gives him a jocular push toward the fountain. He falls upon his belly and thrusts his hands into the dried-up basin. Then he staggers to his feet with a despairing cry.

THE SURVIVOR:
La fuente está seca!

[*Rosita laughs madly but the other Street People moan. A dry gourd rattles.*]

ROSITA:
The fountain is dry, but there's plenty to drink in the Siete Mares!

[*She shoves him toward the hotel. The proprietor, Gutman, steps out, smoking a thin cigar, fanning himself with a palm leaf. As the Survivor advances, Gutman whistles. A man in military dress comes out upon the low terrace.*]

OFFICER:
Go back!

[*The Survivor stumbles forward. The Officer fires at him. He lowers his hands to his stomach, turns slowly about with a lost expression, looking up at the sky, and stumbles toward the fountain. During the scene that follows, until the entrance of La Madrecita and her Son, the Survivor drags*

182

*himself slowly about the concrete rim of the fountain,
almost entirely ignored, as a dying pariah dog in a starving
country. Jacques Casanova comes out upon the terrace of
the Siete Mares. Now he passes the hotel proprietor's impassive figure, descending a step beneath and a little in
advance of him, and without looking at him.*]

JACQUES [*with infinite weariness and disgust*]:
What has happened?

GUTMAN [*serenely*]:

We have entered the second in a progress of sixteen blocks on
the Camino Real. It's five o'clock. That angry old lion, the
Sun, looked back once and growled and then went switching
his tail toward the cool shade of the Sierras. Our guests have
taken their afternoon siestas . . .

[*The Survivor has come out upon the forestage, now, not
like a dying man but like a shy speaker who has forgotten
the opening line of his speech. He is only a little crouched
over with a hand obscuring the red stain over his belly. Two
or three Street People wander about calling their wares:
"Tacos, tacos, fritos . . ."—"Lotería, lotería"—Rosita shuffles
around, calling "Love? Love?"—pulling down the filthy
décolletage of her blouse to show more of her sagging
bosom. The Survivor arrives at the top of the stairs descending into the orchestra of the theatre, and hangs onto it,
looking out reflectively as a man over the rail of a boat
coming into a somewhat disturbingly strange harbor.*]

GUTMAN [*continuing*]:
—They suffer from extreme fatigue, our guests at the Siete
Mares, all of them have a degree or two of fever. Questions
are passed amongst them like something illicit and shameful,
like counterfeit money or drugs or indecent postcards—

183

[*He leans forward and whispers:*]

—"What is this place? Where are we? What is the meaning of—*Shhhh!*"—Ha ha . . .

THE SURVIVOR [*very softly to the audience*]:
I once had a pony named Peeto. He caught in his nostrils the scent of thunderstorms coming even before the clouds had crossed the Sierra . . .

VENDOR:
Tacos, tacos, fritos . . .

ROSITA:
Love? Love?

LADY MULLIGAN [*to waiter on terrace*]:
Are you sure no one called me? I was expecting a call . . .

GUTMAN [*smiling*]:
My guests are confused and exhausted but at this hour they pull themselves together, and drift downstairs on the wings of gin and the lift, they drift into the public rooms and ex-change notes again on fashionable couturiers and custom tailors, restaurants, vintages of wine, hair-dressers, plastic surgeons, girls and young men susceptible to offers . . .

[*There is a hum of light conversation and laughter within.*]

—Hear them? They're exchanging notes . . .

JACQUES [*striking the terrace with his cane*]:
I asked you what has happened in the plaza!

GUTMAN:
Oh, in the plaza, ha ha!—Happenings in the plaza don't concern us . . .

184

JACQUES:

I heard shots fired.

GUTMAN:

Shots were fired to remind you of your good fortune in staying here. The public fountains have gone dry, you know, but the Siete Mares was erected over the only perpetual never-dried-up spring in Tierra Caliente, and of course that advantage has to be—protected—sometimes by—martial law . . .

[*The guitar resumes.*]

THE SURVIVOR:

When Peeto, my pony, was born—he stood on his four legs at once, and accepted the world!—He was wiser than I . . .

VENDOR:

Fritos, fritos, tacos!

ROSITA:

Love!

THE SURVIVOR:

—When Peeto was one year old he was wiser than God!

[*A wind sings across the plaza; a dry gourd rattles.*]

"Peeto, Peeto!" the Indian boys call after him, trying to stop him—trying to stop the wind!

[*The Survivor's head sags forward. He sits down as slowly as an old man on a park bench. Jacques strikes the terrace again with his cane and starts toward the Survivor. The Guard seizes his elbow.*]

JACQUES:

Don't put your hand on *me*!

185

GUARD:
Stay here.

GUTMAN:
Remain on the terrace, please, Signor Casanova.

JACQUES [*fiercely*]:
—*Cognac!*

[*The Waiter whispers to Gutman. Gutman chuckles.*]

GUTMAN:
The Maître 'D' tells me that your credit has been discontinued in the restaurant and bar, he says that he has enough of your tabs to pave the terrace with!

JACQUES:
What a piece of impertinence! I told the man that the letter that I'm expecting has been delayed in the mail. The postal service in this country is fantastically disorganized, and you know it! You also know that Mlle. Gautier will guarantee my tabs!

GUTMAN:
Then let her pick them up at dinner tonight if you're hungry!

JACQUES:
I'm not accustomed to this kind of treatment on the *Camino Real!*

GUTMAN:
Oh, you'll be, you'll be, after a single night at the "Ritz Men Only." That's where you'll have to transfer your patronage if the letter containing the remittance check doesn't arrive tonight.

JACQUES:

I assure you that I shall do nothing of the sort!—Tonight or ever!

GUTMAN:

Watch out, old hawk, the wind is ruffling your feathers!

[*Jacques sinks trembling into a chair.*]

—Give him a thimble of brandy before he collapses . . . Fury is a luxury of the young, their veins are resilient, but his are brittle . . .

JACQUES:

Here I sit, submitting to insult for a thimble of brandy— while directly in front of me—

[*The singer, La Madrecita, enters the plaza. She is a blind woman led by a ragged Young Man. The Waiter brings Jacques a brandy.*]

—a man in the plaza dies like a pariah dog!—I take the brandy! I sip it!—My heart is too tired to break, my heart is too tired to—break . . .

[*La Madrecita chants softly. She slowly raises her arm to point at the Survivor crouched on the steps from the plaza.*]

GUTMAN [*suddenly*]:

Give me the phone! Connect me with the Palace. Get me the Generalissimo, quick, quick, quick!

[*The Survivor rises feebly and shuffles very slowly toward the extended arms of "The Little Blind One."*]

Generalissimo? Gutman speaking! Hello, sweetheart. There has been a little incident in the plaza. You know that party of

187

young explorers that attempted to cross the desert on foot? Well, one of them's come back. He was very thirsty. He found the fountain dry. He started toward the hotel. He was politely advised to advance no further. But he disregarded this advice. Action had to be taken. And now, and now—that old blind woman they call "La Madrecita"?—She's come into the plaza with the man called "The Dreamer" . . .

SURVIVOR:
Donde?

THE DREAMER:
Aquí!

GUTMAN [*continuing*]:
You remember those two! I once mentioned them to you. You said "They're harmless dreamers and they're loved by the people."—"What," I asked you, "is harmless about a dreamer, and what," I asked you, "is harmless about the love of the people?—Revolution only needs good dreamers who remember their dreams, and the love of the people belongs safely only to you—their Generalissimo!"—Yes, now the blind woman has recovered her sight and is extending her arms to the wounded Survivor, and the man with the guitar is leading him to her . . .

[*The described action is being enacted.*]

Wait one moment! There's a possibility that the forbidden word may be spoken! Yes! The forbidden word is about to be spoken!

[*The Dreamer places an arm about the blinded Survivor, and cries out:*]

THE DREAMER:
Hermano!

[*The cry is repeated like springing fire and a loud murmur sweeps the crowd. They push forward with cupped hands extended and the gasping cries of starving people at the sight of bread. Two Military Guards herd them back under the colonnades with clubs and drawn revolvers. La Madrecita chants softly with her blind eyes lifted. A Guard starts toward her. The People shout "NO!"*]

LA MADRECITA [*chanting*]:
"Rojo está el sol! Rojo está el sol de sangre! Blanca está la luna! Blanca está la luna de miedo!"

[*The crowd makes a turning motion.*]

GUTMAN [*to the waiter*]:
Put up the ropes!

[*Velvet ropes are strung very quickly about the terrace of the Siete Mares. They are like the ropes on decks of steamers in rough waters. Gutman shouts into the phone again:*]

The word was spoken. The crowd is agitated. Hang on!

[*He lays down instrument.*]

JACQUES [*hoarsely, shaken*]:
He said "Hermano." That's the word for brother.

GUTMAN [*calmly*]:
Yes, the most dangerous word in any human tongue is the word for brother. It's inflammatory.—I don't suppose it can be struck out of the language altogether but it must be reserved for strictly private usage in back of soundproof walls. Otherwise it disturbs the population . . .

JACQUES:
The people need the word. They're thirsty for it!

189

GUTMAN:

What are these creatures? Mendicants. Prostitutes. Thieves and petty vendors in a bazaar where the human heart is a part of the bargain.

JACQUES:

Because they need the word and the word is forbidden!

GUTMAN:

The word is said in pulpits and at tables of council where its volatile essence can be contained. But on the lips of these creatures, what is it? A wanton incitement to riot, without understanding. For what is a brother to them but someone to get ahead of, to cheat, to lie to, to undersell in the market. Brother, you say to a man whose wife you sleep with!—But now, you see, the word has disturbed the people and made it necessary to invoke martial law!

[*Meanwhile the Dreamer has brought the Survivor to La Madrecita, who is seated on the cement rim of the fountain. She has cradled the dying man in her arms in the attitude of a* Pietà. *The Dreamer is crouched beside them, softly playing a guitar. Now he springs up with a harsh cry:*]

THE DREAMER:
Muerto!

[*The Streetcleaners' piping commences at a distance. Gutman seizes the phone again.*]

GUTMAN [*into phone*]:
Generalissimo, the Survivor is no longer surviving. I think we'd better have some public diversion right away. Put the Gypsy on! Have her announce the Fiesta!

LOUDSPEAKER [*responding instantly*]:
Damas y Caballeros! The next voice you hear will be the voice of—the Gypsy!

GYPSY [*over loudspeaker*]:
Hoy! Noche de Fiesta! Tonight the moon will restore the virginity of my daughter!

GUTMAN:
Bring on the Gypsy's daughter, Esmeralda. Show the virgin-to-be!

[*Esmeralda is led from the Gypsy's stall by a severe duenna, "Nursie," out upon the forestage. She is manacled by the wrist to the duenna. Her costume is vaguely Levantine.*]

[*Guards are herding the crowd back again.*]

GUTMAN:
Ha ha! Ho ho ho! Music!

[*There is gay music. Rosita dances.*]

Abdullah! You're on!

[*Abdullah skips into the plaza, shouting histrionically.*]

ABDULLAH:
Tonight the moon will restore the virginity of my sister, Esmeralda!

GUTMAN:
Dance, boy!

[*Esmeralda is led back into the stall. Throwing off his burnoose, Abdullah dances with Rosita. Behind their dance, armed Guards force La Madrecita and the Dreamer to retreat from the fountain, leaving the lifeless body of the*

191

survivor. All at once there is a discordant blast of brass instruments.

[*Kilroy comes into the plaza. He is a young American vagrant, about twenty-seven. He wears dungarees and a skivvy shirt, the pants faded nearly white from long wear and much washing, fitting him as closely as the clothes of sculpture. He has a pair of golden boxing gloves slung about his neck and he carries a small duffle bag. His belt is ruby-and-emerald-studded with the word CHAMP in bold letters. He stops before a chalked inscription on a wall downstage which says: "Kilroy Is Coming!" He scratches out "Coming" and over it prints "Here!"*]

GUTMAN:

Ho ho!—a clown! The Eternal Punchinella! That's exactly what's needed in a time of crisis!

Block Three on the Camino Real.

BLOCK THREE

KILROY [*genially, to all present*]:
Ha ha!

[*Then he walks up to the Officer by the terrace of the Siete Mares.*]

Buenas dias, señor.

[*He gets no response—barely even a glance.*]

Habla Inglesia? Usted?

OFFICER:
What is it you want?

KILROY:
Where is Western Union or Wells-Fargo? I got to send a wire to some friends in the States.

OFFICER:
No hay Western Union, no hay Wells-Fargo.

KILROY:
That is very peculiar. I never struck a town yet that didn't have one or the other. I just got off a boat. Lousiest frigging tub I ever shipped on, one continual hell it was, all the way up from Rio. And me sick, too. I picked up one of those tropical fevers. No sick-bay on that tub, no doctor, no medicine or nothing, not even one quinine pill, and I was burning up with Christ knows how much fever. I couldn't make them understand I was sick. I got a bad heart, too. I had to retire from the prize ring because of my heart. I was the light heavyweight champion of the West Coast, won these gloves! —before my ticker went bad.—Feel my chest! Go on, feel it! Feel it. I've got a heart in my chest as big as the head of a baby. Ha ha! They stood me in front of a screen that makes

193

you transparent and that's what they seen inside me, a heart in my chest as big as the head of a baby! With something like that you don't need the Gypsy to tell you, "Time is short, Baby —get ready to hitch on wings!" The medics wouldn't okay me for no more fights. They said to give up liquor and smoking and sex!—To give up sex!—I used to believe a man couldn't live without sex—but he can—if he wants to! My real true woman, my wife, she would of stuck with me, but it was all spoiled with her being scared and me, too, that a real hard kiss would kill me!—So one night while she was sleeping I wrote her good-bye . . .

[*He notices a lack of attention in the Officer: he grins.*]

No comprendo the lingo?

OFFICER:
What is it you want?

KILROY:
Excuse my ignorance, but what place is this? What is this country and what is the name of this town? I know it seems funny of me to ask such a question. Loco! But I was so glad to get off that rotten tub that I didn't ask nothing of no one except my pay—and I got short-changed on that. I have trouble counting these pesos or Whatzit-you-call-'em.

[*He jerks out his wallet.*]

All-a-this-here. In the States that pile of lettuce would make you a plutocrat!—But I bet you this stuff don't add up to fifty dollars American coin. Ha ha!

OFFICER:
Ha ha.

194

KILROY:
Ha ha!

OFFICER [*making it sound like a death-rattle*]:
Ha-ha-ha-ha-ha.

[*He turns and starts into the cantina. Kilroy grabs his arm.*]

KILROY:
Hey!

OFFICER:
What is it you want?

KILROY:
What is the name of this country and this town?

[*The Officer thrusts his elbow in Kilroy's stomach and twists his arm loose with a Spanish curse. He kicks the swinging doors open and enters the cantina.*]

Brass hats are the same everywhere.

[*As soon as the Officer goes, the Street People come forward and crowd about Kilroy with their wheedling cries.*]

STREET PEOPLE:
Dulces, dulces! Lotería! Lotería! Pasteles, café con leche!

KILROY:
No caree, no caree!

[*The Prostitute creeps up to him and grins.*]

ROSITA:
Love? Love?

KILROY:
What did you say?

ROSITA:
Love?

KILROY:
Sorry—I don't feature that. [*To audience*] I have ideals.

[*The Gypsy appears on the roof of her establishment with Esmeralda whom she secures by handcuffs to the iron railing.*]

GYPSY:
Stay there while I give the pitch!

[*She then advances with a portable microphone.*]

Testing! One, two, three, four!

NURSIE [*from offstage*]:
You're on the air!

GYPSY'S LOUDSPEAKER:
Are you perplexed by something? Are you tired out and confused? Do you have a fever?

[*Kilroy looks around for the source of the voice.*]

Do you feel yourself to be spiritually unprepared for the age of exploding atoms? Do you distrust the newspapers? Are you suspicious of governments? Have you arrived at a point on the Camino Real where the walls converge not in the distance but right in front of your nose? Does further progress appear impossible to you? Are you afraid of anything at all? Afraid of your heartbeat? Or the eyes of strangers! Afraid of breathing? Afraid of not breathing? Do you wish that things could be straight and simple again as they were in your childhood? Would you like to go back to Kindy Garten?

196

[*Rosita has crept up to Kilroy while he listens. She reaches out to him. At the same time a Pickpocket lifts his wallet.*]

KILROY [*catching the whore's wrist*]:
Keep y'r hands off me, y' dirty ole bag! No caree putas! No loteria, no dulces, nada—so get away! Vamoose! All of you! Quit picking at me!

[*He reaches in his pocket and jerks out a handful of small copper and silver coins which he flings disgustedly down the street. The grotesque people scramble after it with their inhuman cries. Kilroy goes on a few steps—then stops short —feeling the back pocket of his dungarees. Then he lets out a startled cry.*]

Robbed! My God, I've been robbed!

[*The Street People scatter to the walls.*]

Which of you got my wallet? *Which* of you dirty—? Shh--Uh!

[*They mumble with gestures of incomprehension. He marches back to the entrance to the hotel.*]

Hey! Officer! Official!—General!

[*The Officer finally lounges out of the hotel entrance and glances at Kilroy.*]

Tiende? One of them's got my wallet! Picked it out of my pocket while that old whore there was groping me! Don't you comprendo?

OFFICER:
Nobody rob you. You don't have no pesos.

KILROY:
Huh?

OFFICER:

You just dreaming that you have money. You don't ever have money. Nunca! Nada!

[*He spits between his teeth.*]

Loco . . .

[*The Officer crosses to the fountain. Kilroy stares at him, then bawls out:*]

KILROY [*to the Street People*]:

We'll see what the American Embassy has to say about this! I'll go to the American Consul. Whichever of you rotten spivs lifted my wallet is going to jail—calaboose! I hope I have made myself plain. If not, I will make myself plainer!

[*There are scattered laughs among the crowd. He crosses to the fountain. He notices the body of the no longer Survivor, kneels beside it, shakes it, turns it over, springs up and shouts:*]

Hey! This guy is dead!

[*There is the sound of the Streetcleaners' piping. They trundle their white barrel into the plaza from one of the downstage arches. The appearance of these men undergoes a progressive alteration through the play. When they first appear they are almost like any such public servants in a tropical country; their white jackets are dirtier than the musicians' and some of the stains are red. They have on white caps with black visors. They are continually exchanging sly jokes and giggling unpleasantly together. Lord Mulligan has come out upon the terrace and as they pass him, they pause for a moment, point at him, snicker. He is extremely discomfited by this impertinence, touches his chest as if he felt a palpitation and turns back inside.*]

[*Kilroy yells to the advancing Streetcleaners.*]

There's a dead man layin' here!

[*They giggle again. Briskly they lift the body and stuff it into the barrel; then trundle it off, looking back at Kilroy, giggling, whispering. They return under the downstage arch through which they entered. Kilroy, in a low, shocked voice:*]

What *is* this place? What kind of a hassle have I got myself into?

LOUDSPEAKER:
If anyone on the Camino is bewildered, come to the Gypsy. A poco dinero will tickle the Gypsy's palm and give her visions!

ABDULLAH [*giving Kilroy a card*]:
If you got a question, ask my mama, the Gypsy!

KILROY:
Man, whenever you see those three brass balls on a street, you don't have to look a long ways for a Gypsy. Now le' me think. I am faced with three problems. One: I'm hungry. Two: I'm lonely. Three: I'm in a place where I don't know what it is or how I got there! First action that's indicated is to—cash in on something—Well ... let's see ...

[*Honky-tonk music fades in at this point and the Skid Row façade begins to light up for the evening. There is the Gypsy's stall with its cabalistic devices, its sectional cranium and palm, three luminous brass balls overhanging the entrance to the Loan Shark and his window filled with a vast assortment of hocked articles for sale: trumpets, banjos, fur coats, tuxedos, a gown of scarlet sequins, loops of pearls and rhinestones. Dimly behind this display is a neon sign*]

199

in three pastel colors, pink, green, and blue. It fades softly in and out and it says: "Magic Tricks Jokes." There is also the advertisement of a flea-bag hotel or flophouse called "Ritz Men Only." This sign is also pale neon or luminous paint, and only the entrance is on the street floor, the rooms are above the Loan Shark and Gypsy's stall. One of the windows of this upper story is practical. Figures appear in it sometimes, leaning out as if suffocating or to hawk and spit into the street below. This side of the street should have all the color and animation that are permitted by the resources of the production. There may be moments of dancelike action (a fight, a seduction, sale of narcotics, arrest, etc.).]

KILROY [*to the audience from the apron*]:
What've I got to cash in on? My golden gloves? Never! I'll say that once more, never! The silver-framed photo of my One True Woman? Never! Repeat that! Never! What else have I got of a detachable and a negotiable nature? Oh! My ruby-and-emerald-studded belt with the word CHAMP on it.

[*He whips it off his pants.*]

This is not necessary to hold on my pants, but this is a precious reminder of the sweet used-to-be. Oh, well. Sometimes a man has got to hock his sweet used-to-be in order to finance his present situation . . .

[*He enters the Loan Shark's. A Drunken Bum leans out the practical window of the "Ritz Men Only" and shouts:*]

200

BUM:

O Jack o' Diamonds, you robbed my pockets, you robbed my pockets of silver and gold!

[*He jerks the window shade down.*]

GUTMAN [*on the terrace*]:
Block Four on the Camino Real!

There is a phrase of light music as the Baron de Charlus, an elderly foppish sybarite in a light silk suit, a carnation in his lapel, crosses from the Siete Mares to the honky-tonk side of the street. On his trail is a wild-looking young man of startling beauty called Lobo. Charlus is aware of the follower and, during his conversation with A. Ratt, he takes out a pocket mirror to inspect him while pretending to comb his hair and point his moustache. As Charlus approaches, the Manager of the flea-bag puts up a vacancy sign and calls out:

A. RATT:

Vacancy here! A bed at the "Ritz Men Only"! A little white ship to sail the dangerous night in ...

THE BARON:

Ah, bon soir, Mr. Ratt.

A. RATT:

Cruising?

THE BARON:

No, just—walking!

A. RATT:

That's all you need to do.

THE BARON:

I sometimes find it suffices. You have a vacancy, do you?

A. RATT:

For you?

THE BARON:

And a possible guest. You know the requirements. An iron bed with no mattress and a considerable length of stout knotted rope. No! Chains this evening, metal chains. I've been very bad, I have a lot to atone for ...

A. RATT:
Why don't you take these joy-rides at the Siete Mares?

THE BARON [*with the mirror focused on Lobo*]:
They don't have Ingreso Libero at the Siete Mares. Oh, I don't like places in the haute saison, the alta staggione, and yet if you go between the fashionable seasons, it's too hot or too damp or appallingly overrun by all the wrong sort of people who rap on the wall if canaries sing in your bed-springs after midnight. I don't know why such people don't stay at home. Surely a Kodak, a Brownie, or even a Leica works just as well in Milwaukee or Sioux City as it does in these places they do on their whirlwind summer tours, and don't look now, but I think I am being followed!

A. RATT:
Yep, you've made a pickup!

THE BARON:
Attractive?

A. RATT:
That depends on who's driving the bicycle, Dad.

THE BARON:
Ciao, Caro! Expect me at ten.

[*He crosses elegantly to the fountain.*]

A. RATT:
Vacancy here! A little white ship to sail the dangerous night in!

203

[*The music changes. Kilroy backs out of the Loan Shark's, belt unsold, engaged in a violent dispute. The Loan Shark is haggling for his golden gloves. Charlus lingers, intrigued by the scene.*]

LOAN SHARK:
I don't want no belt! I want the gloves! Eight-fifty!

KILROY:
No dice.

LOAN SHARK:
Nine, nine-fifty!

KILROY:
Nah, nah, nah!

LOAN SHARK:
Yah, yah, yah.

KILROY:
I say nah.

LOAN SHARK:
I say yah.

KILROY:
The nahs have it.

LOAN SHARK:
Don't be a fool. What can you do with a pair of golden gloves?

KILROY:
I can remember the battles I fought to win them! I can remember that I used to be—CHAMP!

[*Fade in Band Music: "March of the Gladiators"—ghostly cheers, etc.*]

LOAN SHARK:

You can remember that you *used to be*—Champ?

KILROY:

Yes! I used to be—CHAMP!

THE BARON:

Used to be is the past tense, meaning useless.

KILROY:

Not to me, Mister. These are my gloves, these gloves are gold, and I fought a lot of hard fights to win 'em! I broke clean from the clinches. I never hit a low blow, the referee never told me to mix it up! And the fixers never got to me!

LOAN SHARK:

In other words, a sucker!

KILROY:

Yep, I'm a sucker that won the golden gloves!

LOAN SHARK:

Congratulations. My final offer is a piece of green paper with Alexander Hamilton's picture on it. Take it or leave it.

KILROY:

I leave it for you to *stuff* it! I'd hustle my heart on this street, I'd peddle my heart's true blood before I'd leave my golden gloves hung up in a loan shark's window between a rusted trombone and some poor lush's long ago mildewed tuxedo!

LOAN SHARK:

So you say but I will see you later.

THE BARON:

The name of the Camino is not unreal!

[*The Bum sticks his head out the window and shouts:*]

BUM:
Pa dam, Pa dam, Pa dam!

THE BARON [*continuing the Bum's song*]:
Echoes the beat of my heart!
Pa dam, Pa dam—*hello!*

[*He has crossed to Kilroy as he sings and extends his hand to him.*]

KILROY [*uncertainly*]:
Hey, mate. It's wonderful to see you.

THE BARON.
Thanks, but why?

KILROY:
A normal American. In a clean white suit.

THE BARON:
My suit is pale yellow. My nationality is French, and my normality has been often subject to question.

KILROY:
I still say your suit is clean.

THE BARON:
Thanks. That's more than I can say for your apparel.

KILROY:
Don't judge a book by the covers. I'd take a shower if I could locate the "Y."

THE BARON:
What's the "Y"?

KILROY:
Sort of a Protestant church with a swimmin' pool in it. Some-

times it also has an employment bureau. It does good in the community.

THE BARON:

Nothing in this community does much good.

KILROY:

I'm getting the same impression. This place is confusing to me. I think it must be the aftereffects of fever. Nothing seems real. Could you give me the scoop?

THE BARON:

Serious questions are referred to the Gypsy. Once upon a time. Oh, once upon a time. I used to wonder. Now I simply wander. I stroll about the fountain and hope to be followed. Some people call it corruption. I call it—simplification . . .

BUM [*very softly at the window*]:
I wonder what's become of Sally, that old gal of mine?

[*He lowers the blind.*]

KILROY:
Well, anyhow . . .

THE BARON:
Well, anyhow?

KILROY:
How about the hot-spots in this town?

THE BARON:

Oh, the hot-spots, ho ho! There's the Pink Flamingo, the Yellow Pelican, the Blue Heron, and the Prothonotary Warbler! They call it the Bird Circuit. But I don't care for such places. They stand three-deep at the bar and look at themselves in the mirror and what they see is depressing. One sailor comes in—they faint! My own choice of resorts is the

207

Bucket of Blood downstairs from the "Ritz Men Only."—
How about a match?

KILROY:
Where's your cigarette?

THE BARON [*gently and sweetly*]:
Oh, I don't smoke. I just wanted to see your eyes more
clearly . . .

KILROY:
Why?

THE BARON:
The eyes are the windows of the soul, and yours are too gentle
for someone who has as much as I have to atone for.

[*He starts off.*]
Au revoir . . .

KILROY:
—A very unusual type character . . .

[*Casanova is on the steps leading to the arch, looking out
at the desert beyond. Now he turns and descends a few
steps, laughing with a note of tired incredulity. Kilroy
crosses to him.*]

Gee, it's wonderful to see you, a normal American in a—

[*There is a strangulated outcry from the arch under which
the Baron has disappeared.*]

Excuse me a minute!

[*He rushes toward the source of the outcry. Jacques crosses
to the bench before the fountain. Rhubarb is heard through
the arch. Jacques shrugs wearily as if it were just a noisy*]

radio. Kilroy comes plummeting out backwards, all the way to Jacques.]

I tried to interfere, but what's th' use?!

KILROY:
No use at all!

[*The Streetcleaners come through the arch with the Baron doubled up in their barrel. They pause and exchange sibilant whispers, pointing and snickering at Kilroy.*]

KILROY:
Who are they pointing at? At me, Kilroy?

[*The Bum laughs from the window. A. Ratt laughs from his shadowy doorway. The Loan Shark laughs from his.*]

Kilroy is here and he's not about to be there!—If he can help it . . .

[*He snatches up a rock and throws it at the Streetcleaners. Everybody laughs louder and the laughter seems to reverberate from the mountains. The light changes, dims a little in the plaza.*]

Sons a whatever you're sons of! Don't look at me, I'm not about to take no ride in the barrel!

[*The Baron, his elegant white shoes protruding from the barrel, is wheeled up the Alleyway Out. Figures in the square resume their dazed attitudes and one or two Guests return to the terrace of the Siete Mares as—*]

GUTMAN:
Block Five on the Camino Real!

[*He strolls off.*]

KILROY [*to Jacques*]:
Gee, the blocks go fast on this street!

JACQUES:
Yes. The blocks go fast.

KILROY:
My name's Kilroy. I'm here.

JACQUES:
Mine is Casanova. I'm here, too.

KILROY:
But you been here longer than me and maybe could brief me on it. For instance, what do they do with a stiff picked up in this town?

[*The Guard stares at them suspiciously from the terrace.*

[*Jacques whistles "La Golondrina" and crosses downstage. Kilroy follows.*]

Did I say something untactful?

JACQUES [*smiling into a sunset glow*]:
The exchange of serious questions and ideas, especially between persons from opposite sides of the plaza, is regarded unfavorably here. You'll notice I'm talking as if I had acute laryngitis. I'm gazing into the sunset. If I should start to whistle "La Golondrina" it means we're being overheard by the Guards on the terrace. Now you want to know what is done to a body from which the soul has departed on the Camino Real!—Its disposition depends on what the Street-cleaners happen to find in its pockets. If its pockets are empty as the unfortunate Baron's turned out to be, and as mine are at this moment—the "stiff" is wheeled straight off to the

Laboratory. And there the individual becomes an undistinguished member of a collectivist state. His chemical components are separated and poured into vats containing the corresponding elements of countless others. If any of his vital organs or parts are at all unique in size or structure, they're placed on exhibition in bottles containing a very foul-smelling solution called formaldehyde. There is a charge of admission to this museum. The proceeds go to the maintenance of the military police.

[*He whistles "La Golondrina" till the Guard turns his back again. He moves toward the front of the stage.*]

KILROY [*following*]:
—I guess that's—sensible . . .

JACQUES:
Yes, but not romantic. And romance is important. Don't you think?

KILROY:
Nobody thinks romance is more important than me!

JACQUES:
Except possibly me!

KILROY:
Maybe that's why fate has brung us together! We're buddies under the skin!

JACQUES:
Travelers born?

KILROY:
Always looking for something!

JACQUES:
Satisfied by nothing!

211

KILROY:
Hopeful?

JACQUES:
Always!

OFFICER:
Keep moving!

[*They move apart till the Officer exits.*]

KILROY:
And when a joker on the Camino gets fed up with one continual hassle—how does he get *off* it?

JACQUES:
You see the narrow and very steep stairway that passes under what is described in the travel brochures as a "Magnificent Arch of Triumph"?—Well, that's the Way Out!

KILROY:
That's the way out?

[*Kilroy without hesitation plunges right up to almost the top step; then pauses with a sound of squealing brakes. There is a sudden loud wind.*]

JACQUES [*shouting with hand cupped to mouth*]:
Well, how does the prospect please you, Traveler born?

KILROY [*shouting back in a tone of awe*]:
It's too unknown for my blood. Man, I seen nothing like it except through a telescope once on the pier on Coney Island. "Ten cents to see the craters and plains of the moon!"—And here's the same view in three dimensions for nothing!

[*The desert wind sings loudly: Kilroy mocks it.*]

JACQUES:

Are you—ready to cross it?

KILROY:

Maybe sometime with someone but not right now and alone!
How about you?

JACQUES:

I'm not alone.

KILROY:

You're with a party?

JACQUES:

No, but I'm sweetly encumbered with a—lady . . .

KILROY:

It wouldn't do with a lady. I don't see nothing but nothing—
and then more nothing. And then I see some mountains. But
the mountains are covered with snow.

JACQUES:

Snowshoes would be useful!

[*He observes Gutman approaching through the passage at
upper left. He whistles "La Golondrina" for Kilroy's attention and points with his cane as he exits.*]

KILROY [*descending steps disconsolately*]:
Mush, mush.

[*The Bum comes to his window. A. Ratt enters his doorway. Gutman enters below Kilroy.*]

BUM:

It's sleepy time down South!

GUTMAN [*warningly as Kilroy passes him*]:
Block Six in a progress of sixteen blocks on the Camino Real.

KILROY [*from the stairs*]:
Man, I could use a bed now.—I'd like to make me a cool pad on this camino now and lie down and sleep and dream of being with someone—friendly ...

[*He crosses to the "Ritz Men Only."*]

A. RATT [*softly and sleepily*]:
Vacancy here! I got a single bed at the "Ritz Men Only," a little white ship to sail the dangerous night in.

[*Kilroy crosses down to his doorway.*]

KILROY:
—You got a vacancy here?

A. RATT:
I got a vacancy here if you got the one-fifty there.

KILROY:
Ha ha! I been in countries where money was not legal tender. I mean it was legal but it wasn't tender.

[*There is a loud groan from offstage above.*]

—Somebody dying on you or just drunk?

A. RATT:
Who knows or cares in this pad, Dad?

KILROY:
I heard once that a man can't die while he's drunk. Is that a fact or a fiction?

A. RATT:
Strictly a fiction.

VOICE ABOVE:
Stiff in number seven! Call the Streetcleaners!

A. RATT [*with absolutely no change in face or voice*]:
Number seven is vacant.

[*Streetcleaners' piping is heard.*]

[*The Bum leaves the window.*]

KILROY:
Thanks, but tonight I'm going to sleep under the stars.

[*A. Ratt gestures "Have it your way" and exits.*]

[*Kilroy, left alone, starts downstage. He notices that La Madrecita is crouched near the fountain, holding something up, inconspicuously, in her hand. Coming to her he sees that it's a piece of food. He takes it, puts it in his mouth, tries to thank her but her head is down, muffled in her rebozo and there is no way for him to acknowledge the gift. He starts to cross. Street People raise up their heads in their Pit and motion him invitingly to come in with them. They call softly, "Sleep, sleep . . ."*]

GUTMAN [*from his chair on the terrace*]:
Hey, Joe.

[*The Street People duck immediately.*]

KILROY:
Who? Me?

GUTMAN:
Yes, you, Candy Man. Are you disocupado?

KILROY:
—That means—unemployed, don't it?

[*He sees Officers converging from right.*]

GUTMAN:
Jobless. On the bum. Carrying the banner!

KILROY:
—Aw, no, aw, no, don't try to hang no vagrancy rap on me! I was robbed on this square and I got plenty of witnesses to prove it.

GUTMAN [*with ironic courtesy*]:
Oh?

[*He makes a gesture asking "Where?"*]

KILROY [*coming down to apron left and crossing to the right*]:

Witnesses! Witness! Witnesses!

[*He comes to La Madrecita.*]

You were a witness!

[*A gesture indicates that he realizes her blindness. Opposite the Gypsy's balcony he pauses for a second.*]

Hey, Gypsy's daughter!

[*The balcony is dark. He continues up to the Pit. The Street People duck as he calls down:*]

You were witnesses!

[*An Officer enters with a Patsy outfit. He hands it to Gutman.*]

GUTMAN:
Here, Boy! Take these.

[*Gutman displays and then tosses on the ground at Kilroy's feet the Patsy outfit—the red fright wig, the big crimson*

216

nose that lights up and has horn rimmed glasses attached, a pair of clown pants that have a huge footprint on the seat.]

KILROY:

What is this outfit?

GUTMAN:

The uniform of a Patsy.

KILROY:

I know what a Patsy is—he's a clown in the circus who takes prat-falls but *I'm no Patsy!*

GUTMAN:

Pick it up.

KILROY:

Don't give me orders. Kilroy is a free agent—

GUTMAN [*smoothly*]:

But a Patsy isn't. Pick it up and put it on, Candy Man. You are now the Patsy.

KILROY:

So you say but you are completely mistaken.

[*Four Officers press in on him.*]

And don't crowd me with your torpedoes! I'm a stranger here but I got a clean record in all the places I been, I'm not in the books for nothin' but vagrancy and once when I was hungry I walked by a truck-load of pineapples without picking one, because I was brought up good—

[*Then, with a pathetic attempt at making friends with the Officer to his right.*]

and there was a cop on the corner!

217

OFFICER:

Ponga selo!

KILROY:

What'd you say? [*Desperately to audience he asks:*] What did he say?

OFFICER:

Ponga selo!

KILROY:

What'd you say?

[*The Officer shoves him down roughly to the Patsy outfit. Kilroy picks up the pants, shakes them out carefully as if about to step into them and says very politely:*]

Why, surely. I'd be delighted. My fondest dreams have come true.

[*Suddenly he tosses the Patsy dress into Gutman's face and leaps into the aisle of the theatre.*]

GUTMAN:

Stop him! Arrest that vagrant! Don't let him get away!

LOUDSPEAKER:

Be on the lookout for a fugitive Patsy. The Patsy has escaped. Stop him, stop that Patsy!

[*A wild chase commences. The two Guards rush madly down either side to intercept him at the back of the house. Kilroy wheels about at the top of the center aisle, and runs back down it, panting, gasping out questions and entreaties to various persons occupying aisle seats, such as:*]

KILROY:

How do I git out? Which way do I go, which way do I get out? Where's the Greyhound depot? Hey, do you know where the Greyhound bus depot is? What's the best way out, if there is any way out? I got to find one. I had enough of this place. I had too much of this place. I'm free. I'm a free man with equal rights in this world! You better believe it because that's news for you and you had better believe it! Kilroy's a free man with equal rights in this world! All right, now, help me, somebody, help me find a way out, I got to find one, I don't like this place! It's not for me and I am not buying any! Oh! Over there! I see a sign that says EXIT. That's a sweet word to me, man, that's a lovely word, EXIT! That's the entrance to paradise for Kilroy! Exit, I'm coming, Exit, I'm coming!

[*The Street People have gathered along the forestage to watch the chase. Esmeralda, barefooted, wearing only a slip, bursts out of the Gypsy's establishment like an animal broken out of a cage, darts among the Street People to the front of the Crowd which is shouting like the spectators at the climax of a corrida. Behind her, Nursie appears, a male actor, wigged and dressed austerely as a duenna, crying out in both languages.*]

NURSIE:
Esmeralda! Esmeralda!

GYPSY:
Police!

NURSIE:
Come back here, Esmeralda!

GYPSY:
Catch her, idiot!

NURSIE:
Where is my lady bird, where is my precious treasure?

GYPSY:

Idiot! I told you to keep her door locked!

NURSIE:

She jimmied the lock, Esmeralda!

[*These shouts are mostly lost in the general rhubarb of the chase and the shouting Street People. Esmeralda crouches on the forestage, screaming encouragement in Spanish to the fugitive. Abdullah catches sight of her, seizes her wrist, shouting:*]

ABDULLAH:

Here she is! I got her!

[*Esmeralda fights savagely. She nearly breaks loose, but Nursie and the Gypsy close upon her, too, and she is overwhelmed and dragged back, fighting all the way, toward the door from which she escaped.*

[*Meanwhile—timed with the above action—shots are fired in the air by Kilroy's Pursuers. He dashes, panting, into the boxes of the theatre, darting from one box to another, shouting incoherently, now, sobbing for breath, crying out:*]

KILROY:

Mary, help a Christian! Help a Christian, Mary!

ESMERALDA:

Yankee! Yankee, jump!

[*The Officers close upon him in the box nearest the stage. A dazzling spot of light is thrown on him. He lifts a little gilded chair to defend himself. The chair is torn from his grasp. He leaps upon the ledge of the box.*]

Jump! Jump, Yankee!

[*The Gypsy is dragging the girl back by her hair.*]

KILROY:

Watch out down there! Geronimo!

[*He leaps onto the stage and crumples up with a twisted ankle. Esmeralda screams demoniacally, breaks from her mother's grasp and rushes to him, fighting off his pursuers who have leapt after him from the box. Abdullah, Nursie and the Gypsy seize her again, just as Kilroy is seized by his pursuers. The Officers beat him to his knees. Each time he is struck, Esmeralda screams as if she received the blow herself. As his cries subside into sobbing, so do hers, and at the end, when he is quite helpless, she is also overcome by her captors and as they drag her back to the Gypsy's she cries to him:*]

ESMERALDA:

They've got you! They've got me!

[*Her mother slaps her fiercely.*]

Caught! Caught! We're caught!

[*She is dragged inside. The door is slammed shut on her continuing outcries. For a moment nothing is heard but Kilroy's hoarse panting and sobbing. Gutman takes command of the situation, thrusting his way through the crowd to face Kilroy who is pinioned by two Guards.*]

GUTMAN [*smiling serenely*]:

Well, well, how do you do! I understand that you're seeking employment here. We need a Patsy and the job is yours for the asking!

KILROY:

I don't. Accept. This job. I been. Shanghied!

[*Kilroy dons Patsy outfit.*]

221

GUTMAN:

Hush! The Patsy doesn't talk. He lights his nose, that's all!

GUARD:

Press the little button at the end of the cord.

GUTMAN:

That's right. Just press the little button at the end of the cord!

[*Kilroy lights his nose. Everybody laughs.*]

GUTMAN:

Again, ha ha! Again, ha ha! Again!

[*The nose goes off and on like a firefly as the stage dims out.*

[*The curtain falls. There is a short intermission.*]

BLOCK SEVEN

The Dreamer is singing with mandolin, "Noche de Ronde."
The Guests murmur, "cool—cool . . ." Gutman stands on the
podiumlike elevation downstage right, smoking a long thin
cigar, signing an occasional tab from the bar or café. He is
standing in an amber spot. The rest of the stage is filled with
blue dusk. At the signal the song fades to a whisper and
Gutman speaks.

GUTMAN:
Block Seven on the Camino Real—
I like this hour.

[*He gives the audience a tender gold-toothed smile.*]

The fire's gone out of the day but the light of it lingers . . .
In Rome the continual fountains are bathing stone heroes with
silver, in Copenhagen the Tivoli gardens are lighted, they're
selling the lottery on San Juan de Latrene . . .

[*The Dreamer advances a little, playing the mandolin*
softly.]

LA MADRECITA [*holding up glass beads and shell necklaces*]:
Recuerdos, recuerdos?

GUTMAN:
And these are the moments when we look into ourselves and
ask with a wonder which never is lost altogether: "Can this
be all? Is there nothing more? Is this what the glittering
wheels of the heavens turn for?"

[*He leans forward as if conveying a secret.*]

—Ask the Gypsy! Un poco dinero will tickle the Gypsy's palm
and give her visions!

[*Abdullah emerges with a silver tray, calling:*]

ABDULLAH:
Letter for Signor Casanova, letter for Signor Casanova!

[*Jacques springs up but stands rigid.*]

GUTMAN:
Casanova, you have received a letter. Perhaps it's the letter with the remittance check in it!

JACQUES [*in a hoarse, exalted voice*]:
Yes! It is! The letter! With the remittance check in it!

GUTMAN:
Then why don't you take it so you can maintain your residence at the Siete Mares and so avoid the more somber attractions of the "Ritz Men Only"?

JACQUES:
My hand is—

GUTMAN:
Your hand is paralyzed? . . . By what? *Anxiety? Apprehension?* . . . Put the letter in Signor Casanova's pocket so he can open it when he recovers the use of his digital extremities. Then give him a shot of brandy on the house before he falls on his face!

[*Jacques has stepped down into the plaza. He looks down at Kilroy crouched to the right of him and wildly blinking his nose.*]

JACQUES:
Yes. I know the Morse code.

[*Kilroy's nose again blinks on and off.*]

Thank you, brother.

[*This is said as if acknowledging a message.*]

I knew without asking the Gypsy that something of this sort would happen to you. You have a spark of anarchy in your spirit and that's not to be tolerated. Nothing wild or honest is tolerated here! It has to be extinguished or used only to light up your nose for Mr. Gutman's amusement . . .

[*Jacques saunters around Kilroy whistling "La Golondrina." Then satisfied that no one is suspicious of this encounter . . .*]

Before the final block we'll find some way out of here! Meanwhile, patience and courage, little brother!

[*Jacques feeling he's been there too long starts away giving Kilroy a reassuring pat on the shoulder and saying:*]

Patience! . . . Courage!

LADY MULLIGAN [*from the Mulligans' table*]:
Mr. Gutman!

GUTMAN:
Lady Mulligan! And how are you this evening, Lord Mulligan?

LADY MULLIGAN [*interrupting Lord Mulligan's rumblings*]:
He's not at all well. This . . . climate is so enervating!

LORD MULLIGAN:
I was so weak this morning . . . I couldn't screw the lid on my tooth paste!

LADY MULLIGAN:
Raymond, tell Mr. Gutman about those two impertinent workmen in the square! . . . These two idiots pushing a white barrel! Pop up every time we step outside the hotel!

LORD MULLIGAN:
—point and giggle at me!

LADY MULLIGAN:
Can't they be discharged?

GUTMAN:
They can't be discharged, disciplined nor bribed! All you can do is pretend to ignore them.

LADY MULLIGAN:
I can't eat! . . . Raymond, stop stuffing!

LORD MULLIGAN:
Shut up!

GUTMAN [*to the audience*]:
When the big wheels crack on this street it's like the fall of a capital city, the destruction of Carthage, the sack of Rome by the white-eyed giants from the North! I've seen them fall! I've seen the destruction of them! Adventurers suddenly frightened of a dark room! Gamblers unable to choose between odd and even! Con men and pitchmen and plume-hatted cavaliers turned baby-soft at one note of the Street-cleaners' pipes! When I observe this change, I say to myself: "Could it happen to ME?"—The answer is "YES!" And that's what curdles my blood like milk on the doorstep of someone gone for the summer!

[*A Hunchback Mummer somersaults through his hoop of silver bells, springs up and shakes it excitedly toward a downstage arch which begins to flicker with a diamond-blue radiance; this marks the advent of each legendary character in the play. The music follows: a waltz from the time of Camille in Paris.*]

GUTMAN [*downstage to the audience*]:
Ah, there's the music of another legend, one that everyone knows, the legend of the sentimental whore, the courtesan

226

who made the mistake of love. But now you see her coming into this plaza not as she was when she burned with a fever that cast a thin light over Paris, but changed, yes, faded as lanterns and legends fade when they burn into day!

[*He turns and shouts:*]

Rosita, sell her a flower!

[*Marguerite has entered the plaza. A beautiful woman of indefinite age. The Street People cluster about her with wheedling cries, holding up glass beads, shell necklaces and so forth. She seems confused, lost, half-awake. Jacques has sprung up at her entrance but has difficulty making his way through the cluster of vendors. Rosita has snatched up a tray of flowers and cries out:*]

ROSITA:
Camellias, camellias! Pink or white, whichever a lady finds suitable to the moon!

GUTMAN:
That's the ticket!

MARGUERITE:
Yes, I would like a camellia.

ROSITA [*in a bad French accent*]:
Rouge ou blanc ce soir?

MARGUERITE:
It's always a white one, now . . . but there used to be five evenings out of the month when a pink camellia, instead of the usual white one, let my admirers know that the moon those nights was unfavorable to pleasure, and so they called me—Camille . . .

227

JACQUES:
Mia cara!

[*Imperiously, very proud to be with her, he pushes the Street People aside with his cane.*]

Out of the way, make way, let us through, please!

MARGUERITE:
Don't push them with your cane.

JACQUES:
If they get close enough they'll snatch your purse.

[*Marguerite utters a low, shocked cry.*]

What is it?

MARGUERITE:
My purse is gone! It's lost! My papers were in it!

JACQUES:
Your passport was in it?

MARGUERITE:
My passport and my permiso de residencia!

[*She leans faint against the arch during the following scene.*

[*Abdullah turns to run. Jacques catches him.*]

JACQUES [*seizing Abdullah's wrist*]:
Where did you take her?

ABDULLAH:
Oww!—P'tit Zoco.

JACQUES:
The Souks?

ABDULLAH:
The Souks!

JACQUES:
Which cafés did she go to?

ABDULLAH:
Ahmed's, she went to—

JACQUES:
Did she smoke at Ahmed's?

ABDULLAH:
Two kif pipes!

JACQUES:
Who was it took her purse? Was it *you*? We'll see!

[*He strips off the boy's burnoose. He crouches whimpering, shivering in a ragged slip.*]

MARGUERITE:
Jacques, let the boy go, he didn't take it!

JACQUES:
He doesn't have it on him but knows who does!

ABDULLAH:
No, no, I don't know!

JACQUES:
You little son of a Gypsy! Senta! . . . You know who I am?
I am Jacques Casanova! I belong to the Secret Order of the
Rose-colored Cross! . . . Run back to Ahmed's. Contact the
spiv that took the lady's purse. Tell him to keep it but give her
back her papers! There'll be a large reward.

[*He thumps his cane on the ground to release Abdullah*

from the spell. The boy dashes off. Jacques laughs and turns triumphantly to Marguerite.]

LADY MULLIGAN:
Waiter! That adventurer and his mistress must not be seated next to Lord Mulligan's table!

JACQUES [*loudly enough for Lady Mulligan to hear*]:
This hotel has become a mecca for black marketeers and their expensively kept women!

LADY MULLIGAN:
Mr. Gutman!

MARGUERITE:
Let's have dinner upstairs!

WAITER [*directing them to terrace table*]:
This way, M'sieur.

JACQUES:
We'll take our usual table.

[*He indicates one.*]

MARGUERITE:
Please!

WAITER [*overlapping Marguerite's "please!"*]:
This table is reserved for Lord Byron!

JACQUES [*masterfully*]:
This table is always our table.

MARGUERITE:
I'm not hungry.

JACQUES:
Hold out the lady's chair, cretino!

GUTMAN [*darting over to Marguerite's chair*]:
Permit me!

[*Jacques bows with mock gallantry to Lady Mulligan as he turns to his chair during seating of Marguerite.*]

LADY MULLIGAN:
We'll move to *that* table!

JACQUES:
—You must learn how to carry the banner of Bohemia into the enemy camp.

[*A screen is put up around them.*]

MARGUERITE:
Bohemia has no banner. It survives by discretion.

JACQUES:
I'm glad that you value discretion. *Wine list!* Was it discretion that led you through the bazaars this afternoon wearing your cabochon sapphire and diamond ear-drops? You were fortunate that you lost only your purse and papers!

MARGUERITE:
Take the wine list.

JACQUES:
Still or sparkling?

MARGUERITE:
Sparkling.

GUTMAN:
May I make a suggestion, Signor Casanova?

JACQUES:
Please do.

231

GUTMAN:

It's a very cold and dry wine from only ten metres below the snowline in the mountains. The name of the wine is Quando! —meaning when! Such as "When are remittances going to be received?" "When are accounts to be settled?" Ha ha ha! Bring Signor Casanova a bottle of Quando with the compliments of the house!

JACQUES:

I'm sorry this had to happen in—your presence . . .

MARGUERITE:

That doesn't matter, my dear. But why don't you *tell* me when you are short of money?

JACQUES:

I thought the fact was apparent. It is to everyone else.

MARGUERITE:

The letter you were expecting, it still hasn't come?

JACQUES [*removing it from his pocket*]:
It came this afternoon—Here it is!

MARGUERITE:

You haven't opened the letter!

JACQUES:

I haven't had the nerve to! I've had so many unpleasant surprises that I've lost faith in my luck.

MARGUERITE:

Give the letter to me. Let me open it for you.

JACQUES:

Later, a little bit later, after the—wine . . . ·

232

MARGUERITE:
Old hawk, anxious old hawk!

[*She clasps his hand on the table: he leans toward her: she kisses her fingertips and places them on his lips.*]

JACQUES:
Do you call that a kiss?

MARGUERITE:
I call it the ghost of a kiss. It will have to do for now.

[*She leans back, her blue-tinted eyelids closed.*]

JACQUES:
Are you tired? Are you tired, Marguerite? You know you should have rested this afternoon.

MARGUERITE:
I looked at silver and rested.

JACQUES:
You looked at silver at Ahmed's?

MARGUERITE:
No, I rested at Ahmed's, and had mint-tea.

[*The Dreamer accompanies their speech with his guitar. The duologue should have the style of an antiphonal poem, the cues picked up so that there is scarcely a separation between the speeches, and the tempo quick and the voices edged.*]

JACQUES:
You had mint-tea downstairs?

MARGUERITE:
No, upstairs.

233

JACQUES:

Upstairs where they burn the poppy?

MARGUERITE:

Upstairs where it's cool and there's music and the haggling of the bazaar is soft as the murmur of pigeons.

JACQUES:

That sounds restful. Reclining among silk pillows on a divan, in a curtained and perfumed alcove above the bazaar?

MARGUERITE:

Forgetting for a while where I am, or that I don't know where I am . . .

JACQUES:

Forgetting alone or forgetting with some young companion who plays the lute or the flute or who had silver to show you? Yes. That sounds very restful. And yet you do seem tired.

MARGUERITE:

If I seem tired, it's your insulting solicitude that I'm tired of!

JACQUES:

Is it insulting to feel concern for your safety in this place?

MARGUERITE:

Yes, it is. The implication is.

JACQUES:

What is the implication?

MARGUERITE:

You know what it is: that I am one of those *aging—voluptuaries*—who used to be paid for pleasure but now have to pay!—Jacques, I won't be followed, I've gone too far to be followed!—*What is it?*

[*The Waiter has presented an envelope on a salver.*]

WAITER:
A letter for the lady.

MARGUERITE:
How strange to receive a letter in a place where nobody knows I'm staying! Will you open it for me?

[*The Waiter withdraws. Jacques takes the letter and opens it.*]

Well! What is it?

JACQUES:
Nothing important. An illustrated brochure from some resort in the mountains.

MARGUERITE:
What is it called?

JACQUES:
Bide-a-While.

[*A chafing dish bursts into startling blue flame at the Mulligans' table. Lady Mulligan clasps her hands and exclaims with affected delight, the Waiter and Mr. Gutman laugh agreeably. Marguerite springs up and moves out upon the forestage. Jacques goes to her.*]

Do you know this resort in the mountains?

MARGUERITE:
Yes. I stayed there once. It's one of those places with open sleeping verandahs, surrounded by snowy pine woods. It has rows and rows of narrow white iron beds as regular as tombstones. The invalids smile at each other when axes flash across valleys, ring, flash, ring again! Young voices shout across

valleys Hola! And mail is delivered. The friend that used to write you ten-page letters contents himself now with a post-card bluebird that tells you to "Get well Quick!"

[*Jacques throws the brochure away.*]

—And when the last bleeding comes, not much later nor earlier than expected, you're wheeled discreetly into a little tent of white gauze, and the last thing you know of this world, of which you've known so little and yet so much, is the smell of an empty ice box.

[*The blue flame expires in the chafing dish. Gutman picks up the brochure and hands it to the Waiter, whispering something.*]

JACQUES:
You won't go back to that place.

[*The Waiter places the brochure on the salver again and approaches behind them.*]

MARGUERITE:
I wasn't released. I left without permission. They sent me this to remind me.

WAITER [*presenting the salver*]:
You dropped this.

JACQUES:
We threw it away!

WAITER:
Excuse me.

JACQUES:
Now, from now on, Marguerite, you must take better care of yourself. Do you hear me?

236

MARGUERITE:

I hear you. No more distractions for me? No more entertainers in curtained and perfumed alcoves above the bazaar, no more young men that a pinch of white powder or a puff of gray smoke can almost turn to someone devoutly remembered?

JACQUES:

No, from now on—

MARGUERITE:

What "from now on," old hawk?

JACQUES:

Rest. Peace.

MARGUERITE:

Rest in peace is that final bit of advice they carve on gravestones, and I'm not ready for it! Are you? Are *you* ready for it?

[*She returns to the table. He follows her.*]

Oh, Jacques, when are we going to leave here, how are we going to leave here, you've got to tell me!

JACQUES:

I've told you all I know.

MARGUERITE:

Nothing, you've given up hope!

JACQUES:

I haven't, that's not true.

[*Gutman has brought out the white cockatoo which he shows to Lady Mulligan at her table.*]

GUTMAN [*his voice rising above the murmurs*]:
Her name is Aurora.

LADY MULLIGAN:
Why do you call her Aurora?

GUTMAN:
She cries at daybreak.

LADY MULLIGAN:
Only at daybreak?

GUTMAN:
Yes, at daybreak only.

[*Their voices and laughter fade under.*]

MARGUERITE:
How long is it since you've been to the travel agencies?

JACQUES:
This morning I made the usual round of Cook's, American Express, Wagon-lits Universal, and it was the same story. There are no flights out of here till further orders from someone higher up.

MARGUERITE:
Nothing, nothing at all?

JACQUES:
Oh, there's a rumor of something called the Fugitivo, but—

MARGUERITE:
The What!!! ?

JACQUES:
The Fugitivo. It's one of those non-scheduled things that—

MARGUERITE:
When, when, when?

JACQUES:

I told you it was non-scheduled. Non-scheduled means it comes and goes at no predictable—

MARGUERITE:

Don't give me the dictionary! I want to know how does one get on it? Did you bribe them? Did you offer them money? No. Of course you didn't! And I know why! You really don't want to leave here. You *think* you don't want to go because you're brave as an old hawk. But the truth of the matter—the real not the royal truth—is that you're terrified of the Terra Incognita outside that wall.

JACQUES:

You've hit upon the truth. I'm terrified of the unknown country inside or outside this wall or any place on earth without you with me! The only country, known or unknown that I can breathe in, or care to, is the country in which we breathe together, as we are now at this table. And later, a little while later, even closer than this, the sole inhabitants of a tiny world whose limits are those of the light from a rose-colored lamp— beside the sweetly, completely known country of your cool bed!

MARGUERITE:

The little comfort of love?

JACQUES:

Is that comfort so little?

MARGUERITE:

Caged birds accept each other but flight is what they long for.

JACQUES:

I want to stay here with you and love you and guard you

until the time or way comes that we both can leave with honor.

MARGUERITE:

"Leave with honor"? Your vocabulary is almost as out-of-date as your cape and your cane. How could anyone quit this field with honor, this place where there's nothing but the gradual wasting away of everything decent in us . . . the sort of desperation that comes after even desperation has been worn out through long wear! . . . Why have they put these screens around the table?

[*She springs up and knocks one of them over.*]

LADY MULLIGAN:

There! You see? I don't understand why you let such people stay here.

GUTMAN:

They pay the price of admission the same as you.

LADY MULLIGAN:

What price is that?

GUTMAN:

Desperation!—With cash here!

[*He indicates the Siete Mares.*]

Without cash there!

[*He indicates Skid Row.*]

Block Eight on the Camino Real!

BLOCK EIGHT

There is the sound of loud desert wind and a flamenco cry followed by a dramatic phrase of music.

A flickering diamond blue radiance floods the hotel entrance. The crouching, grimacing Hunchback shakes his hoop of bells which is the convention for the appearance of each legendary figure.

Lord Byron appears in the doorway readied for departure. Gutman raises his hand for silence.

GUTMAN:
You're leaving us, Lord Byron?

BYRON:
Yes, I'm leaving you, Mr. Gutman.

GUTMAN:
What a pity! But this is a port of entry and departure. There are no permanent guests. Possibly you are getting a little restless?

BYRON:
The luxuries of this place have made me soft. The metal point's gone from my pen, there's nothing left but the feather.

GUTMAN:
That may be true. But what can you do about it?

BYRON:
Make a departure!

GUTMAN:
From yourself?

BYRON:
From my present self to myself as I used to be!

GUTMAN:

That's the *furthest* departure a man could make! I guess you're sailing to Athens? There's another war there and like all wars since the beginning of time it can be interpreted as a —struggle for *what?*

BYRON:

—For *freedom!* You may laugh at it, but it still means something to *me!*

GUTMAN:

Of course it does! I'm not laughing a bit, I'm beaming with admiration.

BYRON:

I've allowed myself many distractions.

GUTMAN:

Yes, indeed!

BYRON:

But I've never altogether forgotten my old devotion to the—

GUTMAN:

—To the *what,* Lord Byron?

[*Byron passes nervous fingers through his hair.*]

You can't remember the object of your one-time devotion?

[*There is a pause. Byron limps away from the terrace and goes toward the fountain.*]

BYRON:

When Shelley's corpse was recovered from the sea . . .

[*Gutman beckons the Dreamer who approaches and accompanies Byron's speech.*]

—It was burned on the beach at Viareggio.—I watched the spectacle from my carriage because the stench was revolting . . . Then it—fascinated me! I got out of my carriage. Went nearer, holding a handkerchief to my nostrils!—I saw that the front of the skull had broken away in the flames, and there—

[*He advances out upon the stage apron, followed by Abdullah with the pine torch or lantern.*]

And there was the brain of Shelley, indistinguishable from a cooking stew!—*boiling, bubbling, hissing!*—in the *blackening* —*cracked—pot*—of his skull!

[*Marguerite rises abruptly. Jacques supports her.*]

—Trelawney, his friend, Trelawney, threw salt and oil and frankincense in the flames and finally the almost intolerable stench—

[*Abdullah giggles. Gutman slaps him.*]

—was *gone* and the burning was *pure!*—as a man's burning should be . . .

A man's burning *ought* to be pure!—*not* like mine—(a crepe suzette—burned in brandy . . .)

Shelley's burning was finally very *pure!*

But the body, the corpse, split open like a grilled pig!

[*Abdullah giggles irrepressibly again. Gutman grips the back of his neck and he stands up stiff and assumes an expression of exaggerated solemnity.*]

—And then Trelawney—as the ribs of the corpse unlocked— reached into them as a baker reaches quickly into an oven!

243

[*Abdullah almost goes into another convulsion.*]

—And snatched out—as a baker would a biscuit!—the *heart* of Shelley! Snatched the heart of Shelley out of the blistering corpse!—Out of the purifying—blue-flame . . .

[*Marguerite resumes her seat; Jacques his.*]

—And it was *over!*—I thought—

[*He turns slightly from the audience and crosses upstage from the apron. He faces Jacques and Marguerite.*]

—I thought it was a disgusting thing to do, to snatch a man's heart from his body! What can one man do with another man's heart?

[*Jacques rises and strikes the stage with his cane.*]

JACQUES [*passionately*]:
He can do this with it!

[*He seizes a loaf of bread on his table, and descends from the terrace.*]

He can twist it like this!

[*He twists the loaf.*]

He can tear it like this!

[*He tears the loaf in two.*]

He can crush it under his foot!

[*He drops the bread and stamps on it.*]

—*And kick it away—like this!*

[*He kicks the bread off the terrace. Lord Byron turns away from him and limps again out upon the stage apron and speaks to the audience.*]

BYRON:

That's very true, Señor. But a poet's vocation, which used to be my vocation, is to influence the heart in a gentler fashion than you have made your mark on that loaf of bread. He ought to purify it and lift it above its ordinary level. For what is the heart but a sort of—

[*He makes a high, groping gesture in the air.*]

—A sort of—*instrument!*—that translates *noise* into *music,* chaos into—*order* . . .

[*Abdullah ducks almost to the earth in an effort to stifle his mirth. Gutman coughs to cover his own amusement.*]

—a *mysterious order!*

[*He raises his voice till it fills the plaza.*]

—That was my vocation once upon a time, before it was obscured by vulgar plaudits!—Little by little it was lost among gondolas and palazzos!—masked balls, glittering salons, huge shadowy courts and torch-lit entrances!—Baroque façades, canopies and carpets, candelabra and gold plate among snowy damask, ladies with throats as slender as flower-stems, bending and breathing toward me their fragrant breath—

—Exposing their breasts to me!

Whispering, half-smiling!—And everywhere marble, the visible grandeur of marble, pink and gray marble, veined and tinted as flayed corrupting flesh,—all these provided agreeable distractions from the rather frightening solitude of a poet. Oh, I wrote many cantos in Venice and Constantinople and in Ravenna and Rome, on all of those Latin and Levantine excursions that my twisted foot led me into—but I wonder about them a little. They seem to improve as the wine in the

245

bottle—dwindles . . . *There is a passion for declivity in this world!*

And lately I've found myself listening to hired musicians behind a row of artificial palm trees—instead of the single—pure-stringed instrument of my heart . . .

Well, then, it's time to leave here!

[*He turns back to the stage.*]

—There is a time for departure even when there's no certain place to go!

I'm going to look for one, now. I'm sailing to Athens. At least I can look up at the Acropolis, I can stand at the foot of it and look up at broken columns on the crest of a hill—if not purity, at least its recollection . . .

I can sit quietly looking for a long, long time in absolute silence, and possibly, yes, *still* possibly—

The old pure music will come to me again. Of course on the other hand I may hear only the little noise of insects in the grass . . .

But I am sailing to Athens! *Make voyages!—Attempt them!—* there's nothing else . . .

MARGUERITE [*excitedly*]:
Watch where he goes!

[*Lord Byron limps across the plaza with his head bowed, making slight, apologetic gestures to the wheedling Beggars who shuffle about him. There is music. He crosses toward the steep Alleyway Out. The following is played with a quiet intensity so it will be in a lower key than the later Fugitivo Scene.*]

246

Watch him, watch him, see which way he goes. Maybe he knows of a way that we haven't found out.

JACQUES:
Yes, I'm watching him, Cara.

[*Lord and Lady Mulligan half rise, staring anxiously through monocle and lorgnon.*]

MARGUERITE:
Oh, my God, I believe he's going up that alley.

JACQUES:
Yes, he is. He has.

LORD and LADY MULLIGAN:
Oh, the fool, the idiot, he's going under the arch!

MARGUERITE:
Jacques, run after him, warn him, tell him about the desert he has to cross.

JACQUES:
I think he knows what he's doing.

MARGUERITE:
I can't look!

[*She turns to the audience, throwing back her head and closing her eyes. The desert wind sings loudly as Byron climbs to the top of the steps.*]

BYRON [*to several porters carrying luggage—which is mainly caged birds*]:
THIS WAY!

[*He exits.*

[*Kilroy starts to follow. He stops at the steps, cringing and looking at Gutman. Gutman motions him to go ahead. Kilroy rushes up the stairs. He looks out, loses his nerve and sits—blinking his nose. Gutman laughs as he announces—]*

GUTMAN:
Block Nine on the Camino Real!

[He goes into the hotel.]

Abdullah runs back to the hotel with the billowing flambeau.
A faint and far away humming sound becomes audible . . .
Marguerite opens her eyes with a startled look. She searches
the sky for something. A very low percussion begins with the
humming sound, as if excited hearts are beating.

MARGUERITE:
Jacques! I hear something in the sky!

JACQUES:
I think what you hear is—

MARGUERITE [*with rising excitement*]:
—No, it's a plane, a great one, I see the lights of it, now!

JACQUES:
Some kind of fireworks, Cara.

MARGUERITE:
Hush! LISTEN!

[*She blows out the candle to see better above it. She rises,*
peering into the sky.]

I see it! I see it! There! It's circling over us!

LADY MULLIGAN:
Raymond, Raymond, sit down, your face is flushed!

HOTEL GUESTS [*overlapping*]:
—What is it?
—The FUGITIVO!
—THE FUGITIVO! THE FUGITIVO!
—Quick, get my jewelry from the hotel safe!
—Cash a check!

—Throw some things in a bag! I'll wait here!
—Never mind luggage, we have our money and papers!
—Where is it now?
—There, there!
—It's turning to land!
—To go like this?
—Yes, go anyhow, just go anyhow, just go!
—Raymond! Please!
—Oh, it's rising again!
—Oh, it's—*SHH! MR. GUTMAN!*

[*Gutman appears in the doorway. He raises a hand in a commanding gesture.*]

GUTMAN:

Signs in the sky should not be mistaken for wonders!

[*The Voices modulate quickly.*]

Ladies, gentlemen, please resume your seats!

[*Places are resumed at tables, and silver is shakily lifted. Glasses are raised to lips, but the noise of concerted panting of excitement fills the stage and a low percussion echoes frantic heart beats.*

[*Gutman descends to the plaza, shouting furiously to the Officer.*]

Why wasn't I told the Fugitivo was coming?

[*Everyone, almost as a man, rushes into the hotel and reappears almost at once with hastily collected possessions. Marguerite rises but appears stunned.*

[*There is a great whistling and screeching sound as the aerial transport halts somewhere close by, accompanied by rainbow splashes of light and cries like children's on a roller-coaster. Some incoming Passengers approach the stage down an aisle of the theatre, preceded by Redcaps with luggage.*]

PASSENGERS:
—What a heavenly trip!
—The scenery was thrilling!
—It's so quick!
—The only way to travel! Etc., etc.

[*A uniformed man, the Pilot, enters the plaza with a megaphone.*]

PILOT [*through the megaphone*]:
Fugitivo now loading for departure! Fugitivo loading immediately for departure! Northwest corner of the plaza!

MARGUERITE:
Jacques, it's the Fugitivo, it's the non-scheduled thing you heard of this afternoon!

PILOT:
All out-going passengers on the Fugitivo are requested to present their tickets and papers immediately at this station.

MARGUERITE:
He said "out-going passengers"!

PILOT:
Out-going passengers on the Fugitivo report immediately at this station for customs inspection.

MARGUERITE [*with a forced smile*]:
Why are you just standing there?

JACQUES [*with an Italian gesture*]:
Che cosa possa fare!

MARGUERITE:
Move, move, do something!

JACQUES:
What!

MARGUERITE:
Go to them, ask, find out!

JACQUES:
I have no idea what the damned thing is!

MARGUERITE:
I do, I'll tell you! It's a way to escape from this abominable place!

JACQUES:
Forse, forse, non so!

MARGUERITE:
It's a way *out* and *I'm* not going to miss it!

PILOT:
Ici la Douane! Customs inspection here!

MARGUERITE:
Customs. That means luggage. Run to my room! Here! Key! Throw a few things in a bag, my jewels, my furs, but hurry! Vite, vite, vite! I don't believe there's much time! No, everybody is—

[*Outgoing Passengers storm the desk and table.*]

—Clamoring for tickets! There must be limited space! Why don't you do what I tell you?

[*She rushes to a man with a rubber stamp and a roll of tickets.*]

Monsieur! Señor! Pardonnez-moi! I'm going, I'm going out!
I want my ticket!

PILOT [*coldly*]:
Name, please.

MARGUERITE:
Mademoiselle—Gautier—but I—

PILOT:
Gautier? Gautier? We have no Gautier listed.

MARGUERITE:
I'm—*not* listed! I mean I'm—traveling under another name.

TRAVEL AGENT:
What name are you traveling under?

[*Prudence and Olympe rush out of the hotel half dressed,
dragging their furs. Meanwhile Kilroy is trying to make a
fast buck or two as a Redcap. The scene gathers wild momentum, is punctuated by crashes of percussion. Grotesque
mummers act as demon custom inspectors and immigration
authorities, etc. Baggage is tossed about, ripped open, smuggled goods seized, arrests made, all amid the wildest im-
portunities, protests, threats, bribes, entreaties; it is a scene
for improvisation.*]

PRUDENCE:
Thank God I woke up!

OLYMPE:
Thank God I wasn't asleep!

PRUDENCE:
I knew it was non-scheduled but I *did* think they'd give you
time to get in your girdle.

OLYMPE:

Look who's trying to crash it! I know damned well *she* don't have a reservation!

PILOT [*to Marguerite*]:

What name did you say, Mademoiselle? Please! People are waiting, you're holding up the line!

MARGUERITE:

I'm so confused! Jacques! What name did you make my reservation under?

OLYMPE:

She has no reservation!

PRUDENCE:

I have, I got mine!

OLYMPE:

I got mine!

PRUDENCE:

I'm next!

OLYMPE:

Don't push *me*, you old bag!

MARGUERITE:

I was here first! I was here before anybody! Jacques, quick! Get my money from the hotel safe!

[*Jacques exits.*]

AGENT:

Stay in line!

[*There is a loud warning whistle.*]

PILOT:

Five minutes. The Fugitivo leaves in five minutes. Five, five minutes only!

[*At this announcement the scene becomes riotous.*]

TRAVEL AGENT:

Four minutes! The Fugitivo leaves in four minutes!

[*Prudence and Olympe are shrieking at him in French. The warning whistle blasts again.*]

Three minutes, the Fugitivo leaves in three minutes!

MARGUERITE [*topping the turmoil*]:

Monsieur! Please! I was here first, I was here before anybody! Look!

[*Jacques returns with her money.*]

I have thousands of francs! Take whatever you want! Take all of it, it's yours!

PILOT:

Payment is only accepted in pounds sterling or dollars. Next, please.

MARGUERITE:

You don't accept francs? They do at the hotel! They accept my francs at the Siete Mares!

PILOT:

Lady, don't argue with me, I don't make the rules!

MARGUERITE [*beating her forehead with her fist*]:

Oh, God, Jacques! Take these back to the cashier!

[*She thrusts the bills at him.*]

255

Get them changed to dollars or—*Hurry! Tout de suite!* I'm—going to faint . . .

JACQUES:
But Marguerite—

MARGUERITE:
Go! Go! Please!

PILOT:
Closing, we're closing now! The Fugitivo leaves in two minutes!

[*Lord and Lady Mulligan rush forward.*]

LADY MULLIGAN:
Let Lord Mulligan through.

PILOT [*to Marguerite*]:
You're standing in the way.

[*Olympe screams as the Customs Inspector dumps her jewels on the ground. She and Prudence butt heads as they dive for the gems: the fight is renewed.*]

MARGUERITE [*detaining the Pilot*]:
Oh, look, Monsieur! Regardez ça! My diamond, a solitaire—two carats! Take that as security!

PILOT:
Let me go. The Loan Shark's across the plaza!

[*There is another warning blast. Prudence and Olympe seize hat boxes and rush toward the whistle.*]

MARGUERITE [*clinging desperately to the Pilot*]:
You don't understand! Señor Casanova has gone to change money! He'll be here in a second. And I'll pay five, ten, twenty

times the price of—*JACQUES! JACQUES! WHERE ARE YOU?*

VOICE [*back of auditorium*]:
We're closing the gate!

MARGUERITE:
You can't close the gate!

PILOT:
Move, Madame!

MARGUERITE:
I won't move!

LADY MULLIGAN:
I tell you, Lord Mulligan is the Iron & Steel man from Cobh! Raymond! They're closing the gate!

LORD MULLIGAN:
I can't seem to get through!

GUTMAN:
Hold the gate for Lord Mulligan!

PILOT [*to Marguerite*]:
Madame, stand back or I will have to use force!

MARGUERITE:
Jacques! Jacques!

LADY MULLIGAN:
Let us through! We're clear!

PILOT:
Madame! Stand back and let these passengers through!

MARGUERITE:
No, No! I'm first! I'm next!

257

LORD MULLIGAN:
Get her out of our way! That woman's a whore!

LADY MULLIGAN:
How dare you stand in our way?

PILOT:
Officer, take this woman!

LADY MULLIGAN:
Come on, Raymond!

MARGUERITE [*as the Officer pulls her away*]:
Jacques! Jacques! Jacques!

[*Jacques returns with changed money.*]

Here! Here is the money!

PILOT:
All right, give me your papers.

MARGUERITE:
—My papers? Did you say my papers?

PILOT:
Hurry, hurry, your passport!

MARGUERITE:
—Jacques! He wants my papers! Give him my papers,
Jacques!

JACQUES:
—The lady's papers are lost!

MARGUERITE [*wildly*]:
No, no, no, THAT IS NOT TRUE! HE WANTS TO
KEEP ME HERE! HE'S LYING ABOUT IT!

258

JACQUES:

Have you forgotten that your papers were stolen?

MARGUERITE:

I gave you my papers, I gave you my papers to keep, you've got my papers.

[*Screaming, Lady Mulligan breaks past her and descends the stairs.*]

LADY MULLIGAN:

Raymond! Hurry!

LORD MULLIGAN [*staggering on the top step*]:

I'm sick! I'm sick!

[*The Streetcleaners disguised as expensive morticians in swallowtail coats come rapidly up the aisle of the theatre and wait at the foot of the stairway for the tottering tycoon.*]

LADY MULLIGAN:

You cannot be sick till we get on the Fugitivo!

LORD MULLIGAN:

Forward all cables to Guaranty Trust in Paris.

LADY MULLIGAN:

Place de la Concorde.

LORD MULLIGAN:

Thank you! All purchases C.O.D. to Mulligan Iron & Steel Works in Cobh—Thank you!

LADY MULLIGAN:

Raymond! Raymond! Who are these men?

LORD MULLIGAN:

I know these men! I recognize their faces!

LADY MULLIGAN:

Raymond! They're the Streetcleaners!

[*She screams and runs up the aisle screaming repeatedly, stopping half-way to look back. The Two Streetcleaners seize Lord Mulligan by either arm as he crumples.*]

Pack Lord Mulligan's body in dry ice! Ship Air Express to Cobh care of Mulligan Iron & Steel Works, in Cobh!

[*She runs sobbing out of the back of the auditorium as the whistle blows repeatedly and a Voice shouts.*]

I'm coming! I'm coming!

MARGUERITE:

Jacques! Jacques! Oh, God!

PILOT:

The Fugitivo is leaving, all aboard!

[*He starts toward the steps. Marguerite clutches his arm.*]

Let go of me!

MARGUERITE:

You can't go without me!

PILOT:

Officer, hold this woman!

JACQUES:

Marguerite, let him go!

[*She releases the Pilot's arm and turns savagely on Jacques. She tears his coat open, seizes a large envelope of papers and rushes after the Pilot who has started down the steps over the orchestra pit and into a center aisle of the house. Timpani build up as she starts down the steps, screaming—*]

MARGUERITE:

Here! I have them here! Wait! I have my papers now, I have my papers!

[*The Pilot runs cursing up the center aisle as the Fugitivo whistle gives repeated short, shrill blasts; timpani and dissonant brass are heard.*]

[*Outgoing Passengers burst into hysterical song, laughter, shouts of farewell. These can come over a loudspeaker at the back of the house.*]

VOICE IN DISTANCE:

Going! Going! Going!

MARGUERITE [*attempting as if half-paralyzed to descend the steps*]:

NOT WITHOUT ME, NO, NO, NOT WITHOUT ME!

[*Her figure is caught in the dazzling glacial light of the follow-spot. It blinds her. She makes violent, crazed gestures, clinging to the railing of the steps; her breath is loud and hoarse as a dying person's, she holds a blood-stained handkerchief to her lips.*

[*There is a prolonged, gradually fading, rocketlike roar as the Fugitivo takes off. Shrill cries of joy from departing passengers; something radiant passes above the stage and streams of confetti and tinsel fall into the plaza. Then there is a great calm, the ship's receding roar diminished to the hum of an insect.*]

GUTMAN [*somewhat compassionately*]:

Block Ten on the Camino Real.

There is something about the desolation of the plaza that suggests a city devastated by bombardment. Reddish lights flicker here and there as if ruins were smoldering and wisps of smoke rise from them.

LA MADRECITA [*almost inaudibly*]:
Donde?

THE DREAMER:
Aquí. Aquí, Madrecita.

MARGUERITE:
Lost! Lost! Lost! Lost!

[*She is still clinging brokenly to the railing of the steps. Jacques descends to her and helps her back up the steps.*]

JACQUES:
Lean against me, Cara. Breathe quietly, now.

MARGUERITE:
Lost!

JACQUES:
Breathe quietly, quietly, and look up at the sky.

MARGUERITE:
Lost . . .

JACQUES:
These tropical nights are so clear. There's the Southern Cross. Do you see the Southern Cross, Marguerite?

[*He points through the proscenium. They are now on the bench before the fountain; she is resting in his arms.*]

And there, over there, is Orion, like a fat, golden fish swimming North in the deep clear water, and we are together, breathing quietly together, leaning together, quietly, quietly together, completely, sweetly together, not frightened, now, not alone, but completely quietly together ...

[*La Madrecita, led into the center of the plaza by her son, has begun to sing very softly; the reddish flares dim out and the smoke disappears.*]

All of us have a desperate bird in our hearts, a memory of—some distant mother with—wings ...

MARGUERITE:
I would have—left—without you ...

JACQUES:
I know, I know!

MARGUERITE:
Then how can you—still—?

JACQUES:
Hold you?

[*Marguerite nods slightly.*]

Because you've taught me that part of love which is tender. I never knew it before. Oh, I had—mistresses that circled me like moons! I scrambled from one bed-chamber to another bed-chamber with shirttails always aflame, from girl to girl, like buckets of coal-oil poured on a conflagration! But never loved until now with the part of love that's tender ...

MARGUERITE:
—We're used to each other. That's what you think is love ... You'd better leave me now, you'd better go and let me go because there's a cold wind blowing out of the mountains and over the desert and into my heart, and if you stay with me now, I'll say cruel things, I'll wound your vanity, I'll taunt you with the decline of your male vigor!

263

JACQUES:

Why does disappointment make people unkind to each other?

MARGUERITE:

Each of us is very much alone.

JACQUES:

Only if we distrust each other.

MARGUERITE:

We have to distrust each other. It is our only defense against betrayal.

JACQUES:

I think our defense is love.

MARGUERITE:

Oh, Jacques, we're used to each other, we're a pair of captive hawks caught in the same cage, and so we've grown used to each other. That's what passes for love at this dim, shadowy end of the Camino Real . . .

What are we sure of? Not even of our existence, dear comforting friend! And whom can we ask the questions that torment us? "What is this place?" "Where are we?"—a fat old man who gives sly hints that only bewilder us more, a fake of a Gypsy squinting at cards and tea-leaves. What else are we offered? The never-broken procession of little events that assure us that we and strangers about us are still going on! Where? Why? and the perch that we hold is unstable! We're threatened with eviction, for this is a port of entry and departure, there are no permanent guests! And where else have we to go when we leave here? Bide-a-While? "Ritz Men Only"? Or under that ominous arch into Terra Incognita? We're lonely. We're frightened. We hear the Streetcleaners' piping not far away. So now and then, although we've wounded each other time and again—we stretch out hands to each other in the dark that we can't escape from— we huddle together for some dim-communal comfort—and that's what passes for love on this terminal stretch of the road that used to be royal. What is it, this feeling between us? When you feel my exhausted weight against your shoulder— when I clasp your anxious old hawk's head to my breast, what is it we feel in whatever is left of our hearts? Something, yes, something—delicate, unreal, bloodless! The sort of violets that could grow on the moon, or in the crevices of those far away mountains, fertilized by the droppings of carrion birds. Those birds are familiar to us. Their shadows inhabit the plaza. I've heard them flapping their wings like old charwomen beating worn-out carpets with gray brooms . . .

But tenderness, the violets in the mountains—can't break the rocks!

JACQUES:
The violets in the mountains can break the rocks if you believe in them and allow them to grow!

[*The plaza has resumed its usual aspect. Abdullah enters through one of the downstage arches.*]

ABDULLAH:
Get your carnival hats and noisemakers here! Tonight the moon will restore the virginity of my sister!

MARGUERITE [*almost tenderly touching his face*]:
Don't you know that tonight I am going to betray you?

JACQUES:
—Why would you do that?

MARGUERITE:
Because I've out-lived the tenderness of my heart. Abdullah,

265

come here! I have an errand for you! Go to Ahmed's and deliver a message!

ABDULLAH:

I'm working for Mama, making the Yankee dollar! Get your carnival hats and—

MARGUERITE:

Here, boy!

[*She snatches a ring off her finger and offers it to him.*]

JACQUES:

—Your cabochon sapphire?

MARGUERITE:

Yes, my cabochon sapphire!

JACQUES:

Are you mad?

MARGUERITE:

Yes, I'm mad, or nearly! The specter of lunacy's at my heels tonight!

[*Jacques drives Abdullah back with his cane.*]

Catch, boy! The other side of the fountain! Quick!

[*The guitar is heard molto vivace. She tosses the ring across the fountain. Jacques attempts to hold the boy back with his cane. Abdullah dodges in and out like a little terrier, laughing. Marguerite shouts encouragement in French. When the boy is driven back from the ring, she snatches it up and tosses it to him again, shouting:*]

Catch, boy! Run to Ahmed's! Tell the charming young man that the French lady's bored with her company tonight! Say that the French lady missed the Fugitivo and wants to forget

266

she missed it! Oh, and reserve a room with a balcony so I can watch your sister appear on the roof when the moonrise makes her a virgin!

[*Abdullah skips shouting out of the plaza. Jacques strikes the stage with his cane. She says, without looking at him:*]

Time betrays us and we betray each other.

JACQUES:
Wait, Marguerite.

MARGUERITE:
No! I can't! The wind from the desert is sweeping me away!

[*A loud singing wind sweeps her toward the terrace, away from him. She looks back once or twice as if for some gesture of leave-taking but he only stares at her fiercely, striking the stage at intervals with his cane, like a death-march. Gutman watches, smiling, from the terrace, bows to Marguerite as she passes into the hotel. The drum of Jacques' cane is taken up by other percussive instruments, and almost unnoticeably at first, weird-looking celebrants or carnival mummers creep into the plaza, silently as spiders descending a wall.*]

[*A sheet of scarlet and yellow rice paper bearing some cryptic device is lowered from the center of the plaza. The percussive effects become gradually louder. Jacques is oblivious to the scene behind him, standing in front of the plaza, his eyes closed.*]

GUTMAN:
Block Eleven on the Camino Real.

BLOCK ELEVEN

GUTMAN:

The Fiesta has started. The first event is the coronation of the King of Cuckolds.

[*Blinding shafts of light are suddenly cast upon Casanova on the forestage. He shields his face, startled, as the crowd closes about him. The blinding shafts of light seem to strike him like savage blows and he falls to his knees as—*

[*The Hunchback scuttles out of the Gypsy's stall with a crown of gilded antlers on a velvet pillow. He places it on Jacques' head. The celebrants form a circle about him chanting.*]

JACQUES:

What is this?—a crown—

GUTMAN:

A crown of horns!

CROWD:

Cornudo! Cornudo! Cornudo! Cornudo! Cornudo!

GUTMAN:

Hail, all hail, the King of Cuckolds on the Camino Real!

[*Jacques springs up, first striking out at them with his cane. Then all at once he abandons self-defense, throws off his cape, casts away his cane, and fills the plaza with a roar of defiance and self-derision.*]

JACQUES:

Si, si, sono cornudo! Cornudo! Cornudo! Casanova is the King of Cuckolds on the Camino Real! Show me crowned to the world! Announce the honor! Tell the world of the honor bestowed on Casanova, Chevalier·de Seingalt! Knight

of the Golden Spur by the Grace of His Holiness the Pope
. . . Famous adventurer! Con man Extraordinary! Gambler!
Pitch-man par excellence! Shill! Pimp! Spiv! *And—great—
lover . . .*

[*The Crowd howls with applause and laughter but his voice
rises above them with sobbing intensity.*]

Yes, I said GREAT LOVER! The greatest lover wears the
longest horns on the Camino! GREAT! LOVER!

GUTMAN:

Attention! Silence! The moon is rising! The restoration is
about to occur!

[*A white radiance is appearing over the ancient wall of the
town. The mountains become luminous. There is music.
Everyone, with breathless attention, faces the light.*

[*Kilroy crosses to Jacques and beckons him out behind the
crowd. There he snatches off the antlers and returns him his
fedora. Jacques reciprocates by removing Kilroy's fright
wig and electric nose. They embrace as brothers. In a Chap-
linesque dumb-play, Kilroy points to the wildly flickering
three brass balls of the Loan Shark and to his golden gloves:
then with a terrible grimace he removes the gloves from
about his neck, smiles at Jacques and indicates that the two
of them together will take flight over the wall. Jacques
shakes his head sadly, pointing to his heart and then to the
Siete Mares. Kilroy nods with regretful understanding of a
human and manly folly. A Guard has been silently approaching them in a soft shoe dance. Jacques whistles "La
Golondrina." Kilroy assumes a very nonchalant pose. The
Guard picks up curiously the discarded fright wig and
electric nose. Then glancing suspiciously at the pair, he
advances. Kilroy makes a run for it. He does a baseball*

269

slide into the Loan Shark's welcoming doorway. The door slams. The Cop is about to crash it when a gong sounds and Gutman shouts:]

GUTMAN:
SILENCE! ATTENTION! THE GYPSY!

GYPSY [*appearing on the roof with a gong*]:
The moon has restored the virginity of my daughter Esmeralda!

[*The gong sounds.*]

STREET PEOPLE:
Ahh!

GYPSY:
The moon in its plenitude has made her a virgin!

[*The gong sounds.*]

STREET PEOPLE:
Ahh!

GYPSY:
Praise her, celebrate her, give her suitable homage!

[*The gong sounds.*]

STREET PEOPLE:
Ahh!

GYPSY:
Summon her to the roof!

[*She shouts:*]

ESMERALDA!

[*Dancers shout the name in rhythm.*]

RISE WITH THE MOON, MY DAUGHTER! CHOOSE
THE HERO!

[*Esmeralda appears on the roof in dazzling light. She seems
to be dressed in jewels. She raises her jeweled arms with a
harsh flamenco cry.*]

ESMERALDA:
OLE!

DANCERS:
OLE!

[*The details of the Carnival are a problem for director and
choreographer but it has already been indicated in the script
that the Fiesta is a sort of serio-comic, grotesque-lyric "Rites
of Fertility" with roots in various pagan cultures.*

[*It should not be over-elaborated or allowed to occupy much
time. It should not be more than three minutes from the
appearance of Esmeralda on the Gypsy's roof till the return
of Kilroy from the Loan Shark's.*

[*Kilroy emerges from the Pawn Shop in grotesque disguise, a
turban, dark glasses, a burnoose and an umbrella or sun-
shade.*]

KILROY [*to Jacques*]:

So long, pal, I wish you could come with me.

[*Jacques clasps his cross in Kilroy's hands.*]

ESMERALDA:
Yankee!

KILROY [*to the audience*]:
So long, everybody. Good luck to you all on the Camino! I

271

hocked my golden gloves to finance this expedition. I'm going. Hasta luega. I'm going. I'm gone!

ESMERALDA:
Yankee!

[*He has no sooner entered the plaza than the riotous women strip off everything but the dungarees and skivvy which he first appeared in.*]

KILROY [*to the women*]:
Let me go. Let go of me! Watch out for my equipment!

ESMERALDA:
Yankee! Yankee!

[*He breaks away from them and plunges up the stairs of the ancient wall. He is half-way up them when Gutman shouts out:*]

GUTMAN:
Follow-spot on that gringo, light the stairs!

[*The light catches Kilroy. At the same instant Esmeralda cries out to him:*]

ESMERALDA:
Yankee! Yankee!

GYPSY:
What's goin' on down there?

[*She rushes into the plaza.*]

KILROY:
Oh, no, I'm on my way out!

ESMERALDA:
Espere un momento!

[*The Gypsy calls the police, but is ignored in the crowd.*]

KILROY:

Don't tempt me, baby! I hocked my golden gloves to finance
this expedition!

ESMERALDA:

Querido!

KILROY:

Querido means sweetheart, a word which is hard to resist but
I must resist it.

ESMERALDA:

Champ!

KILROY:

I used to be Champ but why remind me of it?

ESMERALDA:

Be champ again! Contend in the contest! Compete in the
competition!

GYPSY [*shouting*]:
Naw, naw, not eligible!

ESMERALDA:
Pl-eeeeeeze!

GYPSY:

Slap her, Nursie, she's flippin'.

[*Esmeralda slaps Nursie instead.*]

ESMERALDA:

Hero! Champ!

KILROY:

I'm not in condition!

ESMERALDA:

You're still the Champ, the undefeated Champ of the golden gloves!

KILROY:

Nobody's called me that in a long, long time!

ESMERALDA:

Champ!

KILROY:

My resistance is crumbling!

ESMERALDA:

Champ!

KILROY:

It's crumbled!

ESMERALDA:

Hero!

KILROY:

GERONIMO!

[*He takes a flying leap from the stairs into the center of the plaza. He turns toward Esmeralda and cries:*]

DOLL!!

[*Kilroy surrounded by cheering Street People goes into a triumphant eccentric dance which reviews his history as fighter, traveler and lover.*

[*At finish of the dance, the music is cut off, as Kilroy lunges, arm uplifted towards Esmeralda, and cries:*]

KILROY:

Kilroy the Champ!

ESMERALDA:

KILROY the Champ!

[*She snatches a bunch of red roses from the stunned Nursie and tosses them to Kilroy.*]

CROWD [*sharply*]:

OLE!

[*The Gypsy, at the same instant, hurls her gong down, creating a resounding noise.*

[*Kilroy turns and comes down towards the audience, saying to them:*]

KILROY:

Y'see?

[*Cheering Street People surge towards him and lift him in the air. The lights fade as the curtain descends.*]

CROWD [*in a sustained yell*]:

OLE!

[*The curtain falls. There is a short intermission.*]

BLOCK TWELVE

The stage is in darkness except for a spot light which picks out Esmeralda on the Gypsy's roof.

ESMERALDA:

Mama, what happened? —Mama, the lights went out!— Mama, where are you? It's so dark I'm scared!—MAMA!

[*The lights are turned on displaying a deserted plaza. The Gypsy is seated at a small table before her stall.*]

GYPSY:

Come on downstairs, Doll. The mischief is done. You've chosen your hero!

GUTMAN [*from the balcony of the Siete Mares*]:
Block Twelve on the Camino Real.

NURSIE [*at the fountain*]:
Gypsy, the fountain is still dry!

GYPSY:

What d'yuh expect? There's nobody left to uphold the old traditions! You raise a girl. She watches television. Plays be-bop. Reads *Screen Secrets*. Comes the Big Fiesta. The moonrise makes her a virgin—which is the neatest trick of the week! And what does she do? Chooses a Fugitive Patsy for the Chosen Hero! Well, show him in! Admit the joker and get the virgin ready!

NURSIE:

You're going through with it?

GYPSY:

Look, Nursie! I'm operating a legitimate joint! This joker'll get the same treatment he'd get if he breezed down the

Camino in a blizzard of G-notes! Trot, girl! Lubricate your means of locomotion!

[*Nursie goes into the Gypsy's stall. The Gypsy rubs her hands together and blows on the crystal ball, spits on it and gives it the old one-two with a "shammy" rag . . . She mutters "Crystal ball, tell me all . . . crystal ball tell me all" . . . as:*

[*Kilroy bounds into the plaza from her stall . . . a rose between his teeth.*]

GYPSY:
Siente se, por favor.

KILROY:
No comprendo the lingo.

GYPSY:
Put it down!

NURSIE [*offstage*]:
Hey, Gypsy!

GYPSY:
Address me as Madam!

NURSIE [*entering*]:
Madam! Winchell has scooped you!

GYPSY:
In a pig's eye!

NURSIE:
The Fugitivo has *"fftt . . ."*!

GYPSY:
In Elizabeth, New Jersey . . . ten fifty seven P.M. . . . Eastern Standard Time—while you were putting them kiss-me-quicks in your hair-do! Furthermore, my second exclusive is that the

277

solar system is drifting towards the constellation of Hercules:
Skiddoo!

[*Nursie exits. Stamping is heard offstage.*]

Quiet, back there! God damn it!

NURSIE [*offstage*]:
She's out of control!

GYPSY:
Give her a double-bromide!

[*To Kilroy:*]

Well, how does it feel to be the Chosen Hero?

KILROY:
I better explain something to you.

GYPSY:
Save your breath. You'll need it.

KILROY:
I want to level with you. Can I level with you?

GYPSY [*rapidly stamping some papers*]:
How could you help but level with the Gypsy?

KILROY:
I don't know what the hero is chosen for

[*Esmeralda and Nursie shriek offstage.*]

GYPSY:
Time will brief you . . . Aw, I hate paper work! . . . NURS-
EHH!

[*Nursie comes out and stands by the. table.*]

This filing system is screwed up six ways from Next Sunday ... File this crap under crap!—

[*To Kilroy:*]

The smoking lamp is lit. Have a stick on me!

[*She offers him a cigarette.*]

KILROY:
No thanks.

GYPSY:
Come on, indulge yourself. You got nothing to lose that won't be lost.

KILROY:
If that's a professional opinion, I don't respect it.

GYPSY:
Resume your seat and give me your full name.

KILROY:
Kilroy.

GYPSY [*writing all this down*]:
Date of birth and place of that disaster?

KILROY:
Both unknown.

GYPSY:
Address?

KILROY:
Traveler.

GYPSY:
Parents?

KILROY:
Anonymous.

GYPSY:
Who brought you up?

KILROY:
I was brought up and down by an eccentric old aunt in Dallas.

GYPSY:
Raise both hands simultaneously and swear that you have not come here for the purpose of committing an immoral act.

ESMERALDA [*from offstage*]:
Hey, Chico!

GYPSY:
QUIET! Childhood diseases?

KILROY:
Whooping cough, measles and mumps.

GYPSY:
Likes and dislikes?

KILROY:
I like situations I can get out of. I don't like cops and—

GYPSY:
Immaterial! Here! Signature on this!

[*She hands him a blank.*]

KILROY:
What is it?

GYPSY:
You always sign something, don't you?

KILROY:

Not till I know what it is.

GYPSY:

It's just a little formality to give a tone to the establishment and make an impression on our out-of-town trade. Roll up your sleeve.

KILROY:

What for?

GYPSY:

A shot of some kind.

KILROY:

What kind?

GYPSY:

Any kind. Don't they always give you some kind of a shot?

KILROY:

"They"?

GYPSY:

Brass-hats, Americanos!

[*She injects a hypo.*]

KILROY:

I am no guinea pig!

GYPSY:

Don't kid yourself. We're all of us guinea pigs in the laboratory of God. Humanity is just a work in progress.

KILROY:

I don't make it out.

GYPSY:

Who does? The Camino Real is a funny paper read backwards!

[*There is weird piping outside. Kilroy shifts on his seat. The Gypsy grins.*]

Tired? The altitude makes you sleepy?

KILROY:

It makes me nervous.

GYPSY:

I'll show you how to take a slug of tequila! It dilates the capillaries. First you sprinkle salt on the back of your hand. Then lick it off with your tongue. Now then you toss the shot down!

[*She demonstrates.*]

—And then you bite into the lemon. That way it goes down easy, but what a bang! —You're next.

KILROY:

No, thanks, I'm on the wagon.

GYPSY:

There's an old Chinese proverb that says, "When your goose is cooked you might as well have it cooked with plenty of gravy."

[*She laughs.*]

Get up, baby. Let's have a look at yuh!—You're not a bad-looking boy. Sometimes working for the Yankee dollar isn't a painful profession. Have you ever been attracted by older women?

KILROY:

Frankly, no, ma'am.

GYPSY:

Well, there's a first time for everything.

KILROY:

That is a subject I cannot agree with you on.

GYPSY:

You think I'm an old bag?

[*Kilroy laughs awkwardly. The Gypsy slaps his face.*]

Will you take the cards or the crystal?

KILROY:

It's immaterial.

GYPSY:

All right, we'll begin with the cards.

[*She shuffles and deals.*]

Ask me a question.

KILROY:

Has my luck run out?

GYPSY:

Baby, your luck ran out the day you were born. Another question.

KILROY:

Ought I to leave this town?

GYPSY:

It don't look to me like you've got much choice in the matter ... Take a card.

283

[*Kilroy takes one.*]

GYPSY:
Ace?

KILROY:
Yes, ma'am.

GYPSY:
What color?

KILROY:
Black.

GYPSY:
Oh, oh—That does it. How big is your heart?

KILROY:
As big as the head of a baby.

GYPSY:
It's going to **break.**

KILROY:
That's what I was afraid of.

GYPSY:
The Streetcleaners are waiting for you outside the door.

KILROY:
Which door, the front one? I'll slip out the back!

GYPSY:
Leave us face it frankly, your number is up! You must've known a long time that the name of Kilroy was on the Streetcleaners' list.

KILROY:
Sure. But not on top of it!

GYPSY:

It's always a bit of a shock. Wait a minute! Here's good news. The Queen of Hearts has turned up in proper position.

KILROY:

What's that mean?

GYPSY:

Love, Baby!

KILROY:

Love?

GYPSY:

The Booby Prize! —Esmeralda!

[*She rises and hits a gong. A divan is carried out. The Gypsy's Daughter is seated in a reclining position, like an odalisque, on this low divan. A spangled veil covers her face. From this veil to the girdle below her navel, that supports her diaphanous bifurcated skirt, she is nude except for a pair of glittering emerald snakes coiled over her breasts. Kilroy's head moves in a dizzy circle and a canary warbles inside it.*]

KILROY:

WHAT'S—WHAT'S *HER* SPECIALTY?—Tea-leaves?

[*The Gypsy wags a finger.*]

GYPSY:

You know what curiosity did to the tom cat!—Nursie, give me my glamour wig and my forty-five. I'm hitting the street! I gotta go down to Walgreen's for change.

KILROY:

What change?

GYPSY:

The change from that ten-spot you're about to give me.

NURSIE:

Don't argue with her. She has a will of iron.

KILROY:

I'm not arguing!

[*He reluctantly produces the money.*]

But let's be *fair* about this! I hocked my golden gloves for this saw-buck!

NURSIE:

All of them Yankee bastids want something for nothing!

KILROY:

I want a receipt for this bill.

NURSIE:

No one is gypped at the Gypsy's!

KILROY:

That's wonderful! How do I know it?

GYPSY:

It's in the cards, it's in the crystal ball, it's in the tea-leaves! Absolutely no one is gypped at the Gypsy's!

[*She snatches the bill. The wind howls.*]

Such changeable weather! I'll slip on my summer furs! Nursie, break out my summer furs!

NURSIE [*leering grotesquely*]:
Mink or sable?

GYPSY:

Ha ha, that's a doll! Here! Clock him!

[*Nursie tosses her a greasy blanket, and the Gypsy tosses Nursie an alarm clock. The Gypsy rushes through the beaded string curtains.*]

Adios! Ha ha!!

[*She is hardly offstage when two shots ring out. Kilroy starts.*]

ESMERALDA [*plaintively*]:
Mother has such an awful time on the street.

KILROY:
You mean that she is insulted on the street?

ESMERALDA:
By strangers.

KILROY [*to the audience*]:
I shouldn't think acquaintances would do it.

[*She curls up on the low divan. Kilroy licks his lips.*]

—You seem very different from—this afternoon . . .

ESMERALDA:
This afternoon?

KILROY:
Yes, in the plaza when I was being roughed up by them gorillas and you was being dragged in the house by your Mama!

[*Esmeralda stares at him blankly.*]

You don't remember?

ESMERALDA:
I never remember what happened before the moonrise makes me a virgin.

KILROY:
—That—comes as a shock to you, huh?

ESMERALDA:
Yes. It comes as a shock.

KILROY [*smiling*]:
You have a little temporary amnesia they call it!

ESMERALDA:
Yankee . . .

KILROY:
Huh?

ESMERALDA:
I'm glad I chose you. I'm glad that you were chosen.

[*Her voice trails off.*]

I'm glad. I'm very glad . . .

NURSIE:
Doll!

ESMERALDA:
—What is it, Nursie?

NURSIE:
How are things progressing?

ESMERALDA:
Slowly, Nursie—

[*Nursie comes lumbering in.*]

NURSIE:
I want some light reading matter.

ESMERALDA:

He's sitting on *Screen Secrets.*

KILROY [*jumping up*]:

Aw. Here.

[*He hands her the fan magazine. She lumbers back out, coyly.*]

—I—I feel——self-conscious . .

[*He suddenly jerks out a silver-framed photo.*]

—D'you—like pictures?

ESMERALDA:

Moving pictures?

KILROY:

No, a—motionless—snapshot!

ESMERALDA:

Of you?

KILROY:

Of my—real—true woman . . . She was a platinum blonde the same as Jean Harlow. Do you remember Jean Harlow? No, you wouldn't remember Jean Harlow. It shows you are getting old when you remember Jean Harlow.

[*He puts the snapshot away.*]

. . . They say that Jean Harlow's ashes are kept in a little private cathedral in Forest Lawn . . . Wouldn't it be wonderful if you could sprinkle them ashes over the ground like seeds, and out of each one would spring another Jean Harlow? And when spring comes you could just walk out and pick them off the bush! . . . You don't talk much.

289

ESMERALDA:
You want me to *talk*?

KILROY:
Well, that's the way we do things in the States. A little vino, some records on the victrola, some quiet conversation—and then if both parties are in a mood for romance . . . Romance—

ESMERALDA:
Music!

[*She rises and pours some wine from a slender crystal decanter as music is heard.*]

They say that the monetary system has got to be stabilized all over the world.

KILROY [*taking the glass*]:
Repeat that, please. My radar was not wide open.

ESMERALDA:
I said that *they* said that—uh, skip it! But we couldn't care less as long as we keep on getting the Yankee dollar . . . plus federal tax!

KILROY:
That's for surely!

ESMERALDA:
How do you feel about the class struggle? Do you take sides in that?

KILROY:
Not that I—

ESMERALDA:
Neither do we because of the dialectics.

290

KILROY:

Who! Which?

ESMERALDA:

Languages with accents, I suppose. But Mama don't care as long as they don't bring the Pope over here and put him in the White House.

KILROY:

Who would do that?

ESMERALDA:

Oh, the Bolsheviskies, those nasty old things with whiskers! *Whiskers scratch!* But little moustaches tickle . . .

[*She giggles.*]

KILROY:

I always got a smooth shave . . .

ESMERALDA:

And how do you feel about the Mumbo Jumbo? Do you think they've got the Old Man in the bag yet?

KILROY:

The Old Man?

ESMERALDA:

God. We don't think so. We think there has been so much of the Mumbo Jumbo it's put Him to sleep!

[*Kilroy jumps up impatiently.*]

KILROY:

This is not what I mean by a quiet conversation. I mean this is no where! *No where!*

ESMERALDA:

What sort of talk do you want?

KILROY:

Something more—intimate sort of! You know, like—

ESMERALDA:

—Where did you get those eyes?

KILROY:

PERSONAL! Yeah ...

ESMERALDA:

Well,—where did you get those eyes?

KILROY:

Out of a dead cod-fish!

NURSIE [*shouting offstage*]:

DOLL!

[*Kilroy springs up, pounding his left palm with his right fist.*]

ESMERALDA:

What?

NURSIE:

Fifteen minutes!

KILROY:

I'm no hot-rod mechanic.

[*To the audience:*]

I bet she's out there holding a stop watch to see that I don't over-stay my time in this place!

ESMERALDA [*calling through the string curtains*]:
Nursie, go to bed, Nursie!

KILROY [*in a fierce whisper*]:
That's right, go to bed, Nursie!!

[*There is a loud crash offstage.*]

ESMERALDA:
—Nursie has gone to bed . . .

[*She drops the string curtains and returns to the alcove.*]

KILROY [*with vast relief*]:
—Ahhhhhhhhhh . . .

ESMERALDA:
What've you got your eyes on?

KILROY:
Those green snakes on you—what do you wear them for?

ESMERALDA:
Supposedly for protection, but really for fun.

[*He crosses to the divan.*]

What are you going to do?

KILROY:
I'm about to establish a beach-head on that sofa.

[*He sits down.*]

How about—lifting your veil?

ESMERALDA:
I can't lift it.

KILROY:
Why not?

ESMERALDA:
I promised Mother I wouldn't.

KILROY:
I thought your mother was the broadminded type.

ESMERALDA:

Oh, she is, but you know how mothers are. You can lift it for me, if you say pretty please.

KILROY:

Aww——

ESMERALDA:

Go on, say it! Say pretty please!

KILROY:

No!!

ESMERALDA:

Why not?

KILROY:

It's silly.

ESMERALDA:

Then you can't lift my veil!

KILROY:

Oh, all right. Pretty please.

ESMERALDA:

Say it again!

KILROY:

Pretty please.

ESMERALDA:

Now say it once more like you meant it.

[*He jumps up. She grabs his hand.*]

Don't go away.

KILROY:

You're making a fool out of me.

ESMERALDA:

I was just teasing a little. Because you're so cute. Sit down again, please—*pretty* please!

[*He falls on the couch.*]

KILROY:

What is that wonderful perfume you've got on?

ESMERALDA:

Guess!

KILROY:

Chanel Number Five?

ESMERALDA:

No.

KILROY:

Tabu?

ESMERALDA:

No.

KILROY:

I give up.

ESMERALDA:

It's *Noche en Acapulco!* I'm just dying to go to Acapulco. I wish that you would take me to Acapulco.

[*He sits up.*]

What's the matter?

KILROY:

You gypsies' daughters are invariably reminded of something without which you cannot do—just when it looks like everything has been fixed.

295

ESMERALDA:

That isn't nice at all. I'm not the gold-digger type. Some girls see themselves in silver foxes. I only see myself in Acapulco!

KILROY:

At Todd's Place?

ESMERALDA:

Oh, no, at the Mirador! Watching those pretty boys dive off the Quebrada!

KILROY:

Look again, Baby. Maybe you'll see yourself in Paramount Pictures or having a Singapore Sling at a Statler bar!

ESMERALDA:

You're being sarcastic?

KILROY:

Nope. Just realistic. All of you gypsies' daughters have hearts of stone, and I'm not whistling "Dixie"! But just the same, the night before a man dies, he says, "Pretty please—will you let me lift your veil?"—while the Streetcleaners wait for him right outside the door!—Because to be warm for a little longer is life. And love?—that's a four-letter word which is sometimes no better than one you see printed on fences by kids playing hooky from school!—Oh, well—what's the use of complaining? You gypsies' daughters have ears that only catch sounds like the snap of a gold cigarette case! Or, pretty please, Baby,—we're going to Acapulco!

ESMERALDA:
Are we?

KILROY:
See what I mean?

[*To the audience:*]

Didn't I tell you?!

[*To Esmeralda:*]

Yes! In the morning!

ESMERALDA:
Ohhhh! I'm dizzy with joy! My little heart is going pitty-pat!

KILROY:
My big heart is going boom-boom! Can I lift your veil now?

ESMERALDA:
If you will be gentle.

KILROY:
I would not hurt a fly unless it had on leather mittens.

[*He touches a corner of her spangled veil.*]

ESMERALDA:
Ohhh ...

KILROY:
What?

ESMERALDA:
Ohhhhhh!!

KILROY:
Why! What's the matter?

ESMERALDA:
You are not being gentle!

KILROY:
I *am* being gentle.

ESMERALDA:

You are *not* being gentle.

KILROY:

What was I being, then?

ESMERALDA:

Rough!

KILROY:

I am *not* being rough.

ESMERALDA:

Yes, you *are* being rough. You have to be gentle with me because you're the first.

KILROY:

Are you kidding?

ESMERALDA:

No.

KILROY:

How about all of those other fiestas you've been to?

ESMERALDA:

Each one's the first one. That is the wonderful thing about gypsies' daughters!

KILROY:

You can say that again!

ESMERALDA:

I don't like you when you're like that.

KILROY:

Like what?

ESMERALDA:

Cynical and sarcastic.

KILROY:

I am sincere.

ESMERALDA:

Lots of boys aren't sincere.

KILROY:

Maybe they aren't but I am.

ESMERALDA:

Everyone says he's sincere, but everyone isn't sincere. If every-one was sincere who says he's sincere there wouldn't be half so many insincere ones in the world and there would be lots, lots, lots more really sincere ones!

KILROY:

I think you have got something there. But how about gypsies' daughters?

ESMERALDA:

Huh?

KILROY:

Are they one hundred percent in the really sincere category?

ESMERALDA:

Well, yes, and no, mostly no! But some of them are for a while if their sweethearts are gentle.

KILROY:

Would you believe I am sincere and gentle?

ESMERALDA:

I would believe that you believe that you are . . . For a while . . .

KILROY:

Everything's for a while. For a while is the stuff that dreams are made of, Baby! Now?—Now?

ESMERALDA:

Yes, now, but be gentle!—*gentle* ...

[*He delicately lifts a corner of her veil. She utters a soft cry. He lifts it further. She cries out again. A bit further ... He turns the spangled veil all the way up from her face.*]

KILROY:

I am sincere.

ESMERALDA:

I am sincere.

KILROY:

I am sincere.

ESMERALDA:

I am sincere.

KILROY:

I am sincere.

ESMERALDA:

I am sincere.

KILROY:

I am sincere.

ESMERALDA:

I am sincere.

[*Kilroy leans back, removing his hand from her veil. She opens her eyes.*]

Is that all?

300

KILROY:
I am tired.

ESMERALDA:
—Already?

[*He rises and goes down the steps from the alcove.*]

KILROY:
I am tired, and full of regret ...

ESMERALDA:
Oh!

KILROY:
It wasn't much to give my golden gloves for.

ESMERALDA:
You pity yourself?

KILROY:
That's right, I pity myself and everybody that goes to the Gypsy's daughter. I pity the world and I pity the God who made it.

[*He sits down.*]

ESMERALDA:
It's always like that as soon as the veil is lifted. They're all so ashamed of having degraded themselves, and their hearts have more regret than a heart can hold!

KILROY:
Even a heart that's as big as the head of a baby!

ESMERALDA:
You don't even notice how pretty my face is, do you?

KILROY:
You look like all gypsies' daughters, no better, no worse. But

as long as you get to go to Acapulco, your cup runneth over with ordinary contentment.

ESMERALDA:

—I've never been so insulted in all my life!

KILROY:

Oh, yes, you have, Baby. And you'll be insulted worse if you stay in this racket. You'll be insulted so much that it will get to be like water off *a duck's back!*

[*The door slams. Curtains are drawn apart on the Gypsy. Esmeralda lowers her veil hastily. Kilroy pretends not to notice the Gypsy's entrance. She picks up a little bell and rings it over his head.*]

Okay, Mamacita! I am aware of your presence!

GYPSY:

Ha-ha! I was followed three blocks by some awful man!

KILROY:

Then you caught him.

GYPSY:

Naw, he ducked into a subway! I waited fifteen minutes outside the men's room and he never came out!

KILROY:

Then you went in?

GYPSY:

No! I got myself a sailor!—The streets are brilliant! . . . Have you all been good children?

[*Esmeralda makes a whimpering sound.*]

The pussy will play while the old mother cat is away?

KILROY:

Your sense of humor is wonderful, but how about my change, Mamacita?

GYPSY:

What change are you talking about?

KILROY:

Are you boxed out of your mind? The change from that ten-spot you trotted over to Walgreen's?

GYPSY:
Ohhhhh—

KILROY:
Oh, what?

GYPSY [*counting on her fingers*]:
Five for the works, one dollar luxury tax, two for the house percentage and two more pour la service!—makes ten! Didn't I tell you?

KILROY:
—What kind of a deal is this?

GYPSY [*whipping out a revolver*]:
A rugged one, Baby!

ESMERALDA:
Mama, don't be unkind!

GYPSY:
Honey, the gentleman's friends are waiting outside the door and it wouldn't be nice to detain him! Come on—Get going— Vamoose!

KILROY:
Okay, Mamacita! Me voy!

303

[*He crosses to the beaded string curtains: turns to look back at the Gypsy and her daughter. The piping of the Street-cleaners is heard outside.*]

Sincere?—Sure! That's the wonderful thing about gypsies' daughters!

[*He goes out. Esmeralda raises a wondering fingertip to one eye. Then she cries out:*]

ESMERALDA:
Look, Mama! Look, Mama! A tear!

GYPSY:
You have been watching television too much . . .

[*She gathers the cards and turns off the crystal ball as—*

[*Light fades out on the phony paradise of the Gypsy's.*]

GUTMAN:
Block Thirteen on the Camino Real.

[*He exits.*]

BLOCK THIRTEEN

In the blackout the Streetcleaners place a barrel in the center and then hide in the Pit.

Kilroy, who enters from the right, is followed by a spot light. He sees the barrel and the menacing Streetcleaners and then runs to the closed door of the Siete Mares and rings the bell. No one answers. He backs up so he can see the balcony and calls:

KILROY:

Mr. Gutman! Just gimme a cot in the lobby. I'll do odd jobs in the morning. I'll be the Patsy again. I'll light my nose sixty times a minute. I'll take prat-falls and assume the position for anybody that drops a dime on the street . . . Have a heart! Have just a LITTLE heart. Please!

[*There is no response from Gutman's balcony. Jacques enters. He pounds his cane once on the pavement.*]

JACQUES:

Gutman! Open the door!—*GUTMAN! GUTMAN!*

[*Eva, a beautiful woman, apparently nude, appears on the balcony.*]

GUTMAN [*from inside*]:

Eva darling, you're exposing yourself!

[*He appears on the balcony with a portmanteau.*]

JACQUES:

What are you doing with my portmanteau?

GUTMAN:

Haven't you come for your luggage?

JACQUES:
Certainly not! I haven't checked out of here!

GUTMAN:
Very few do . . . but residences are frequently terminated.

JACQUES:
Open the door!

GUTMAN:
Open the letter with the remittance check in it!

JACQUES:
In the morning!

GUTMAN:
Tonight!

JACQUES:
Upstairs in my room!

GUTMAN:
Downstairs at the entrance!

JACQUES:
I won't be intimidated!

GUTMAN [*raising the portmanteau over his head*]:
What?!

JACQUES:
Wait!—

[*He takes the letter out of his pocket.*]

Give me some light.

[*Kilroy strikes a match and holds it over Jacques' shoulder.*]

Thank you. What does it say?

306

GUTMAN:
—Remittances?

KILROY [*reading the letter over Jacques' shoulder*]:
—discontinued . . .

[*Gutman raises the portmanteau again.*]

JACQUES:
Careful, I have—

[*The portmanteau lands with a crash.*

[*The Bum comes to the window at the crash. A. Ratt comes out to his doorway at the same time.*]

—fragile—mementoes . . .

[*He crosses slowly down to the portmanteau and kneels as . . .*

[*Gutman laughs and slams the balcony door. Jacques turns to Kilroy. He smiles at the young adventurer.*]

—"And so at last it has come, the distinguished thing!"

[*A. Ratt speaks as Jacques touches the portmanteau.*]

A. RATT
Hey, Dad—Vacancy here! A bed at the "Ritz Men Only." A little white ship to sail the dangerous night in.

JACQUES:
Single or double?

A. RATT
There's only singles in this pad.

JACQUES [*to Kilroy*]:
Match you for it.

KILROY:

What the hell, we're buddies, we can sleep spoons! If we can't sleep, we'll push the wash stand against the door and sing old popular songs till the crack of dawn! . . . "Heart of my heart, I love that melody!" . . . You bet your life I do.

[*Jacques takes out a pocket handkerchief and starts to grasp the portmanteau handle.*]

—It looks to me like you could use a Redcap and my rates are non-union!

[*He picks up the portmanteau and starts to cross towards the "Ritz Men Only." He stops at right center.*]

Sorry, buddy. Can't make it! The altitude on this block has affected my ticker! And in the distance which is nearer than further, I hear—the Streetcleaners'—piping!

[*Piping is heard.*]

JACQUES:
COME ALONG!

[*He lifts the portmanteau and starts on.*]

KILROY:
NO. Tonight! I prefer! To sleep! Out! Under! The stars!

JACQUES [*gently*]:
I understand, Brother!

KILROY [*to Jacques as he continues toward the "Ritz Men Only"*]:

Bon Voyage! I hope that you sail the dangerous night to the sweet golden port of morning!

JACQUES [*exiting*]:
Thanks, Brother!

KILROY:
Excuse the *corn!* I'm sincere!

BUM:
Show me the way to go home! ...

GUTMAN [*appearing on the balcony with white parakeet*]:
Block Fourteen on the Camino Real.

BLOCK FOURTEEN

At opening, the Bum is still at the window.

The Streetcleaners' piping continues a little louder. Kilroy climbs, breathing heavily, to the top of the stairs and stands looking out at Terra Incognita as . . .

Marguerite enters the plaza through alleyway at right. She is accompanied by a silent Young Man who wears a domino.

MARGUERITE:

Don't come any further with me. I'll have to wake the night porter. Thank you for giving me safe conduct through the Medina.

[*She has offered her hand. He grips it with a tightness that makes her wince.*]

Ohhhh . . . I'm not sure which is more provocative in you, your ominous silence or your glittering smile or—

[*He's looking at her purse.*]

What do you want? . . . Oh!

[*She starts to open the purse. He snatches it. She gasps as he suddenly strips her cloak off her. Then he snatches off her pearl necklace. With each successive despoilment, she gasps and retreats but makes no resistance. Her eyes are closed. He continues to smile. Finally, he rips her dress and runs his hands over her body as if to see if she had anything else of value concealed on her.*]

—What else do I have that you want?

THE YOUNG MAN [*contemptuously*]:
Nothing.

[*The Young Man exits through the cantina, examining his loot. The Bum leans out his window, draws a deep breath and says:*]

BUM:
Lonely.

MARGUERITE [*to herself*]:
Lonely ...

KILROY [*on the steps*]:
Lonely ...

[*The Streetcleaners' piping is heard.*

[*Marguerite runs to the Siete Mares and rings the bell. Nobody answers. She crosses to the terrace. Kilroy, meanwhile, has descended the stairs.*]

MARGUERITE:
Jacques!

[*Piping is heard.*]

KILROY:
Lady?

MARGUERITE:
What?

KILROY:
—*I'm—safe* ...

MARGUERITE:
I wasn't expecting that music tonight, were you?

[*Piping.*]

KILROY:
It's them Streetcleaners.

311

MARGUERITE:
I know.

[*Piping.*]

KILROY:
You better go on in, lady.

MARGUERITE:
No.

KILROY:
GO ON IN!

MARGUERITE:
NO! I want to stay out here and I do what I want to do!

[*Kilroy looks at her for the first time.*]

Sit down with me please.

KILROY:
They're coming for me. The Gypsy told me I'm on top of their list. Thanks for. Taking my. Hand.

[*Piping is heard.*]

MARGUERITE:
Thanks for taking mine.

[*Piping.*]

KILROY:
Do me one more favor. Take out of my pocket a picture. My fingers are. Stiff.

MARGUERITE:
This one?

KILROY:

My one. True. Woman.

MARGUERITE:

A silver-framed photo! Was she really so fair?

KILROY:

She was so fair and much fairer than they could tint that picture!

MARGUERITE:

Then you have been on the street when the street was royal.

KILROY:

Yeah ... when the street was royal!

[*Piping is heard. Kilroy rises.*]

MARGUERITE:

Don't get up, don't leave me!

KILROY:

I want to be on my feet when the Streetcleaners come for me!

MARGUERITE:

Sit back down again and tell me about your girl.

[*He sits.*]

KILROY:

Y'know what it is you miss most? When you're separated. From someone. You lived. With. And loved? It's waking up in the night! With that—warmness beside you!

MARGUERITE:

Yes, that *warmness* beside you!

KILROY:

Once you get used to that. *Warmness!* It's a hell of a lonely feeling to wake up without it! Specially in some dollar-a-night hotel room on Skid! A hot-water bottle won't do. And a stranger. Won't do. It has to be some one you're used to. And that you. *KNOW LOVES* you!

[*Piping is heard.*]

Can you see them?

MARGUERITE:
I see no one but you.

KILROY:
I looked at my wife one night when she was sleeping and that was the night that the medics wouldn't okay me for no more fights . . . Well . . . My wife was sleeping with a smile like a child's. I kissed her. She didn't wake up. I took a pencil and paper. I wrote her. Good-bye!

MARGUERITE:
That was the night she would have loved you the most!

KILROY:
Yeah, *that* night, but what about *after* that night? Oh, Lady . . . Why should a beautiful girl tie up with a broken-down champ?—The earth still turning and her obliged to turn with it, not out—of dark into light but out of light into dark? Naw, naw, naw, naw!—Washed up!—Finished!

[*Piping.*]

. . . that ain't a word that a man can't look at . . . There ain't no words in the language a man can't look at . . . and know just what they mean. and be. And act. And *go*!

[*He turns to the waiting Streetcleaners.*]

Come on! . . . Come on! . . . COME ON, YOU SONS OF
BITCHES! KILROY IS HERE! HE'S READY!

[*A gong sounds.*

[*Kilroy swings at the Streetcleaners. They circle about him
out of reach, turning him by each of their movements. The
swings grow wilder like a boxer. He falls to his knees still
swinging and finally collapses flat on his face.*

[*The Streetcleaners pounce but La Madrecita throws herself
protectingly over the body and covers it with her shawl.*

[*Blackout.*]

MARGUERITE:
Jacques!

GUTMAN [*on balcony*]:
Block Fifteen on the Camino Real.

BLOCK FIFTEEN

La Madrecita is seated: across her knees is the body of Kilroy.
Up center, a low table on wheels bears a sheeted figure. Beside
the table stands a Medical Instructor addressing Students and
Nurses, all in white surgical outfits.

INSTRUCTOR:
This is the body of an unidentified vagrant.

LA MADRECITA:
This was thy son, America—and now mine.

INSTRUCTOR:
He was found in an alley along the Camino Real.

LA MADRECITA:
Think of him, now, as he was before his luck failed him.
Remember his time of greatness, when he was not faded, not
frightened.

INSTRUCTOR:
More light, please!

LA MADRECITA:
More light!

INSTRUCTOR:
Can everyone see clearly!

LA MADRECITA:
Everyone must see clearly!

INSTRUCTOR:
There is no external evidence of disease.

LA MADRECITA:
He had clear eyes and the body of a champion boxer.

INSTRUCTOR:

There are no marks of violence on the body.

LA MADRECITA:

He had the soft voice of the South and a pair of golden gloves.

INSTRUCTOR:

His death was apparently due to natural causes.

[*The Students make notes. There are keening voices.*]

LA MADRECITA:

Yes, blow wind where night thins! He had many admirers!

INSTRUCTOR:

There are no legal claimants.

LA MADRECITA:

He stood as a planet among the moons of their longing, haughty with youth, a champion of the prize-ring!

INSTRUCTOR:

No friends or relatives having identified him—

LA MADRECITA:

You should have seen the lovely monogrammed robe in which he strode the aisles of the Colosseums!

INSTRUCTOR:

After the elapse of a certain number of days, his body becomes the property of the State—

LA MADRECITA:

Yes, blow wind where night thins—for laurel is not ever-lasting . . .

INSTRUCTOR:

And now is transferred to our hands for the nominal sum of five dollars.

317

LA MADRECITA:
This was thy son,—and now mine ...

INSTRUCTOR:
We will now proceed with the dissection. Knife, please!

LA MADRECITA:
Blow wind!

[*Keening is heard offstage.*]

Yes, blow wind where night thins! You are his passing bell and his lamentation.

[*More keening is heard.*]

Keen for him, all maimed creatures, deformed and mutilated —his homeless ghost is your own!

INSTRUCTOR:
First we will open up the chest cavity and examine the heart for evidence of coronary occlusion.

LA MADRECITA:
His heart was pure gold and as big as the head of a baby.

INSTRUCTOR:
We will make an incision along the vertical line.

LA MADRECITA:
Rise, ghost! Go! Go bird! "Humankind cannot bear very much reality."

[*At the touch of her flowers, Kilroy stirs and pushes himself up slowly from her lap. On his feet again, he rubs his eyes and looks around him.*]

VOICES [*crying offstage*]:
Olé! Olé! Olé!

318

KILROY:

Hey! Hey, somebody! Where am I?

[*He notices the dissection room and approaches.*]

INSTRUCTOR [*removing a glittering sphere from a dummy corpse*]:

Look at this heart. It's as big as the head of a baby.

KILROY:

My heart!

INSTRUCTOR:

Wash it off so we can look for the pathological lesions.

KILROY:

Yes, siree, that's my heart!

GUTMAN:

Block Sixteen!

[*Kilroy pauses just outside the dissection area as a Student takes the heart and dips it into a basin on the stand beside the table. The Student suddenly cries out and holds aloft a glittering gold sphere.*]

INSTRUCTOR:

Look! This heart's solid gold!

BLOCK SIXTEEN

KILROY [*rushing forward*]:
That's mine, you bastards!

[*He snatches the golden sphere from the Medical Instructor. The autopsy proceeds as if nothing had happened as the spot of light on the table fades out, but for Kilroy a ghostly chase commences, a dreamlike re-enactment of the chase that occurred at the end of Block Six. Gutman shouts from his balcony:*]

GUTMAN:
Stop, thief, stop, corpse! That gold heart is the property of the State! Catch him, catch the golden-heart robber!

[*Kilroy dashes offstage into an aisle of the theatre. There is the wail of a siren: the air is filled with calls and whistles, roar of motors, screeching brakes, pistol-shots, thundering footsteps. The dimness of the auditorium is transected by searching rays of light—but there are no visible pursuers.*]

KILROY [*as he runs panting up the aisle*]:
This is my heart! It don't belong to no State, not even the U.S.A. Which way is out? Where's the Greyhound depot? Nobody's going to put my heart in a bottle in a museum and charge admission to support the rotten police! Where are they? Which way are they going? Or coming? Hey, somebody, help me get out of here! Which way do I—which way —which way do I—*go! go! go! go! go!*

[*He has now arrived in the balcony.*]

Gee, I'm lost! I don't know where I am! I'm all turned around, I'm *confused,* I don't understand—what's—happened, it's like a—*dream,* it's—just like a—dream . . . *Mary! Oh, Mary! Mary!*

[*He has entered the box from which he leapt in Act One.*

[*A clear shaft of light falls on him. He looks up into it, crying:*]

Mary, help a Christian!! Help a Christian, Mary!—It's like a dream . . .

[*Esmeralda appears in a childish nightgown beside her gauze-tented bed on the Gypsy's roof. Her Mother appears with a cup of some sedative drink, cooing . . .*]

GYPSY:
Beddy-bye, beddy-bye, darling. It's sleepy-time down South and up North, too, and also East and West!

KILROY [*softly*]:
Yes, it's—like a—*dream* . . .

[*He leans panting over the ledge of the box, holding his heart like a football, watching Esmeralda.*]

GYPSY:
Drink your Ovaltine, Ducks, and the sandman will come on tip-toe with a bag full of dreams . . .

ESMERALDA:
I want to dream of the Chosen Hero, Mummy.

GYPSY:
Which one, the one that's coming or the one that is gone?

ESMERALDA:
The *only* one, *Kilroy! He* was *sincere!*

KILROY:
That's *right! I was,* for a while!

321

GYPSY:

How do you know that Kilroy was sincere?

ESMERALDA:

He said so.

KILROY:

That's the truth, I *was*!

GYPSY:

When did he say that?

ESMERALDA:

When he lifted my veil.

GYPSY:

Baby, they're always sincere when they lift your veil; it's one of those natural reflexes that don't mean a thing.

KILROY [*aside*]:

What a cynical old bitch that Gypsy mama is!

GYPSY:

And there's going to be lots of other fiestas for you, baby doll, and lots of other chosen heroes to lift your little veil when Mamacita and Nursie are out of the room.

ESMERALDA:

No, Mummy, never, I mean it!

KILROY:

I *believe* she means it!

GYPSY:

Finish your Ovaltine and say your Now-I-Lay-Me.

[*Esmeralda sips the drink and hands her the cup.*]

KILROY [*with a catch in his voice*]:

I had one true woman, which I can't go back to, but now I've found another.

[*He leaps onto the stage from the box.*]

ESMERALDA [*dropping to her knees*]:

Now I lay me down to sleep, I pray the Lord my soul to keep. If I should die before I wake, I pray the Lord my soul to take.

GYPSY:

God bless Mummy!

ESMERALDA:

And the crystal ball and the tea-leaves.

KILROY:

Pssst!

ESMERALDA:

What's that?

GYPSY:

A tom-cat in the plaza.

ESMERALDA:

God bless all cats without pads in the plaza tonight.

KILROY:

Amen!

[*He falls to his knees in the empty plaza.*]

ESMERALDA:

God bless all con men and hustlers and pitch-men who hawk their hearts on the street, all two-time losers who're likely to lose once more, the courtesan who made the mistake of love, the greatest of lovers crowned with the longest horns, the poet who wandered far from his heart's green country and possibly will and possibly won't be able to find his way back, look down with a smile tonight on the last cavaliers, the ones with the rusty armor and soiled white plumes, and visit with understanding and something that's almost tender those fading legends that come and go in this plaza like songs not clearly remembered, oh, sometime and somewhere, let there be something to mean the word *honor* again!

QUIXOTE [*hoarsely and loudly, stirring slightly among his verminous rags*]:
Amen!

KILROY:
Amen . . .

GYPSY [*disturbed*]:
—That will do, now.

ESMERALDA:
And, oh, God, let me dream tonight of the Chosen Hero!

GYPSY:
Now, sleep. Fly away on the magic carpet of dreams!

[*Esmeralda crawls into the gauze-tented cot. The Gypsy descends from the roof.*]

KILROY:
Esmeralda! My little Gypsy sweetheart!

ESMERALDA [*sleepily*]:
Go away, cat.

[*The light behind the gauze is gradually dimming.*]

KILROY:
This is no cat. This is the chosen hero of the big fiesta, Kilroy,

the champion of the golden gloves with his gold heart cut from his chest and in his hands to give you!

ESMERALDA:

Go away. Let me dream of the Chosen Hero.

KILROY:

What a hassle! Mistook for a cat! What can I do to convince this doll I'm real?

[*Three brass balls wink brilliantly.*]

—Another transaction seems to be indicated!

[*He rushes to the Loan Shark's. The entrance immediately lights up.*]

My heart is gold! What will you give me for it?

[*Jewels, furs, sequined gowns, etc., are tossed to his feet. He throws his heart like a basketball to the Loan Shark, snatches up the loot and rushes back to the Gypsy's.*]

Doll! Behold this loot! I gave my golden heart for it!

ESMERALDA:

Go away, cat . . .

[*She falls asleep. Kilroy bangs his forehead with his fist, then rushes to the Gypsy's door, pounds it with both fists. The door is thrown open and the sordid contents of a large jar are thrown at him. He falls back gasping, spluttering, retching. He retreats and finally assumes an exaggerated attitude of despair.*]

KILROY:

Had for a button! Stewed, screwed and tattooed on the Camino Real! Baptized, finally, with the contents of a slop-jar!—Did anybody say the deal was rugged?!

[*Quixote stirs against the wall of Skid Row. He hawks and spits and staggers to his feet.*]

GUTMAN:
Why, the old knight's awake, his dream is over!

QUIXOTE [*to Kilroy*]:
Hello! Is that a fountain?

KILROY:
—Yeah, but—

QUIXOTE:
I've got a mouthful of old chicken feathers ...

[*He approaches the fountain. It begins to flow. Kilroy falls back in amazement as the Old Knight rinses his mouth and drinks and removes his jacket to bathe, handing the tattered garment to Kilroy.*]

QUIXOTE [*as he bathes*]:
Qué pasa, mi amigo?

KILROY:
The deal is rugged. D'you know what I mean?

QUIXOTE:
Who knows better than I what a rugged deal is!

[*He produces a tooth brush and brushes his teeth.*]

—Will you take some advice?

KILROY:
Brother, at this point on the Camino I will take anything which is offered!

QUIXOTE:
Don't! Pity! Your! Self!

326

[*He takes out a pocket mirror and grooms his beard and moustache.*]

The wounds of the vanity, the many offenses our egos have to endure, being housed in bodies that age and hearts that grow tired, are better accepted with a tolerant smile—like *this!* —You *see?*

[*He cracks his face in two with an enormous grin.*]

GUTMAN:
Follow-spot on the face of the ancient knight!

QUIXOTE:
Otherwise what you become is a bag full of curdled cream— *leche mala,* we call it!—attractive to nobody, least of all to yourself!

[*He passes the comb and pocket mirror to Kilroy.*]

Have you got any plans?

KILROY [*a bit uncertainly, wistfully*]:
Well, I was thinking of—going *on* from—*here!*

QUIXOTE:
Good! Come with me.

KILROY [*to the audience*]:
Crazy old bastard.

[*Then to the Knight:*]

Donde?

QUIXOTE [*starting for the stairs*]:
Quien sabe!

[*The fountain is now flowing loudly and sweetly. The Street People are moving toward it with murmurs of wonder. Marguerite comes out upon the terrace.*]

KILROY:

Hey, there's—!

QUIXOTE:

Shhh! Listen!

[*They pause on the stairs.*]

MARGUERITE:

Abdullah!

[*Gutman has descended to the terrace.*]

GUTMAN:

Mademoiselle, allow me to deliver the message for you. It would be in bad form if I didn't take some final part in the pageant.

[*He crosses the plaza to the opposite façade and shouts "Casanova!" under the window of the "Ritz Men Only."*

[*Meanwhile Kilroy scratches out the verb "is" and prints the correction "was" in the inscription on the ancient wall.*]

Casanova! Great lover and King of Cuckolds on the Camino Real! The last of your ladies has guaranteed your tabs and is expecting you for breakfast on the terrace!

[*Casanova looks first out of the practical window of the flophouse, then emerges from its scabrous doorway, haggard, unshaven, crumpled in dress but bearing himself as erectly as ever. He blinks and glares fiercely into the brilliant morning light.*

[*Marguerite cannot return his look, she averts her face with a look for which anguish would not be too strong a term, but at the same time she extends a pleading hand toward him. After some hesitation, he begins to move toward her, striking the pavement in measured cadence with his cane, glancing once, as he crosses, out at the audience with a wry smile that makes admissions that would be embarrassing to a vainer man than Casanova now is. When he reaches Marguerite she gropes for his hand, seizes it with a low cry and presses it spasmodically to her lips while he draws her into his arms and looks above her sobbing, dyed-golden head with the serene, clouded gaze of someone mortally ill as the mercy of a narcotic laps over his pain.*

[*Quixote raises his lance in a formal gesture and cries out hoarsely, powerfully from the stairs:*]

QUIXOTE:
The violets in the mountains have broken the rocks!

[*Quixote goes through the arch with Kilroy.*]

GUTMAN [*to the audience*]:
The Curtain Line has been spoken!

[*To the wings:*]

Bring it down!

[*He bows with a fat man's grace as—*

[*The curtain falls.*]

SWEET BIRD OF YOUTH

Relentless caper for all those who step
The legend of their youth into the noon

HART CRANE

To Cheryl Crawford

FOREWORD*

When I came to my writing desk on a recent morning, I found lying on my desk top an unmailed letter that I had written. I began reading it and found this sentence: "We are all civilized people, which means that we are all savages at heart but observing a few amenities of civilized behavior." Then I went on to say: "I am afraid that I observe fewer of these amenities than you do. Reason? My back is to the wall and has been to the wall for so long that the pressure of my back on the wall has started to crumble the plaster that covers the bricks and mortar."

Isn't it odd that I said the wall was giving way, not my back? I think so. Pursuing this course of free association, I suddenly remembered a dinner date I once had with a distinguished colleague. During the course of this dinner, rather close to the end of it, he broke a long, mournful silence by lifting to me his sympathetic gaze and saying to me, sweetly, "Tennessee, don't you feel that you are blocked as a writer?"

I didn't stop to think of an answer; it came immediately off my tongue without any pause for planning. I said, "Oh, yes, I've always been blocked as a writer but my desire to write has been so strong that it has always broken down the block and gone past it."

Nothing untrue comes off the tongue that quickly. It is planned speeches that contain lies or dissimulations, not what you blurt out so spontaneously in one instant.

It was literally true. At the age of fourteen I discovered writing as an escape from a world of reality in which I felt acutely uncomfortable. It immediately became my place of retreat, my cave, my refuge. From what? From being called a

---

* Written prior to the Broadway opening of *Sweet Bird of Youth* and published in the *New York Times* on Sunday, March 8, 1959.

sissy by the neighborhood kids, and Miss Nancy by my father, because I would rather read books in my grandfather's large and classical library than play marbles and baseball and other normal kid games, a result of a severe childhood illness and of excessive attachment to the female members of my family, who had coaxed me back into life.

I think no more than a week after I started writing I ran into the first block. It's hard to describe it in a way that will be understandable to anyone who is not a neurotic. I will try. All my life I have been haunted by the obsession that to desire a thing or to love a thing intensely is to place yourself in a vulnerable position, to be a possible, if not a probable, loser of what you most want. Let's leave it like that. That block has always been there and always will be, and my chance of getting, or achieving, anything that I long for will always be gravely reduced by the interminable existence of that block.

I described it once in a poem called "The Marvelous Children."

"He, the demon, set up barricades of gold and purple tinfoil, labeled Fear (and other august titles), which they, the children, would leap lightly over, always tossing backwards their wild laughter."

But having, always, to contend with this adversary of fear, which was sometimes terror, gave me a certain tendency toward an atmosphere of hysteria and violence in my writing, an atmosphere that has existed in it since the beginning.

In my first published work, for which I received the big sum of thirty-five dollars, a story published in the July or August issue of Weird Tales in the year 1928, I drew upon a paragraph in the ancient histories of Herodotus to create a story of how the Egyptian queen, Nitocris, invited all of her enemies to a lavish banquet in a subterranean hall on the shores of the Nile, and how, at the height of this banquet, she excused herself from the table and opened sluice gates admitting the waters of the Nile into the locked banquet hall, drowning her unloved guests like so many rats.

I was sixteen when I wrote this story, but already a confirmed writer, having entered upon this vocation at the age of fourteen, and, if you're well acquainted with my writings since then, I don't have to tell you that it set the keynote for most of the work that has followed.

My first four plays, two of them performed in St. Louis, were correspondingly violent or more so. My first play professionally produced and aimed at Broadway was *Battle of Angels* and it was about as violent as you can get on the stage.

During the nineteen years since then I have only produced five plays that are *not* violent: *The Glass Menagerie, You Touched Me, Summer and Smoke, The Rose Tattoo* and, recently in Florida, a serious comedy called *Period of Adjustment,* which is still being worked on.

What surprises me is the degree to which both critics and audience have accepted this barrage of violence. I think I was surprised, most of all, by the acceptance and praise of *Suddenly Last Summer.* When it was done off Broadway, I thought I would be critically tarred and feathered and ridden on a fence rail out of the New York theatre, with no future haven except in translation for theatres abroad, who might mistakenly construe my work as a castigation of American morals, not understanding that I write about violence in American life only because I am not so well acquainted with the society of other countries.

Last year I thought it might help me as a writer to undertake psychoanalysis and so I did. The analyst, being acquainted with my work and recognizing the psychic wounds expressed in it, asked me, soon after we started, "Why are you so full of hate, anger and envy?"

Hate was the word I contested. After much discussion and argument, we decided that "hate" was just a provisional term and that we would only use it till we had discovered the more precise term. But unfortunately I got restless and started hopping back and forth between the analyst's couch and some Caribbean beaches. I think before we called it quits I had persuaded the doctor that hate was not the right word, that there was some other thing, some other word for it, which we had not yet uncovered, and we left it like that.

Anger, oh yes! And envy, yes! But not hate. I think that hate is a thing, a feeling, that can only exist where there is no understanding. Significantly, good physicians never have it. They never hate their patients, no matter how hateful their patients may seem to be, with their relentless, maniacal concentration on their own tortured egos.

Since I am a member of the human race, when I attack its behavior toward fellow members I am obviously including myself in the attack, unless I regard myself as not human but superior to humanity. I don't. In fact, I can't expose a human weakness on the stage unless I know it through having it myself. I have exposed a good many human weaknesses and brutalities and consequently I have them.

I don't even think that I am more conscious of mine than any of you are of yours. Guilt is universal. I mean a strong sense of guilt. If there exists any area in which a man can rise above his moral condition, imposed upon him at birth and long before birth, by the nature of his breed, then I think it is only a willingness to know it, to face its existence in him, and I think that at least below the conscious level, we all face it. Hence guilty feelings, and hence defiant aggressions, and hence the deep dark of despair that haunts our dreams, our creative work, and makes us distrust each other.

Enough of these philosophical abstractions, for now. To

get back to writing for the theatre, if there is any truth in the Aristotelian idea that violence is purged by its poetic representation on a stage, then it may be that my cycle of violent plays have had a moral justification after all. I know that I have felt it. I have always felt a release from the sense of meaninglessness and death when a work of tragic intention has seemed to me to have achieved that intention, even if only approximately, nearly.

I would say that there is something much bigger in life and death than we have become aware of (or adequately recorded) in our living and dying. And, further, to compound this shameless romanticism, I would say that our serious theatre is a search for that something that is not yet successful but is still going on.

Synopsis of Scenes

ACT ONE

SCENE ONE: A bedroom in the Royal Palms Hotel, somewhere on the Gulf Coast.

SCENE TWO: The same. Later.

ACT TWO

SCENE ONE: The terrace of Boss Finley's house in St. Cloud.

SCENE TWO: The cocktail lounge and Palm Garden of the Royal Palms Hotel.

ACT THREE

The bedroom again.

TIME: Modern, an Easter Sunday, from late morning till late night.

SETTING and "SPECIAL EFFECTS": The stage is backed by a cyclorama that should give a poetic unity of mood to the several specific settings. There are nonrealistic projections on this "cyc," the most important and constant being a grove of royal palm trees. There is nearly always a wind among these very tall palm trees, sometimes loud, sometimes just a whisper, and sometimes it blends into a thematic music which will be identified, when it occurs, as "The Lament."

During the daytime scenes the cyclorama projection is a poetic abstraction of semitropical sea and sky in fair spring weather. At night it is the palm garden with its branches among the stars.

The specific settings should be treated as freely and sparingly as the sets for *Cat on a Hot Tin Roof* or *Summer and Smoke.* They'll be described as you come to them in the script.

Sweet Bird of Youth was presented at the Martin Beck Theatre in New York on March 10, 1959, by Cheryl Crawford. It was directed by Elia Kazan; the stage settings and lighting were by Jo Mielziner, the costumes by Anna Hill Johnstone, and the music by Paul Bowles; production stage manager, David Pardoll. The cast was as follows:

CHANCE WAYNE	PAUL NEWMAN
THE PRINCESS KOSMONOPOLIS	GERALDINE PAGE
FLY	MILTON J. WILLIAMS
MAID	PATRICIA RIPLEY
GEORGE SCUDDER	LOGAN RAMSEY
HATCHER	JOHN NAPIER
BOSS FINLEY	SIDNEY BLACKMER
TOM JUNIOR	RIP TORN
AUNT NONNIE	MARTINE BARTLETT
HEAVENLY FINLEY	DIANA HYLAND
CHARLES	EARL SYDNOR
STUFF	BRUCE DERN
MISS LUCY	MADELEINE SHERWOOD
THE HECKLER	CHARLES TYNER
VIOLET	MONICA MAY
EDNA	HILDA BRAWNER
SCOTTY	CHARLES MC DANIEL
BUD	JIM JETER
MEN IN BAR	DUKE FARLEY, RON HARPER, KENNETH BLAKE
PAGE	GLENN STENSEL

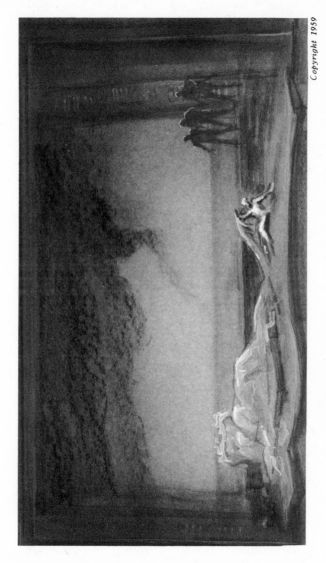

PAINTING OF STAGE SETTING FOR THE NEW YORK PRODUCTION BY JO MIELZINER

ACT ONE

A bedroom of an old-fashioned but still fashionable hotel somewhere along the Gulf Coast in a town called St. Cloud. I think of it as resembling one of those "Grand Hotels" around Sorrento or Monte Carlo, set in a palm garden. The style is vaguely "Moorish." The principal set-piece is a great double bed which should be raked toward the audience. In a sort of Moorish corner backed by shuttered windows, is a wicker tabouret and two wicker stools, over which is suspended a Moorish lamp on a brass chain. The windows are floor length and they open out upon a gallery. There is also a practical door frame, opening onto a corridor: the walls are only suggested.

On the great bed are two figures, a sleeping woman, and a young man awake, sitting up, in the trousers of white silk pajamas. The sleeping woman's face is partly covered by an eyeless black satin domino to protect her from morning glare. She breathes and tosses on the bed as if in the grip of a nightmare. The young man is lighting his first cigarette of the day.

Outside the windows there is heard the soft, urgent cries of birds, the sound of their wings. Then a colored waiter, FLY, appears at door on the corridor, bearing coffee-service for two. He knocks. CHANCE rises, pauses a moment at a mirror in the fourth wall to run a comb through his slightly thinning blond hair before he crosses to open the door.

CHANCE: Aw, good, put it in there.

FLY: Yes, suh.

CHANCE: Give me the Bromo first. You better mix it for me, I'm—

FLY: Hands kind of shaky this mawnin'?

CHANCE [*shuddering after the Bromo*]: Open the shutters a little. Hey, I said a little, not much, not that much!

[*As the shutters are opened we see him clearly for the first time: he's in his late twenties and his face looks slightly older than that; you might describe it as a "ravaged young face" and yet it is still exceptionally good-looking. His body shows no decline, yet it's the kind of a body that white silk pajamas are, or ought to be, made for. A church bell tolls, and from another church, nearer, a choir starts singing The Hallelujah Chorus. It draws him to the window, and as he crosses, he says:*]

I didn't know it was—Sunday.

FLY: Yes, suh, it's *Easter* Sunday.

CHANCE [*leans out a moment, hands gripping the shutters*]: Uh-huh. . . .

FLY: That's the Episcopal Church they're singin' in. The bell's from the Catholic Church.

CHANCE: I'll put your tip on the check.

FLY: Thank you, Mr. Wayne.

CHANCE [*as FLY starts for the door*]: Hey. How did you know my name?

FLY: I waited tables in the Grand Ballroom when you used to come to the dances on Saturday nights, with that real pretty girl you used to dance so good with, Mr. Boss Finley's daughter?

CHANCE: I'm increasing your tip to five dollars in return for a favor which is not to remember that you have recognized me or anything else at all. Your name is Fly—Shoo, Fly. Close the door with no noise.

342

VOICE OUTSIDE: Just a minute.

CHANCE: Who's that?

VOICE OUTSIDE: George Scudder.

[*Slight pause.* FLY *exits.*]

CHANCE: How did you know I was here?

[GEORGE SCUDDER *enters: a coolly nice-looking, business-like young man who might be the head of the Junior Chamber of Commerce but is actually a young doctor, about thirty-six or -seven.*]

SCUDDER: The assistant manager that checked you in here last night phoned me this morning that you'd come back to St. Cloud.

CHANCE: So you came right over to welcome me home?

SCUDDER: Your lady friend sounds like she's coming out of ether.

CHANCE: The Princess had a rough night.

SCUDDER: You've latched onto a Princess? [*mockingly*] Gee.

CHANCE: She's traveling incognito.

SCUDDER: Golly, I should think she would, if she's checking in hotels with *you.*

CHANCE: George, you're the only man I know that still says "gee," "golly," and "gosh."

SCUDDER: Well, I'm not the sophisticated type, Chance.

CHANCE: That's for sure. Want some coffee?

SCUDDER: Nope. Just came for a talk. A quick one.

343

CHANCE: Okay. Start talking, man.

SCUDDER: Why've you come back to St. Cloud?

CHANCE: I've still got a mother and a girl in St. Cloud. How's Heavenly, George?

SCUDDER: We'll get around to that later. [*He glances at his watch.*] I've got to be in surgery at the hospital in twenty-five minutes.

CHANCE: You operate now, do you?

SCUDDER [*opening doctor's bag*]: I'm chief-of-staff there now.

CHANCE: Man, you've got it made.

SCUDDER: Why have you come back?

CHANCE: I heard that my mother was sick.

SCUDDER: But you said, "How's Heavenly," not "How's my mother," Chance. [CHANCE *sips coffee.*] Your mother died a couple of weeks ago. . . .

[CHANCE *slowly turns his back on the man and crosses to the window. Shadows of birds sweep the blind. He lowers it a little before he turns back to* SCUDDER.]

CHANCE: Why wasn't I notified?

SCUDDER: You were. A wire was sent you three days before she died at the last address she had for you which was General Delivery, Los Angeles. We got no answer from that and another wire was sent you after she died, the same day of her death and we got no response from that either. Here's the Church Record. The church took up a collection for her hospital and funeral expenses. She was buried nicely in your family plot and the church has also given her a very nice

344

headstone. I'm giving you these details in spite of the fact that I know and everyone here in town knows that you had no interest in her, less than people who knew her only slightly, such as myself.

CHANCE: How did she go?

SCUDDER: She had a long illness, Chance. You know about that.

CHANCE: Yes. She was sick when I left here the last time.

SCUDDER: She was sick at heart as well as sick in her body at that time, Chance. But people were very good to her, especially people who knew her in church, and the Reverend Walker was with her at the end.

[CHANCE *sits down on the bed. He puts out his unfinished cigarette and immediately lights another. His voice becomes thin and strained.*]

CHANCE: She never had any luck.

SCUDDER: Luck? Well, that's all over with now. If you want to know anything more about that, you can get in touch with Reverend Walker about it, although I'm afraid he won't be likely to show much cordiality to you.

CHANCE: She's gone. Why talk about it?

SCUDDER: I hope you haven't forgotten the letter I wrote you soon after you last left town.

CHANCE: No. I got no letter.

SCUDDER: I wrote you in care of an address your mother gave me about a very important private matter.

CHANCE: I've been moving a lot.

SCUDDER: I didn't even mention names in the letter.

CHANCE: What was the letter about?

SCUDDER: Sit over here so I don't have to talk loud about this. Come over here. I can't talk loud about this. [SCUDDER *indicates the chair by the tabouret.* CHANCE *crosses and rests a foot on the chair.*] In this letter I just told you that a certain girl we know had to go through an awful experience, a tragic ordeal, because of past contact with you. I told you that I was only giving you this information so that you would know better than to come back to St. Cloud, but you didn't know better.

CHANCE: I told you I got no letter. Don't tell me about a letter, I didn't get any letter.

SCUDDER: I'm telling you what I told you in this letter.

CHANCE: All right. Tell me what you told me, don't— don't talk to me like a club, a chamber of something. What did you tell me? What ordeal? What girl? Heavenly? Heavenly? George?

SCUDDER: I see it's not going to be possible to talk about this quietly and so I . . .

CHANCE [*rising to block* SCUDDER'S *way*]: Heavenly? What ordeal?

SCUDDER: We will not mention names. Chance, I rushed over here this morning as soon as I heard you were back in St. Cloud, before the girl's father and brother could hear that you were back in St. Cloud, to stop you from trying to get in touch with the girl and to get out of here. That is absolutely all I have to say to you in this room at this moment. . . . But I hope I have said it in a way to impress you with the vital urgency of it, so you will leave. . . .

CHANCE: Jesus! If something's happened to Heavenly, will you please tell me—what?

SCUDDER: I said no names. We are not alone in this room. Now when I go downstairs now, I'll speak to Dan Hatcher, assistant manager here . . . he told me you'd checked in here . . . and tell him you want to check out, so you'd better get Sleeping Beauty and yourself ready to travel, and I suggest that you keep on traveling till you've crossed the State line. . . .

CHANCE: You're not going to leave this room till you've explained to me what you've been hinting at about my girl in St. Cloud.

SCUDDER: There's a lot more to this which we feel ought not to be talked about to anyone, least of all to you, since you have turned into a criminal degenerate, the only right term for you, but, Chance, I think I ought to remind you that once long ago. the father of this girl wrote out a prescription for you, a sort of medical prescription, which is castration. You'd better think about that, that would deprive you of all you've got to get by on. [*He moves toward the steps.*]

CHANCE: I'm used to that threat. I'm not going to leave St. Cloud without my girl.

SCUDDER [*on the steps*]: You don't have a girl in St. Cloud. Heavenly and I are going to be married next month. [*He leaves abruptly.*]

[CHANCE, *shaken by what he has heard, turns and picks up phone, and kneels on the floor.*]

CHANCE: Hello? St. Cloud 525. Hello, Aunt Nonnie? This is Chance, yes Chance. I'm staying at the Royal Palms

347

and I . . . what's the matter, has something happened to Heavenly? Why can't you talk now? George Scudder was here and . . . Aunt Nonnie? Aunt Nonnie?

[*The other end hangs up. The sleeping woman suddenly cries out in her sleep.* CHANCE *drops the phone on its cradle and runs to the bed.*]

CHANCE [*bending over her as she struggles out of a nightmare*]: Princess! Princess! Hey, *Princess Kos!* [*He removes her eyemask; she sits up gasping and staring wild-eyed about her.*]

PRINCESS: Who are you? Help!

CHANCE [*on the bed*]: Hush now. . . .

PRINCESS: Oh . . . I . . . had . . . a *terrible* dream.

CHANCE: It's all right. Chance's with you.

PRINCESS: Who?

CHANCE: Me.

PRINCESS: I don't know who you are!

CHANCE: You'll remember soon, Princess.

PRINCESS: I don't know, I don't know. . . .

CHANCE: It'll come back to you soon. What are you reachin' for, honey?

PRINCESS: Oxygen! Mask!

CHANCE: Why? Do you feel short-winded?

PRINCESS Yes! I have . . . air . . . shortage!

CHANCE [*looking for the correct piece of luggage*]: Which bag is your oxygen in? I can't remember which bag we packed it in. Aw, yeah, the crocodile case, the one with the combination lock. Wasn't the first number zero . . . [*He comes back to the bed and reaches for a bag under its far side.*]

PRINCESS [*as if with her dying breath*]: Zero, zero. Two zeros to the right and then back around to . . .

CHANCE: Zero, three zeros, two of them to the right and the last one to the left. . . .

PRINCESS: Hurry! I can't breathe, I'm dying!

CHANCE: I'm getting it, Princess.

PRINCESS: HURRY!

CHANCE: Here we are, I've got it. . . .

[*He has extracted from case a small oxygen cylinder and mask. He fits the inhalator over her nose and mouth. She falls back on the pillow. He places the other pillow under her head. After a moment, her panicky breath subsiding, she growls at him.*]

PRINCESS: Why in hell did you lock it up in that case?

CHANCE [*standing at the head of the bed*]: You said to put all your valuables in that case.

PRINCESS: I meant my jewelry, and you know it, you, bastard!

CHANCE: Princess, I didn't think you'd have these attacks any more. I thought that having me with you to protect you would stop these attacks of panic, I . . .

PRINCESS: Give me a pill.

CHANCE: Which pill?

PRINCESS: A pink one, a pinkie, and vodka . . .

349

[*He puts the tank on the floor, and goes over to the trunk. The phone rings.* CHANCE *gives the* PRINCESS *a pill, picks up the vodka bottle and goes to the phone. He sits down with the bottle between his knees.*]

CHANCE [*pouring a drink, phone held between shoulder and ear*]: Hello? Oh, hello, Mr. Hatcher——Oh? But Mr. Hatcher, when we checked in here last night we weren't told that, and Miss Alexandra Del Lago . . .

PRINCESS [*shouting*]: *Don't use my name!*

CHANCE: . . . is suffering from exhaustion, she's not at all well, Mr. Hatcher, and certainly not in any condition to travel. . . . I'm sure you don't want to take the responsibility for what might happen to Miss Del Lago . . .

PRINCESS [*shouting again*]: *Don't use my name!*

CHANCE: . . . if she attempted to leave here today in the condition she's in . . . do you?

PRINCESS: *Hang up!* [*He does. He comes over with his drink and the bottle to the* PRINCESS.] I want to forget everything, I want to forget who I am. . . .

CHANCE [*handing her the drink*]: He said that . . .

PRINCESS [*drinking*]: Please shut up, I'm *forgetting!*

CHANCE [*taking the glass from her*]: Okay, go on forget. There's nothing better than that, I wish I could do it. . . .

PRINCESS: I can, I will. I'm forgetting . . . I'm forgetting. . . .

[*She lies down.* CHANCE *moves to the foot of the bed, where he seems to be struck with an idea. He puts the bottle down on the floor, runs to the chaise and picks up*]

350

a tape recorder. Taking it back to the bed, he places the recorder on the floor. As he plugs it in, he coughs.]

What's going on?

CHANCE: Looking for my toothbrush.

PRINCESS [*throwing the oxygen mask on the bed*]: Will you please take that away.

CHANCE: Sure you've had enough of it?

PRINCESS [*laughs breathlessly*]: Yes, for God's sake, take it away. I must look hideous in it.

CHANCE [*taking the mask*]: No, no, you just look exotic, like a Princess from Mars or a big magnified insect.

PRINCESS: Thank you, check the cylinder please.

CHANCE: For what?

PRINCESS: Check the air left in it; there's a gauge on the cylinder that gives the pressure. . . .

CHANCE: You're still breathing like a quarter horse that's been run a full mile. Are you sure you don't want a doctor?

PRINCESS: No, for God's sake . . . no!

CHANCE: Why are you so scared of doctors?

PRINCESS [*hoarsely, quickly*]: I don't need them. What happened is nothing at all. It happens frequently to me. Something disturbs me . . . adrenalin's pumped in my blood and I get short-winded, that's all, that's all there is to it . . . I woke up, I didn't know where I was or who I was with, I got panicky . . . adrenalin was released and I got short-winded. . . .

CHANCE: Are you okay now, Princess? Huh? [*He kneels on the bed, and helps straighten up the pillows.*]

351

PRINCESS: Not quite yet, but I will be. I will be.

CHANCE: You're full of complexes, plump lady.

PRINCESS: What did you call me?

CHANCE: Plump lady.

PRINCESS: Why do you call me that? Have I let go of my figure?

CHANCE: You put on a good deal of weight after that disappointment you had last month.

PRINCESS [*hitting him with a small pillow*]: What disappointment? I don't remember any.

CHANCE: Can you control your memory like that?

PRINCESS: Yes. I've had to learn to. What is this place, a hospital? And you, what are you, a male nurse?

CHANCE: I take care of you but I'm not your nurse.

PRINCESS: But you're employed by me, aren't you? For some purpose or other?

CHANCE: I'm not on salary with you.

PRINCESS: What are you on? Just expenses?

CHANCE: Yep. You're footing the bills.

PRINCESS: I see. Yes, I see.

CHANCE: Why're you rubbing your eyes?

PRINCESS: My vision's so cloudy! Don't I wear glasses, don't I have any glasses?

CHANCE: You had a little accident with your glasses.

PRINCESS: What was that?

CHANCE: You fell on your face with them on.

PRINCESS: Were they completely demolished?

CHANCE: One lens cracked.

PRINCESS: Well, please give me the remnants. I don't mind waking up in an intimate situation with someone, but I like to see who it's with, so I can make whatever adjustment seems called for. . . .

CHANCE [*rises and goes to the trunk, where he lights cigarette*]: You know what I look like.

PRINCESS: No, I don't.

CHANCE: You did.

PRINCESS: I tell you I don't remember, it's all gone away!

CHANCE: I don't believe in amnesia.

PRINCESS: Neither do I. But you have to believe a thing that happens to you.

CHANCE: Where did I put your glasses?

PRINCESS: Don't ask me. You say I fell on them. If I was in that condition I wouldn't be likely to know where anything is I had with me. What happened last night?

[*He has picked them up but not given them to her.*]

CHANCE: You knocked yourself out.

PRINCESS: Did we sleep here together?

CHANCE: Yes, but I didn't molest you.

PRINCESS: Should I thank you for that, or accuse you of cheating? [*She laughs sadly.*]

353

CHANCE: I like you, you're a nice monster.

PRINCESS: Your voice sounds young. Are you young?

CHANCE: My age is twenty-nine years.

PRINCESS: That's young for anyone but an Arab. Are you very good-looking?

CHANCE: I used to be the best-looking boy in this town.

PRINCESS: How large is the town?

CHANCE: Fair-sized.

PRINCESS: Well, I like a good mystery novel, I read them to put me to sleep and if they don't put me to sleep, they're good; but this one's a little too good for comfort. I wish you would find me my glasses. . . .

[*He reaches over headboard to hand the glasses to her. She puts them on and looks him over. Then she motions him to come nearer and touches his bare chest with her finger tips.*]

Well, I may have done better, but God knows I've done worse.

CHANCE: What are you doing now, Princess?

PRINCESS: The tactile approach.

CHANCE: You do that like you were feeling a piece of goods to see if it was genuine silk or phony. . . .

PRINCESS: It feels like silk. Genuine! This much I do remember, that I like bodies to be hairless, silky-smooth gold!

CHANCE: Do I meet these requirements?

PRINCESS: You seem to meet those requirements. But I still have a feeling that something is not satisfied in the relation between us.

CHANCE [*moving away from her*]: You've had your experiences, I've had mine. You can't expect everything to be settled at once. . . . Two different experiences of two different people. Naturally there's some things that have to be settled between them before there's any absolute agreement.

PRINCESS [*throwing the glasses on the bed*]: Take that splintered lens out before it gets in my eye.

CHANCE [*obeying this instruction by knocking the glasses sharply on the bed table*]: You like to give orders, don't you?

PRINCESS: It's something I seem to be used to.

CHANCE: How would you like to *take* them? To be a slave?

PRINCESS: What time is it?

CHANCE: My watch is in hock somewhere. Why don't you look at yours?

PRINCESS: Where's mine?

[*He reaches lazily over to the table, and hands it to her.*]

CHANCE: It's stopped, at five past seven.

PRINCESS: Surely it's later than that, or earlier, that's no hour when I'm . . .

CHANCE: Platinum, is it?

PRINCESS: No, it's only white gold. I never travel with anything very expensive.

355

CHANCE: Why? Do you get robbed much? Huh? Do you get "rolled" often?

PRINCESS: Get what?

CHANCE: "Rolled." Isn't that expression in your vocabulary?

PRINCESS: Give me the phone.

CHANCE: For what?

PRINCESS: I said give me the phone.

CHANCE: I know. And I said for what?

PRINCESS: I want to enquire where I am and who is with me?

CHANCE: Take it easy.

PRINCESS: Will you give me the phone?

CHANCE: Relax. You're getting short-winded again. . . . [*He takes hold of her shoulders.*]

PRINCESS: Please let go of me.

CHANCE: Don't you feel secure with me? Lean back. Lean back against me.

PRINCESS: Lean back?

CHANCE: This way, this way. There . . .

[*He pulls her into his arms: She rests in them, panting a little like a trapped rabbit.*]

PRINCESS: It gives you an awful trapped feeling this, this memory block. . . . I feel as if someone I loved had died lately, and I don't want to remember who it could be.

CHANCE: Do you remember your name?

PRINCESS: Yes, I do.

CHANCE: What's your name?

PRINCESS: I think there's some reason why I prefer not to tell you.

CHANCE: Well, I happen to know it. You registered under a phony name in Palm Beach but I discovered your real one. And you admitted it to me.

PRINCESS: I'm the Princess Kosmonopolis.

CHANCE: Yes, and you used to be known as . . .

PRINCESS [*sits up sharply*]: No, stop . . . will you let me do it? Quietly, in my own way? The last place I remember . . .

CHANCE: What's the last place you remember?

PRINCESS: A town with the crazy name of Tallahassee.

CHANCE: Yeah. We drove through there. That's where I reminded you that today would be Sunday and we ought to lay in a supply of liquor to get us through it without us being dehydrated too severely, and so we stopped there but it was a college town and we had some trouble locating a package store, open. . . .

PRINCESS: But we did, did we?

CHANCE: [*getting up for the bottle and pouring her a drink*]: Oh, sure, we bought three bottles of Vodka. You curled up in the back seat with one of those bottles and when I looked back you were blotto. I intended to stay on the old Spanish Trail straight through to Texas, where you had some oil wells to look at. I didn't stop here . . . I was stopped.

PRINCESS: What by, a cop? Or . . .

357

CHANCE: No. No cop, but I was arrested by something.

PRINCESS: My car. Where is my car?

CHANCE [*handling her the drink*]: In the hotel parking lot, Princess.

PRINCESS: Oh, then, this is a hotel?

CHANCE: It's the elegant old Royal Palms Hotel in the town of St. Cloud.

[*Gulls fly past window, shadows sweeping the blind: they cry out with soft urgency.*]

PRINCESS: Those pigeons out there sound hoarse. They sound like gulls to me. Of course, they could be pigeons with laryngitis.

[CHANCE *glances at her with his flickering smile and laughs softly.*]

Will you help me please? I'm about to get up.

CHANCE: What do you want? I'll get it.

PRINCESS: I want to go to the window.

CHANCE: What for?

PRINCESS: To look out of it.

CHANCE: I can describe the view to you.

PRINCESS: I'm not sure I'd trust your description. WELL?

CHANCE: Okay, *oopsa-daisy.*

PRINCESS: My God! I said help me up, not . . . toss me onto the carpet! [*Sways dizzily a moment, clutching bed. Then draws a breath and crosses to the window.*]

[*Pauses as she gazes out, squinting into noon's brilliance.*]

CHANCE: Well, what do you see? Give me your description of the view, Princess?

PRINCESS [*faces the audience*]: I see a palm garden.

CHANCE: And a four-lane highway just past it.

PRINCESS [*squinting and shielding her eyes*]: Yes, I see that and a strip of beach with some bathers and then, an infinite stretch of nothing but water and . . . [*She cries out softly and turns away from the window.*]

CHANCE: What? . . .

PRINCESS: Oh God, I remember the thing I wanted not to. The goddam end of my life! [*She draws a deep shuddering breath.*]

CHANCE [*running to her aid*]: What's the matter?

PRINCESS: Help me back to bed. Oh God, no wonder I didn't want to remember, I was no fool!

[*He assists her to the bed. There is an unmistakable sympathy in his manner, however shallow.*]

CHANCE: Oxygen?

PRINCESS [*draws another deep shuddering breath*]: **No!** Where's the stuff? Did you leave it in the car?

CHANCE: Oh, the stuff? Under the mattress. [*Moving to the other side of the bed, he pulls out a small pouch.*]

PRINCESS: A stupid place to put it.

CHANCE [*sits at the foot of the bed*]: What's wrong with under the mattress?

359

PRINCESS [*sits up on the edge of the bed*]: There's such a thing as chambermaids in the world, they make up beds, they come across lumps in a mattress.

CHANCE: This isn't pot. What is it?

PRINCESS: Wouldn't that be pretty? A year in jail in one of those model prisons for distinguished addicts. What is it? Don't you know what it is, you beautiful, stupid young man? It's hashish, Moroccan, the finest.

CHANCE: Oh, hash! How'd you get it through customs when you came back for your come-back?

PRINCESS: I didn't get it through customs. The ship's doctor gave me injections while this stuff was winging over the ocean to a shifty young gentleman who thought he could blackmail me for it. [*She puts on her slippers with a vigorous gesture.*]

CHANCE: Couldn't he?

PRINCESS: Of course not. I called his bluff.

CHANCE: You took injections coming over?

PRINCESS: With my neuritis? I had to. Come on give it to me.

CHANCE: Don't you want it packed right?

PRINCESS: You talk too much. You ask too many questions. I need something quick. [*She rises.*]

CHANCE: I'm a new hand at this.

PRINCESS: I'm sure, or you wouldn't discuss it in a hotel room. . . .

[*She turns to the audience, and intermittently changes the focus of her attention.*]

360

For years they all told me that it was ridiculous of me to feel that I couldn't go back to the screen or the stage as a middle-aged woman. They told me I was an artist, not just a star whose career depended on youth. But I knew in my heart that the legend of Alexandra del Lago couldn't be separated from an appearance of youth. . . .

There's no more valuable knowledge than knowing the right time to go. I knew it. I went at the right time to go. RETIRED! Where to? To what? To that dead planet the moon. . . .

There's nowhere else to retire to when you retire from an art because, believe it or not, I really was once an artist. So I retired to the moon, but the atmosphere of the moon doesn't have any oxygen in it. I began to feel breathless, in that withered, withering country, of time coming after time not meant to come after, and so I discovered . . . Haven't you fixed it yet?

[CHANCE *rises and goes to her with a cigarette he has been preparing.*]

Discovered this!

And other practices like it, to put to sleep the tiger that raged in my nerves. . . . Why the unsatisfied tiger? In the nerves jungle? Why is anything, anywhere, unsatisfied, and raging? . . .

Ask somebody's good doctor. But don't believe his answer because it isn't . . . the answer . . . if I had just been old but you see, I wasn't old. . . .

I just wasn't young, not young, young. I just wasn't young anymore. . . .

CHANCE: Nobody's young anymore. . . .

PRINCESS: But you see, I couldn't get old with that tiger still in me raging.

361

CHANCE: Nobody can get old. . . .

PRINCESS: Stars in retirement sometimes give acting lessons. Or take up painting, paint flowers on pots, or landscapes. I could have painted the landscape of the endless, withering country in which I wandered like a lost nomad. If I could paint deserts and nomads, if I could paint . . . hahaha. . . .

CHANCE: SH-Sh-sh-

PRINCESS: Sorry!

CHANCE: Smoke.

PRINCESS: Yes, smoke! And then the young lovers. . . .

CHANCE: Me?

PRINCESS: You? Yes, finally you. But you come after the come-back. Ha . . . Ha . . . The glorious come-back, when I turned fool and came back. . . . The screen's a very clear mirror. There's a thing called a close-up. The camera advances and you stand still and your head, your face, is caught in the frame of the picture with a light blazing on it and all your terrible history screams while you smile. . . .

CHANCE: How do you know? Maybe it wasn't a failure, maybe you were just scared, just chicken, Princess . . . ha-ha-ha. . . .

PRINCESS: Not a failure . . . after that close-up they gasped. . . . People gasped. . . . I heard them whisper, their shocked whispers. Is that her? Is that her? Her? . . . I made the mistake of wearing a very elaborate gown to the *première,* a gown with a train that had to be gathered up as I rose from my seat and began the interminable retreat

362

from the city of flames, up, up, up the unbearably long theatre aisle, gasping for breath and still clutching up the regal white train of my gown, all the way up the forever . . . length of the aisle, and behind me some small unknown man grabbing at me, saying, stay, stay! At last the top of the aisle, I turned and struck him, then let the train fall, forgot it, and tried to run down the marble stairs, tripped of course, fell and, rolled, rolled, like a sailor's drunk whore to the bottom . . . hands, merciful hands without faces, assisted me to get up. After that? Flight, just flight, not interrupted until I woke up this morning. . . . Oh God it's gone out. . . .

CHANCE: Let me fix you another. Huh? Shall I fix you another?

PRINCESS: Let me finish yours. You can't retire with the out-crying heart of an artist still crying out, in your body, in your nerves, in your what? Heart? Oh, no that's gone, that's . . .

CHANCE [*He goes to her, takes the cigarette out of her hand and gives her a fresh one.*] Here, I've fixed you another one . . . Princess, I've fixed you another. . . . [*He sits on the floor, leaning against the foot of the bed.*]

PRINCESS: Well, sooner or later, at some point in your life, the thing that you lived for is lost or abandoned, and then . . . you die, or find something else. This is my something else. . . . [*She approaches the bed.*] And ordinarily I take the most fantastic precautions against . . . detection. . . . [*She sits on the bed, then lies down on her back, her head over the foot, near his.*] I cannot imagine what possessed me to let you know. Knowing so little about you as I seem to know.

CHANCE: I must've inspired a good deal of confidence in you.

PRINCESS: If that's the case, I've gone crazy. Now tell me something. What is that body of water, that sea, out past the palm garden and four-lane highway? I ask you because I remember now that we turned west from the sea w¹·en we went onto that highway called the Old Spanish Trail.

CHANCE: We've come back to the sea.

PRINCESS: What sea?

CHANCE: The Gulf.

PRINCESS: The Gulf?

CHANCE: The Gulf of misunderstanding between me and you. . . .

PRINCESS: We don't understand each other? And lie here smoking this stuff?

CHANCE: Princess, don't forget that this stuff is yours, that you provided me with it.

PRINCESS: What are you trying to prove? [*Church bells toll.*] Sundays go on a long time.

CHANCE: You don't deny it was yours.

PRINCESS: What's mine?

CHANCE: You brought it into the country, you smuggled it through customs into the U.S.A. and you had a fair supply of it at that hotel in Palm Beach and were asked to check out before you were ready to do so, because its aroma drifted into the corridor one breezy night.

PRINCESS: What are you trying to prove?

CHANCE: You don't deny that you introduced me to it?

PRINCESS: Boy, I doubt very much that I have any vice that I'd need to introduce to you. . . .

CHANCE: Don't call me "boy."

PRINCESS: Why not?

CHANCE: It sounds condescending. And all my vices were caught from other people.

PRINCESS: What are you trying to prove? My memory's come back now. Excessively clearly. It was this mutual practice that brought us together. When you came in my cabana to give me one of those papaya cream rubs, you sniffed, you grinned and said you'd like a stick too.

CHANCE: That's right. I knew the smell of it.

PRINCESS: What are you trying to prove?

CHANCE: You asked me four or five times what I'm trying to prove, the answer is nothing. I'm just making sure that your memory's cleared up now. You do remember me coming in your cabana to give you those papaya cream rubs?

PRINCESS: Of course I do, Carl!

CHANCE: My name is not Carl. It's Chance.

PRINCESS: You called yourself Carl.

CHANCE: I always carry an extra name in my pocket.

PRINCESS: You're not a criminal, are you?

CHANCE: No ma'am, not me. You're the one that's committed a federal offense.

[*She stares at him a moment, and then goes to the door leading to the hall, looks out and listens.*]

365

What did you do that for?

PRINCESS [*closing the door*]: To see if someone was planted outside the door.

CHANCE: You still don't trust me?

PRINCESS: Someone that gives me a false name?

CHANCE: You registered under a phony one in Palm Beach.

PRINCESS: Yes, to avoid getting any reports or condolences on the disaster I ran from. [*She crosses to the window. There is a pause followed by "The Lament."*] And so we've not arrived at any agreement?

CHANCE: No ma'am, not a complete one.

[*She turns her back to the window and gazes at him from there.*]

PRINCESS: What's the gimmick? The hitch?

CHANCE: The usual one.

PRINCESS: What's that?

CHANCE: Doesn't somebody always hold out for something?

PRINCESS: Are you holding out for something?

CHANCE: Uh-huh. . . .

PRINCESS: What?

CHANCE: You said that you had a large block of stock, more than half ownership in a sort of a second-rate Hollywood Studio, and could put me under contract. I doubted your word about that. You're not like any phony I've met before, but phonies come in all types and sizes. So I held out, even after we locked your cabana door for the papaya cream rubs. . . . You wired for some contract papers we signed. It was notarized and witnessed by three strangers found in a bar.

PRINCESS: Then why did you hold out, still?

CHANCE: I didn't have much faith in it. You know, you can buy those things for six bits in novelty stores. I've been conned and tricked too often to put much faith in anything that could still be phony.

PRINCESS: You're wise. However, I have the impression that there's been a certain amount of intimacy between us.

CHANCE: A certain amount. No more. I wanted to hold your interest.

PRINCESS: Well, you miscalculated. My interest always increases with satisfaction.

CHANCE: Then you're unusual in that respect, too.

PRINCESS: In all respects I'm not common.

CHANCE: But I guess the contract we signed is full of loopholes?

PRINCESS: Truthfully, yes, it is. I can get out of it if I wanted to. And so can the studio. Do you have any talent?

CHANCE: For what?

PRINCESS: Acting, baby, ACTING!

CHANCE: I'm not as positive of it as I once was. I've had more chances than I could count on my fingers, and made the grade almost, but not quite, every time. Something always blocks me. . . .

PRINCESS: What? What? Do you *know?* [*He rises. The lamentation is heard very faintly.*] Fear?

CHANCE: No not fear, but terror . . . otherwise would I be your goddam caretaker, hauling you across the country? Picking you up when you fall? Well would I? Except for that block, by anything less than a star?

PRINCESS: CARL!

CHANCE: Chance. . . . Chance Wayne. You're stoned.

PRINCESS: Chance, come back to your youth. Put off this false, ugly hardness and . . .

CHANCE: And be took in by every con-merchant I meet?

PRINCESS: I'm not a phony, believe me.

CHANCE: Well, then, what is it you want? Come on say it, Princess.

PRINCESS: Chance, come here. [*He smiles but doesn't move.*] Come here and let's comfort each other a little. [*He crouches by the bed; she encircles him with her bare arms.*]

CHANCE: Princess! Do you know something? All this conversation has been recorded on tape?

PRINCESS: What are you talking about?

CHANCE: Listen. I'll play it back to you. [*He uncovers the tape recorder; approaches her with the earpiece.*]

PRINCESS: How did you get that thing?

CHANCE: You bought it for me in Palm Beach. I said that I wanted it to improve my diction. . . .

[*He presses the "play" button on the recorder. The follow-ing in the left column can either be on a public address system, or can be cut.*]

(PLAYBACK)

PRINCESS: What is it? Don't you know what it is? You stupid, beautiful young man. It's hashish, Moroccan, the finest.

CHANCE: Oh, hash? How'd you get it through customs when you came back for your "come-back"?

PRINCESS: I didn't get it through customs. The ship's doctor. . . .

PRINCESS: What a smart cookie you are.

CHANCE: How does it feel to be over a great big barrel?

[*He snaps off the recorder and picks up the reels.*]

PRINCESS: This is blackmail is it? Where's my mink stole?

CHANCE: Not stolen.

[*He tosses it to her contemptuously from a chair.*]

PRINCESS: Where is my jewel case?

CHANCE [*picks it up off the floor and throws it on the bed*]: Here.

PRINCESS [*opens it up and starts to put on some jewelry*]: Every piece is insured and described in detail. Lloyd's in London.

CHANCE: *Who's* a smart cookie, Princess? You want your purse now so you can count your money?

369

PRINCESS: I don't carry currency with me, just travelers' checks.

CHANCE: I noted that fact already. But I got a fountain pen you can sign them with.

PRINCESS: Ho, Ho!

CHANCE: "Ho, ho!" What an insincere laugh, if that's how you fake a laugh, no wonder you didn't make good in your come-back picture. . . .

PRINCESS: Are you serious about this attempt to blackmail me?

CHANCE: You'd better believe it. Your trade's turned dirt on you, Princess. You understand that language?

PRINCESS: The language of the gutter is understood anywhere that anyone ever fell in it.

CHANCE: Aw, then you *do* understand.

PRINCESS: And if I shouldn't comply with this order of yours?

CHANCE: You still got a name, you're still a personage, Princess. You wouldn't want "Confidential" or "Whisper" or "Hush-Hush" or the narcotics department of the F.B.I. to get hold of one of these tape-records, would you? And I'm going to make lots of copies. Huh? Princess?

PRINCESS: You are trembling and sweating . . . you see this part doesn't suit you, you just don't play it well, Chance. . . . [CHANCE *puts the reels in a suitcase.*] I hate to think of what kind of desperation has made you try to intimidate me, ME? ALEXANDRA DEL LAGO? with that ridiculous threat. Why it's so silly, it's touching, downright endearing, it makes me feel close to you, Chance.

You were well born, weren't you? Born of good Southern stock, in a genteel tradition, with just one disadvantage, a laurel wreath on your forehead, given too early, without enough effort to earn it . . . where's your scrapbook, Chance? [*He crosses to the bed, takes a travelers' checkbook out of her purse, and extends it to her.*] Where's your book full of little theatre notices and stills that show you in the background of . . .

CHANCE: Here! Here! Start signing . . . or . . .

PRINCESS [*pointing to the bathroom*]: Or WHAT? Go take a shower under cold water. I don't like hot sweaty bodies in a tropical climate. Oh, you, I do want and will accept, still . . . under certain conditions which I will make very clear to you.

CHANCE: Here. [*Throws the checkbook toward the bed.*]

PRINCESS: Put this away. And your leaky fountain pen. . . . When monster meets monster, one monster has to give way, AND IT WILL NEVER BE ME. I'm an older hand at it . . . with much more natural aptitude at it than you have. . . . Now then, you put the cart a little in front of the horse. Signed checks are payment, delivery comes first. Certainly I can afford it, I could deduct you, as my caretaker, Chance, remember that I was a star before big taxes . . . and had a husband who was a great merchant prince. He taught me to deal with money. . . . Now, Chance, please pay close attention while I tell you the very special conditions under which I will keep you in my employment . . . after this miscalculation. . . .

Forget the legend that I was and the ruin of that legend.

Whether or not I do have a disease of the heart that places an early terminal date on my life, no mention of that, no reference to it ever. No mention of death, never, never a word

on that odious subject. I've been accused of having a death
wish but I think it's life that I wish for, terribly, shamelessly,
on any terms whatsoever.

When I say now, the answer must not be later. I have
only one way to forget these things I don't want to remember
and that's through the act of love-making. That's the only
dependable distraction so when I say now, because I need
that distraction, it has to be now, not later.

[*She crosses to the bed: He rises from the opposite side of
the bed and goes to the window: She gazes at his back as
he looks out the window. Pause: Lamentation.*]

[*Princess, finally, softly.*]

Chance, I need that distraction. It's time for me to find
out if you're able to give it to me. You mustn't hang onto
your silly little idea that you can increase your value by
turning away and looking out a window when somebody
wants you. . . . I want you. . . . I say now and I mean now,
then and not until then will I call downstairs and tell the
hotel cashier that I'm sending a young man down with some
travelers' checks to cash for me. . . .

CHANCE [*turning slowly from the window*]: Aren't you
ashamed, a little?

PRINCESS: Of course I am. Aren't you?

CHANCE: More than a little. . . .

PRINCESS: Close the shutters, draw the curtain across them.

[*He obeys these commands.*]

Now get a little sweet music on the radio and come here
to me and make me almost believe that we're a pair of
young lovers without any shame.

As the curtain rises, the PRINCESS *has a fountain pen in hand and is signing checks.* CHANCE, *now wearing dark slacks, socks and shoes of the fashionable loafer type, is putting on his shirt and speaks as the curtain opens.*

CHANCE: Keep on writing, has the pen gone dry?

PRINCESS: I started at the back of the book where the big ones are.

CHANCE: Yes, but you stopped too soon.

PRINCESS: All right, one more from the front of the book as a token of some satisfaction. I said some, not complete.

CHANCE [*picking up the phone*]: Operator—Give me the cashier please.

PRINCESS: What are you doing that for?

CHANCE: You have to tell the cashier you're sending me down with some travelers' checks to cash for you.

PRINCESS: Have to? Did you say have to?

CHANCE: Cashier? Just a moment. The Princess Kosmonopolis. [*He thrusts the phone at her.*]

PRINCESS [*into the phone*]: Who is this? But I don't want the cashier. My watch has stopped and I want to know the right time . . . five after three? Thank you . . . he says it's five after three. [*She hangs up and smiles at* CHANCE.] I'm not ready to be left alone in this room. Now let's not fight any more over little points like that, let's save our strength for the big ones. I'll have the checks cashed for you as soon as I've put on my face. I just don't want to be left alone in this place till I've put on the face that I face the world with, baby. Maybe after we get to know each other,

373

we won't fight over little points any more, the struggle will stop, maybe we won't even fight over big points, baby. Will you open the shutters a little bit please? [*He doesn't seem to hear her. The lament is heard.*] I won't be able to see my face in the mirror. . . . Open the shutters, I won't be able to see my face in the mirror.

CHANCE: Do you want to?

PRINCESS [*pointing*]: Unfortunately I have to! Open the shutters!

[*He does. He remains by the open shutters, looking out as the lament in the air continues.*]

CHANCE: —I was born in this town. I was born in St. Cloud.

PRINCESS: That's a good way to begin to tell your life story. Tell me your life story. I'm interested in it, I really would like to know it. Let's make it your audition, a sort of screen test for you. I can watch you in the mirror while I put my face on. And tell me your life story, and if you hold my attention with your life story, I'll know you have talent, I'll wire my studio on the Coast that I'm still alive and I'm on my way to the Coast with a young man named Chance Wayne that I think is cut out to be a great young star.

CHANCE [*moving out on the forestage*]: Here is the town I was born in, and lived in till ten years ago, in St. Cloud. I was a twelve-pound baby, normal and healthy, but with some kind of quantity "X" in my blood, a wish or a need to be different. . . . The kids that I grew up with are mostly still here and what they call "settled down," gone into business, married and bringing up children, the little crowd I was in with, that I used to be the star of, was the snobset, the

ones with the big names and money. I didn't have either . . .
[*The* PRINCESS *utters a soft laugh in her dimmed-out area.*]
What I had was . . . [*The* PRINCESS *half turns, brush poised
in a faint, dusty beam of light.*]

PRINCESS: BEAUTY! Say it! Say it! What you had was
beauty! I had it! I say it, with pride, no matter how sad,
being gone, now.

CHANCE: Yes, well . . . the others . . . [*The* PRINCESS
*resumes brushing hair and the sudden cold beam of light on
her goes out again.*] . . . are all now members of the young
social set here. The girls are young matrons, bridge-players,
and the boys belong to the Junior Chamber of Commerce and
some of them, clubs in New Orleans such as Rex and Comus
and ride on the Mardi Gras floats. Wonderful? No boring . . .
I wanted, expected, intended to get, something better . . . Yes,
and I did, I got it. I did things that fat-headed gang never
dreamed of. Hell when they were still freshmen at Tulane or
LSU or Ole Miss, I sang in the chorus of the biggest show
in New York, in "Oklahoma," and had pictures in LIFE in
a cowboy outfit, tossin' a ten-gallon hat in the air! YIP . . .
EEEEEE! Ha-ha. . . . And at the same time pursued my other
vocation. . . .

Maybe the only one I was truly meant for, love-making . . .
slept in the social register of New York! Millionaires' widows
and wives and debutante daughters of such famous names
as Vanderbrook and Masters and Halloway and Connaught,
names mentioned daily in columns, whose credit cards are
their faces. . . . And . . .

PRINCESS: What did they pay you?

CHANCE: I gave people more than I took. Middle-aged
people I gave back a feeling of youth. Lonely girls? Understanding, appreciation! An absolutely convincing show of

375

affection. Sad people, lost people? Something light and up-lifting! Eccentrics? Tolerance, even odd things they long for. . . .

But always just at the point when I might get something back that would solve my own need, which was great, to rise to their level, the memory of my girl would pull me back home to her . . . and when I came home for those visits, man oh man how that town buzzed with excitement. I'm telling you, it would blaze with it, and then that thing in Korea came along. I was about to be sucked into the Army so I went into the Navy, because a sailor's uniform suited me better, the uniform was all that suited me, though. . . .

PRINCESS: Ah-ha!

CHANCE [*mocking her*]: Ah-ha. I wasn't able to stand the goddam routine, discipline. . . .

I kept thinking, this stops everything. I was twenty-three, that was the peak of my youth and I knew my youth wouldn't last long. By the time I got out, Christ knows, I might be nearly thirty! Who would remember Chance Wayne? In a life like mine, you just can't stop, you know, can't take time out between steps, you've got to keep going right on up from one thing to the other, once you drop out, it leaves you and goes on without you and you're washed up.

PRINCESS: I don't think I know what you're talking about.

CHANCE: I'm talking about the parade. THE parade! The parade! the boys that go places that's the parade I'm talking about, not a parade of swabbies on a wet deck. And so I ran my comb through my hair one morning and noticed that eight or ten hairs had come out, a warning signal of a future baldness. My hair was still thick. But would it be five years from now, or even three? When the war would be over, that scared me, that speculation. I started to have bad dreams.

Nightmares and cold sweats at night, and I had palpitations, and on my leaves I got drunk and woke up in strange places with faces on the next pillow I had never seen before. My eyes had a wild look in them in the mirror. . . . I got the idea I wouldn't live through the war, that I wouldn't come back, that all the excitement and glory of being Chance Wayne would go up in smoke at the moment of contact between my brain and a bit of hot steel that happened to be in the air at the same time and place that my head was . . . that thought didn't comfort me any. Imagine a whole lifetime of dreams and ambitions and hopes dissolving away in one instant, being blacked out like some arithmetic problem washed off a blackboard by a wet sponge, just by some little accident like a bullet, not even aimed at you but just shot off in space, and so I cracked up, my nerves did. I got a medical discharge out of the service and I came home in civvies, then it was when I noticed how different it was, the town and the people in it. Polite? Yes, but not cordial. No headlines in the papers, just an item that measured one inch at the bottom of page five saying that Chance Wayne, the son of Mrs. Emily Wayne of North Front Street had received an honorable discharge from the Navy as the result of illness and was home to recover . . . that was when Heavenly became more important to me than anything else. . . .

PRINCESS: Is Heavenly a girl's name?

CHANCE: Heavenly is the name of my girl in St. Cloud.

PRINCESS: Is Heavenly why we stopped here?

CHANCE: What other reason for stopping here can you think of?

PRINCESS: So . . . I'm being used. Why not? Even a dead race horse is used to make glue. Is she pretty?

CHANCE [*handing* PRINCESS *a snapshot*]: This is a flash-light photo I took of her, nude, one night on Diamond Key, which is a little sandbar about half a mile off shore which is under water at high tide. This was taken with the tide coming in. The water is just beginning to lap over her body like it desired her like I did and still do and will always, always. [CHANCE *takes back the snapshot*.] Heavenly was her name. You can see that it fits her. This was her at fifteen.

PRINCESS: Did you have her that early?

CHANCE: I was just two years older, we had each other that early.

PRINCESS: Sheer luck!

CHANCE: Princess, the great difference between people in this world is not between the rich and the poor or the good and the evil, the biggest of all differences in this world is between the ones that had or have pleasure in love and those that haven't and hadn't any pleasure in love, but just watched it with envy, sick envy. The spectators and the performers. I don't mean just ordinary pleasure or the kind you can buy, I mean great pleasure, and nothing that's happened to me or to Heavenly since can cancel out the many long nights without sleep when we gave each other such pleasure in love as very few people can look back on in their lives . . .

PRINCESS: No question, go on with your story.

CHANCE: Each time I came back to St. Cloud I had her love to come back to. . . .

PRINCESS: Something permanent in a world of change?

CHANCE: Yes, after each disappointment, each failure at something, I'd come back to her like going to a hospital. . . .

PRINCESS: She put cool bandages on your wounds? Why didn't you marry this Heavenly little physician?

CHANCE: Didn't I tell you that Heavenly is the daughter of Boss Finley, the biggest political wheel in this part of the country? Well, if I didn't I made a serious omission.

PRINCESS: He disapproved?

CHANCE: He figured his daughter rated someone a hundred, a thousand percent better than me, Chance Wayne. . . . The last time I came back here, she phoned me from the drugstore and told me to swim out to Diamond Key, that she would meet me there. I waited a long time, till almost sunset, and the tide started coming in before I heard the put-put of an outboard motor boat coming out to the sandbar. The sun was behind her, I squinted. She had on a silky wet tank suit and fans of water and mist made rainbows about her . . . she stood up in the boat as if she was water-skiing, shouting things at me an' circling around the sandbar, around and around it!

PRINCESS: She didn't come to the sandbar?

CHANCE: No, just circled around it, shouting things at me. I'd swim toward the boat, I would just about reach it and she'd race it away, throwing up misty rainbows, disappearing in rainbows and then circled back and shouting things at me again. . . .

PRINCESS: What things?

CHANCE: Things like, "Chance go away," "Don't come back to St. Cloud." "Chance, you're a liar." "Chance, I'm sick of your lies!" "My father's right about you!" "Chance, you're no good any more." "Chance, stay away from St. Cloud."

379

The last time around the sandbar she shouted nothing, just waved good-by and turned the boat back to shore.

PRINCESS: Is that the end of the story?

CHANCE: Princess, the end of the story is up to you. You want to help me?

PRINCESS: I want to help you. Believe me, not everybody wants to hurt everybody. I don't want to hurt you, can you believe me?

CHANCE: I can if you prove it to me.

PRINCESS: How can I prove it to you?

CHANCE: I have something in mind.

PRINCESS: Yes, what?

CHANCE: Okay I'll give you a quick outline of this project I have in mind. Soon as I've talked to my girl and shown her my contract, we go on, you and me. Not far, just to New Orleans, Princess. But no more hiding away, we check in at the Hotel Roosevelt there as Alexandra Del Lago and Chance Wayne. Right away the newspapers call you and give a press conference. . . .

PRINCESS: Oh?

CHANCE: Yes! The idea briefly, a local contest of talent to find a pair of young people to star as unknowns in a picture you're planning to make to show your faith in YOUTH, Princess. You stage this contest, you invite other judges, but your decision decides it!

PRINCESS: And you and . . . ?

CHANCE: Yes, Heavenly and I win it. We get her out of St. Cloud, we go to the West Coast together.

PRINCESS: And me?

CHANCE: You?

PRINCESS: Have you forgotten, for instance, that any public attention is what I least want in the world?

CHANCE: What better way can you think of to show the public that you're a person with bigger than personal interest?

PRINCESS: Oh, yes, yes, but not true.

CHANCE: You could pretend it was true.

PRINCESS: If I didn't despise pretending!

CHANCE: I understand. Time does it. Hardens people. Time and the world that you've lived in.

PRINCESS: Which you want for yourself. Isn't that what you want? [*She looks at him then goes to the phone.*] [*in phone*] Cashier?
Hello Cashier? This is the Princess Kosmonopolis speaking. I'm sending down a young man to cash some travelers' checks for me. [*She hangs up.*]

CHANCE: And I want to borrow your Cadillac for a while. . . .

PRINCESS: What for, Chance?

CHANCE [*posturing*]: I'm pretentious. I want to be seen in your car on the streets of St. Cloud. Drive all around town in it, blowing those long silver trumpets and dressed in the fine clothes you bought me. . . . Can I?

PRINCESS: Chance, you're a lost little boy that I really would like to help find himself.

CHANCE: I passed the screen test!

PRINCESS: Come here, kiss me, I love you. [*She faces the audience.*] Did I say that? Did I mean it? [*Then to* CHANCE *with arms outstretched.*] What a child you are. . . . Come here. . . . [*He ducks under her arms, and escapes to the chair.*]

CHANCE: I want this big display. Big phony display in your Cadillac around town. And a wad a dough to flash in their faces and the fine clothes you've bought me, on me.

PRINCESS: Did I buy you fine clothes?

CHANCE [*picking up his jacket from the chair*]: The finest. When you stopped being lonely because of my company at that Palm Beach Hotel, you bought me the finest. That's the deal for tonight, to toot those silver horns and drive slowly around in the Cadillac convertible so everybody that thought I was washed up will see me. And I have taken my false or true contract to flash in the faces of various people that called me washed up. All right that's the deal. Tomorrow you'll get the car back and what's left of your money. Tonight's all that counts.

PRINCESS: How do you know that as soon as you walk out of this room I won't call the police?

CHANCE: You wouldn't do that, Princess. [*He puts on his jacket.*] You'll find the car in back of the hotel parking lot, and the left-over dough will be in the glove compartment of the car.

PRINCESS: Where will you be?

CHANCE: With my girl, or nowhere.

PRINCESS: Chance Wayne! This was not necessary, all this. I'm not a phony and I wanted to be your friend.

CHANCE: Go back to sleep. As far as I know you're not a bad person, but you just got into bad company on this occasion.

PRINCESS: I am your friend and I'm not a phony. [CHANCE *turns and goes to the steps.*] When will I see you?

CHANCE [*at the top of the steps*]: I don't know—maybe never.

PRINCESS: Never is a long time, Chance, I'll wait.

[*She throws him a kiss.*]

CHANCE: So long.

[*The* PRINCESS *stands looking after him as the lights dim and the curtain closes.*]

ACT TWO

The terrace of BOSS FINLEY'S *house, which is a frame house of Victorian Gothic design, suggested by a door frame at the right and a single white column. As in the other scenes, there are no walls, the action occurring against the sky and sea cyclorama.*

The Gulf is suggested by the brightness and the gulls crying as in Act One. There is only essential porch furniture, Victorian wicker but painted bone white. The men should also be wearing white or off-white suits: the tableau is all blue and white, as strict as a canvas of Georgia O'Keefe's.

At the rise of the curtain, BOSS FINLEY *is standing in the center and* GEORGE SCUDDER *nearby.*

BOSS FINLEY: Chance Wayne had my daughter when she was fifteen.

SCUDDER: That young.

BOSS: When she was fifteen he had her. Know how I know? Some flashlight photos were made of her, naked, on Diamond Key.

SCUDDER: By Chance Wayne?

BOSS: My little girl was fifteen, barely out of her childhood when— [*calling offstage*] Charles—

[*Charles enters.*]

BOSS: Call Miss Heavenly—

CHARLES [*concurrently*]: Miss Heavenly. Miss Heavenly. Your daddy wants to see you.

[CHARLES *leaves.*]

BOSS [*to* SCUDDER]: By Chance Wayne? Who the hell else do you reckon? I seen them. He had them developed by some studio in Pass Christian that made more copies of them than Chance Wayne ordered and these photos were circulated. I seen them. That was when I first warned the son-of-a-bitch to git and out of St. Cloud. But he's back in St. Cloud right now. I tell you—

SCUDDER: Boss, let me make a suggestion. Call off this rally, I mean your appearance at it, and take it easy tonight. Go out on your boat, you and Heavenly take a short cruise on the Starfish. . . .

BOSS: I'm not about to start sparing myself. Oh, I know, I'll have me a coronary and go like that. But not because Chance Wayne had the unbelievable gall to come back to St. Cloud. [*calling offstage*] Tom Junior!

TOM JUNIOR [*offstage*]: Yes, sir!

BOSS: Has he checked out yet?

TOM JUNIOR [*entering*]: Hatcher says he called their room at the Royal Palms, and Chance Wayne answered the phone, and Hatcher says . . .

BOSS: Hatcher says,—who's Hatcher?

TOM JUNIOR: Dan Hatcher.

BOSS: I hate to expose my ignorance like this but the name Dan Hatcher has no more meaning to me than the name of Hatcher, which is none whatsoever.

SCUDDER [*quietly, deferentially*]: Hatcher, Dan Hatcher, is the assistant manager of the Royal Palms Hotel, and the man that informed me this morning that Chance Wayne was back in St. Cloud.

385

BOSS: Is this Hatcher a talker, or can he keep his mouth shut?

SCUDDER: I think I impressed him how important it is to handle this thing discreetly.

BOSS: Discreetly, like you handled that operation you done on my daughter, so discreetly that a hillbilly heckler is shouting me questions about it wherever I speak?

SCUDDER: I went to fantastic lengths to preserve the secrecy of that operation.

TOM JUNIOR: When Papa's upset he hits out at anyone near him.

BOSS: I just want to know—Has Wayne left?

TOM JUNIOR: Hatcher says that Chance Wayne told him that this old movie star that he's latched on to . . .

SCUDDER: Alexandra Del Lago.

TOM JUNIOR: She's not well enough to travel.

BOSS: Okay, you're a doctor, remove her to a hospital. Call an ambulance and haul her out of the Royal Palms Hotel.

SCUDDER: Without her consent?

BOSS: Say she's got something contagious, typhoid, bubonic plague. Haul her out and slap a quarantine on her hospital door. That way you can separate them. We can remove Chance Wayne from St. Cloud as soon as this Miss Del Lago is removed from Chance Wayne.

SCUDDER: I'm not so sure that's the right way to go about it.

BOSS: Okay, you think of a way. My daughter's no whore, but she had a whore's operation after the last time he had her. I don't want him passin' another night in St. Cloud. Tom Junior.

TOM JUNIOR: Yes, sir.

BOSS: I want him gone by tomorrow—tomorrow commences at midnight.

TOM JUNIOR: I know what to do, Papa. Can I use the boat?

BOSS: Don't ask me, don't tell me nothin'—

TOM JUNIOR: Can I have *The Starfish* tonight?

BOSS: I don't want to know how, just go about it. Where's your sister?

[CHARLES *appears on the gallery, points out* HEAVENLY *lying on the beach to* BOSS *and exits.*]

TOM JUNIOR: She's lyin' out on the beach like a dead body washed up on it.

BOSS [*calling*]: Heavenly!

TOM JUNIOR: Gawge, I want you with me on this boat trip tonight, Gawge.

BOSS [*calling*]: Heavenly!

SCUDDER: I know what you mean, Tom Junior, but I couldn't be involved in it. I can't even know about it.

BOSS [*calling again*]: Heavenly!

TOM JUNIOR: Okay, don't be involved in it. There's a pretty fair doctor that lost his license for helping a girl out

387

of trouble, and he won't be so goddam finicky about doing this absolutely just thing.

SCUDDER: I don't question the moral justification, which is complete without question. . . .

TOM JUNIOR: Yeah, complete without question.

SCUDDER: But I am a reputable doctor, I haven't lost my license. I'm chief of staff at the great hospital put up by your father. . . .

TOM JUNIOR: I said, don't know about it.

SCUDDER: No, sir, I won't know about it . . . [BOSS *starts to cough.*] I can't afford to, and neither can your father. . . . [SCUDDER *goes to gallery writing prescription.*]

BOSS: Heavenly! Come up here, sugar. [*to* SCUDDER] What's that you're writing?

SCUDDER: Prescription for that cough.

BOSS: Tear it up, throw it away. I've hawked and spit all my life, and I'll be hawking and spitting in the hereafter. You all can count on that.

[*Auto horn is heard.*]

TOM JUNIOR [*leaps up on the gallery and starts to leave*]: Papa, he's drivin' back by.

BOSS: Tom Junior.

[TOM JUNIOR *stops.*]

TOM JUNIOR: Is Chance Wayne insane?

SCUDDER: Is a criminal degenerate sane or insane is a question that lots of law courts haven't been able to settle.

BOSS: Take it to the Supreme Court, they'll hand you down a decision on that question. They'll tell you a handsome young criminal degenerate like Chance Wayne is the mental and moral equal of any white man in the country.

TOM JUNIOR: He's stopped at the foot of the drive.

BOSS: Don't move, don't move, Tom Junior.

TOM JUNIOR: I'm not movin', Papa.

CHANCE [offstage]: Aunt Nonnie! Hey, Aunt Nonnie!

BOSS: What's he shouting?

TOM JUNIOR: He's shouting at Aunt Nonnie.

BOSS: Where is she?

TOM JUNIOR: Runnin' up the drive like a dog-track rabbit.

BOSS: He ain't followin', is he?

TOM JUNIOR: Nope. He's drove away.

[AUNT NONNIE appears before the veranda, terribly flustered, rooting in her purse for something, apparently blind to the men on the veranda.]

BOSS: Whatcha lookin' for, Nonnie?

NONNIE [stopping short]: Oh—I didn't notice you, Tom. I was looking for my door-key.

BOSS: Door's open, Nonnie, it's wide open, like a church door.

NONNIE [laughing]: Oh, ha, ha . . .

BOSS: Why didn't you answer that good-lookin' boy in the Cadillac car that shouted at you, Nonnie?

NONNIE: Oh. I hoped you hadn't seen him. [*Draws a deep breath and comes on to the terrace, closing her white purse.*] That was Chance Wayne. He's back in St. Cloud, he's at the Royal Palms, he's—

BOSS: Why did you snub him like that? After all these years of devotion?

NONNIE: I went to the Royal Palms to warn him not to stay here but—

BOSS: He was out showing off in that big white Cadillac with the trumpet horns on it.

NONNIE: I left a message for him, I—

TOM JUNIOR: What was the message, Aunt Nonnie? Love and kisses?

NONNIE: Just get out of St. Cloud right away, Chance.

TOM JUNIOR: He's gonna git out, but not in that fish-tail Caddy.

NONNIE [*to* TOM JUNIOR]: I hope you don't mean violence— [*turning to* BOSS] does he, Tom? Violence don't solve problems. It never solves young people's problems. If you will leave it to me, I'll get him out of St. Cloud. I can, I will, I promise. I don't think Heavenly knows he's back in St. Cloud. Tom, you know, Heavenly says it wasn't Chance that—She says it wasn't Chance.

BOSS: You're like your dead sister, Nonnie, gullible as my wife was. You don't know a lie if you bump into it on a street in the daytime. Now go out there and tell Heavenly I want to see her.

NONNIE: Tom, she's not well enough to—

BOSS: Nonnie, you got a whole lot to answer for.

NONNIE: Have I?

BOSS: Yes, you sure have, Nonnie. You favored Chance Wayne, encouraged, aided and abetted him in his corruption of Heavenly over a long, long time. You go get her. You sure do have a lot to answer for. You got a helluva lot to answer for.

NONNIE: I remember when Chance was the finest, nicest, sweetest boy in St. Cloud, and he stayed that way till you, till you—

BOSS: Go get her, go get her! [*She leaves by the far side of the terrace. After a moment her voice is heard calling,* "HEAVENLY? HEAVENLY?"] It's a curious thing, a mighty peculiar thing, how often a man that rises to high public office is drug back down by every soul he harbors under his roof. He harbors them under his roof, and they pull the roof down on him. Every last living one of them.

TOM JUNIOR: Does that include me, Papa?

BOSS: If the shoe fits, put it on you.

TOM JUNIOR: How does that shoe fit me?

BOSS: If it pinches your foot, just slit it down the sides a little—it'll feel comfortable on you.

TOM JUNIOR: Papa, you are UNJUST.

BOSS: What do you want credit for?

TOM JUNIOR: I have devoted the past year to organizin' the "Youth for Tom Finley" clubs.

BOSS: I'm carryin' Tom Finley Junior on my ticket.

391

TOM JUNIOR: You're lucky to have me on it.

BOSS: How do you figure I'm lucky to have you on it?

TOM JUNIOR: I got more newspaper coverage in the last six months than . . .

BOSS: Once for drunk drivin', once for a stag party you thrown in Capitol City that cost me five thousand dollars to hush it up!

TOM JUNIOR: You are so unjust, it . . .

BOSS: And everyone knows you had to be drove through school like a blazeface mule pullin' a plow uphill: flunked out of college with grades that only a moron would have an excuse for.

TOM JUNIOR: I got re-admitted to college.

BOSS: At my insistence. By fake examinations, answers provided beforehand, stuck in your fancy pockets. And your promiscuity. Why, these Youth for Tom Finley clubs are practically nothin' but gangs of juvenile delinquents, wearin' badges with my name and my photograph on them.

TOM JUNIOR: How about your well known promiscuity, Papa? How about your Miss Lucy?

BOSS: Who is Miss Lucy?

TOM JUNIOR [*laughing so hard he staggers*]: Who is Miss Lucy? You don't even know who she is, this woman you keep in a fifty-dollar a day hotel suite at the Royal Palms, Papa?

BOSS: What're you talkin' about?

TOM JUNIOR: That rides down the Gulf Stream Highway with a motorcycle escort blowin' their sirens like the Queen of Sheba was going into New Orleans for the day. To use her charge accounts there. And you ask who's Miss Lucy? She don't even talk good of you. She says you're too old for a lover.

BOSS: That is a goddam lie. Who says Miss Lucy says that?

TOM JUNIOR: She wrote it with lipstick on the ladies' room mirror at the Royal Palms.

BOSS: Wrote what?

TOM JUNIOR: I'll quote it to you exactly. "Boss Finley," she wrote, "is too old to cut the mustard."

[*Pause: the two stags, the old and the young one, face each other, panting.* SCUDDER *has discreetly withdrawn to a far end of porch.*]

BOSS: I don't believe this story!

TOM JUNIOR: Don't believe it.

BOSS: I will check on it, however.

TOM JUNIOR: I already checked on it. Papa, why don't you get rid of her, huh, Papa?

[BOSS FINLEY *turns away, wounded, baffled: stares out at the audience with his old, bloodshot eyes as if he thought that someone out there had shouted a question at him which he didn't quite hear.*]

BOSS: Mind your own goddam business. A man with a mission, which he holds sacred, and on the strength of which he rises to high public office—crucified in this way, publicly, by his own offspring. [HEAVENLY *has entered on the gallery.*] Ah, here she is, here's my little girl. [*stopping* HEAVENLY] You stay here, honey. I think you all had better leave me

393

alone with Heavenly now, huh—yeah. . . . [TOM JUNIOR *and* SCUDDER *exit.*] Now, honey, you stay here. I want to have a talk with you.

HEAVENLY: Papa, I can't talk now.

BOSS: It's necessary.

HEAVENLY: I can't, I can't talk now.

BOSS: All right, don't talk, just listen.

[*But she doesn't want to listen, starts away: He would have restrained her forcibly if an old colored manservant,* CHARLES, *had not, at that moment, come out on the porch. He carries a stick, a hat, a package, wrapped as a present. Puts them on a table.*]

CHARLES: It's five o'clock, Mister Finley.

BOSS: Huh? Oh—thanks . . .

[CHARLES *turns on a coach lamp by the door. This marks a formal division in the scene. The light change is not realistic; the light doesn't seem to come from the coach lamp but from a spectral radiance in the sky, flooding the terrace.*

[*The sea wind sings.* HEAVENLY *lifts her face to it. Later that night may be stormy, but now there is just a quickness and freshness coming in from the Gulf.* HEAVENLY *is always looking that way, toward the Gulf, so that the light from Point Lookout catches her face with its repeated soft stroke of clarity.*

[*In her father, a sudden dignity is revived. Looking at his very beautiful daughter, he becomes almost stately. He approaches her, soon as the colored man returns inside, like an aged courtier comes deferentially up to a Crown*

Princess or Infanta. It's important not to think of his attitude toward her in the terms of crudely conscious in-cestuous feeling, but just in the natural terms of almost any aging father's feeling for a beautiful young daughter who reminds him of a dead wife that he desired intensely when she was the age of his daughter.

[At this point there might be a phrase of stately, Mozartian music, suggesting a court dance. The flagged terrace may suggest the parquet floor of a ballroom and the two players' movements may suggest the stately, formal movements of a court dance of that time; but if this effect is used, it should be just a suggestion. The change toward "stylization" ought to be held in check.]

BOSS: You're still a beautiful girl.

HEAVENLY: Am I, Papa?

BOSS: Of course you are. Lookin' at you nobody could guess that—

HEAVENLY [*laughs*]: The embalmers must have done a good job on me, Papa. . . .

BOSS: You got to quit talkin' like that. [*then, seeing* CHARLES] Will you get back in the house! [*Phone rings.*]

CHARLES: Yes, sir, I was just—

BOSS: Go on in! If that phone call is for me, I'm in only to the governor of the state and the president of the Tidewater Oil Corporation.

CHARLES [*offstage*]: It's for Miss Heavenly again.

BOSS: Say she ain't in.

CHARLES: Sorry, she ain't in.

[HEAVENLY *has moved upstage to the low parapet or sea
wall that separates the courtyard and lawn from the beach.
It is early dusk. The coach lamp has cast a strange light
on the setting which is neo-romantic:* HEAVENLY *stops by
an ornamental urn containing a tall fern that the salty
Gulf wind has stripped nearly bare. The* BOSS *follows her,
baffled.*]

BOSS: Honey, you say and do things in the presence of
people as if you had no regard of the fact that people have
ears to hear you and tongues to repeat what they hear. And
so you become a issue.

HEAVENLY: Become what, Papa?

BOSS: A issue, a issue, subject of talk, of scandal—which
can defeat the mission that—

HEAVENLY: Don't give me your "Voice of God" speech.
Papa, there was a time when you could have saved me, by
letting me marry a boy that was still young and clean, but
instead you drove him away, drove him out of St. Cloud.
And when he came back, you took me out of St. Cloud, and
tried to force me to marry a fifty-year-old money bag that
you wanted something out of—

BOSS: Now, honey—

HEAVENLY: —and then another, another, all of them ones
that you wanted something out of. I'd gone, so Chance went
away. Tried to compete, make himself big as these big-shots
you wanted to use me for a bond with. He went. He tried.
The right doors wouldn't open, and so he went in the wrong
ones, and—Papa, you married for love, why wouldn't you
let me do it, while I was alive, inside, and the boy still clean,
still decent?

BOSS: Are you reproaching me for—?

HEAVENLY [*shouting*]: Yes, I am, Papa, I am. You married for love, but you wouldn't let me do it, and even though you'd done it, you broke Mama's heart, Miss Lucy had been your mistress—

BOSS: Who is Miss Lucy?

HEAVENLY: Oh, Papa, she was your mistress long before Mama died. And Mama was just a front for you. Can I go in now, Papa? Can I go in now?

BOSS: No, no, not till I'm through with you. What a terrible, terrible thing for my baby to say . . . [*He takes her in his arms.*] Tomorrow, tomorrow morning, when the big after-Easter sales commence in the stores—I'm gonna send you in town with a motorcycle escort, straight to the Maison Blanche. When you arrive at the store, I want you to go directly up to the office of Mr. Harvey C. Petrie and tell him to give you unlimited credit there. Then go down and outfit yourself as if you was—buyin' a trousseau to marry the Prince of Monaco. . . . Purchase a full wardrobe, includin' furs. Keep 'em in storage until winter. Gown? Three, four, five, the most lavish. Slippers? Hell, pairs and pairs of 'em. Not one hat—but a dozen. I made a pile of dough on a deal involvin' the sale of rights to oil under water here lately, and baby, I want you to buy a piece of jewelry. Now about that, you better tell Harvey to call me. Or better still, maybe Miss Lucy had better help you select it. She's wise as a backhouse rat when it comes to a stone,—that's for sure. . . . Now where'd I buy that clip that I give your mama? D'you remember the clip I bought your mama? Last thing I give your mama before she died . . . I knowed she was dyin' when I bought her that clip, and I bought that clip for fifteen thousand dollars mainly to make her think she was

397

going to get well. . . . When I pinned it on her on the night-gown she was wearing, that poor thing started crying. She said, for God's sake, Boss, what does a dying woman want with such a big diamond? I said to her, honey, look at the price tag on it. What does the price tag say? See them five figures, that one and that five and them three aughts on there? Now, honey, make sense, I told her. If you was dying, if there was any chance of it, would I invest fifteen grand in a diamond clip to pin on the neck of a shroud? Ha, haha. That made the old lady laugh. And she sat up as bright as a little bird in that bed with the diamond clip on, receiving callers all day, and laughing and chatting with them, with that diamond clip on inside and she died before midnight, with that diamond clip on her. And not till the very last minute did she believe that the diamonds wasn't a proof that she wasn't dying. [*He moves to terrace, takes off robe and starts to put on tuxedo coat.*]

HEAVENLY: Did you bury her with it?

BOSS: Bury her with it? Hell, no. I took it back to the jewelry store in the morning.

HEAVENLY: Then it didn't cost you fifteen grand after all.

BOSS: Hell, did I care what it cost me? I'm not a small man. I wouldn't have cared one hoot if it cost me a million . . . if at that time I had that kind of loot in my pockets. It would have been worth that money to see that one little smile your mama bird give me at noon of the day she was dying.

HEAVENLY: I guess that shows, demonstrates very clearly, that you have got a pretty big heart after all.

BOSS: Who doubts it then? Who? Who ever? [*He laughs.*]

[HEAVENLY *starts to laugh and then screams hysterically. She starts going toward the house.*]

[BOSS *throws down his cane and grabs her.*]

Just a minute, Missy. Stop it. Stop it. Listen to me, I'm gonna tell you something. Last week in New Bethesda, when I was speaking on the threat of desegregation to white women's chastity in the South, some heckler in the crowd shouted out, "Hey, Boss Finley, how about your daughter? How about that operation you had done on your daughter at the Thomas J. Finley hospital in St. Cloud? Did she put on black in mourning for her appendix?" Same heckler, same question when I spoke in the Coliseum at the state capitol.

HEAVENLY: What was your answer to him?

BOSS: He was removed from the hall at both places and roughed up a little outside it.

HEAVENLY: Papa, you have got an illusion of power.

BOSS: I have power, which is not an illusion.

HEAVENLY: Papa, I'm sorry my operation has brought this embarrassment on you, but can you imagine it, Papa? I felt worse than embarrassed when I found out that Dr. George Scudder's knife had cut the youth out of my body, made me an old childless woman. Dry, cold, empty, like an old woman. I feel as if I ought to rattle like a dead dried-up vine when the Gulf Wind blows, but, Papa—I won't embarrass you any more. I've made up my mind about something. If they'll let me, accept me, I'm going into a convent.

BOSS [*shouting*]: You ain't going into no convent. This state is a Protestant region and a daughter in a convent would politically ruin me. Oh, I know, you took your mama's religion because in your heart you always wished to defy me. Now, tonight, I'm addressing the Youth for Tom Finley clubs in the ballroom of the Royal Palms Hotel. My speech

399

is going out over a national TV network, and Missy, you're going to march in the ballroom on my arm. You're going to be wearing the stainless white of a virgin, with a Youth for Tom Finley button on one shoulder and a corsage of lilies on the other. You're going to be on the speaker's platform with me, you on one side of me and Tom Junior on the other, to scotch these rumors about your corruption. And you're gonna wear a proud happy smile on your face, you're gonna stare straight out at the crowd in the ballroom with pride and joy in your eyes. Lookin' at you, all in white like a virgin, nobody would dare to speak or believe the ugly stories about you. I'm relying a great deal on this campaign to bring in young voters for the crusade I'm leading. I'm all that stands between the South and the black days of Reconstruction. And you and Tom Junior are going to stand there beside me in the grand crystal ballroom, as shining examples of white Southern youth—in danger.

HEAVENLY [*defiant*]: Papa, I'm not going to do it.

BOSS: I didn't say would you, I said you would, and you will.

HEAVENLY: Suppose I still say I won't.

BOSS: Then you won't, that's all. If you won't, you won't. But there would be consequences you might not like. [*Phone rings.*] Chance Wayne is back in St. Cloud.

CHARLES [*offstage*]: Mr. Finley's residence. Miss Heavenly? Sorry, she's not in.

BOSS: I'm going to remove him, he's going to be removed from St. Cloud. How do you want him to leave, in that white Cadillac he's riding around in, or in the scow that totes the garbage out to the dumping place in the Gulf?

HEAVENLY: You wouldn't dare?

BOSS: You want to take a chance on it?

CHARLES [*enters*]: That call was for you again, Miss Heavenly.

BOSS: A lot of people approve of taking violent action against corrupters. And on all of them that want to adulterate the pure white blood of the South. Hell, when I was fifteen, I come down barefoot out of the red clay hills as if the Voice of God called me. Which it did, I believe. I firmly believe He called me. And nothing, nobody, nowhere is gonna stop me, never. . . . [*He motions to* CHARLES *for gift.* CHARLES *hands it to him.*] Thank you, Charles. I'm gonna pay me an early call on Miss Lucy.

[*A sad, uncertain note has come into his voice on this final line. He turns and plods wearily, doggedly off at left.*]

THE CURTAIN FALLS

[*House remains dark for short intermission.*]

A corner of cocktail lounge and of outside gallery of the Royal Palms Hotel. This corresponds in style to the bedroom set: Victorian with Moorish influence. Royal palms are projected on the cyclorama which is deep violet with dusk. There are Moorish arches between gallery and interior: over the single table, inside, is suspended the same lamp, stained glass and ornately wrought metal, that hung in the bedroom. Perhaps on the gallery there is a low stone balustrade that supports, where steps descend into the garden, an electric light standard with five branches and pear-shaped globes of a dim pearly luster. Somewhere out of the sight-lines an entertainer plays a piano or novachord.

The interior table is occupied by two couples that represent society in St. Cloud. They are contemporaries of CHANCE'S. *Behind the bar is* STUFF *who feels the dignity of his recent advancement from drugstore soda-fountain to the Royal Palms cocktail lounge: he has on a white mess-jacket, a scarlet cummerbund and light blue trousers, flatteringly close-fitted.* CHANCE WAYNE *was once barman here:* STUFF *moves with an indolent male grace that he may have unconsciously remembered admiring in* CHANCE.

BOSS FINLEY'S *mistress,* MISS LUCY, *enters the cocktail lounge dressed in a ball gown elaborately ruffled and very bouffant like an antebellum Southern belle's. A single blonde curl is arranged to switch girlishly at one side of her sharp little terrier face. She is outraged over something and her glare is concentrated on* STUFF *who "plays it cool" behind the bar.*

STUFF: Ev'nin', Miss Lucy.

MISS LUCY: I wasn't allowed to sit at the banquet table. No. I was put at a little side table, with a couple of state legislators an' wives. [*She sweeps behind the bar in a pro-*

prietary fashion.] Where's your Grant's twelve-year-old?
Hey! Do you have a big mouth? I used to remember a kid
that jerked sodas at Walgreen's that had a big mouth. . . .
Put some ice in this. . . . Is yours big, huh? I want to tell you
something.

STUFF: What's the matter with your finger?

[*She catches him by his scarlet cummerbund.*]

MISS LUCY: I'm going to tell you just now. The boss came
over to me with a big candy Easter egg for me. The top of
the egg unscrewed. He told me to unscrew it. So I unscrewed
it. Inside was a little blue velvet jewel box, no not little, a
big one, as big as somebody's mouth, too.

STUFF: Whose mouth?

MISS LUCY: The mouth of somebody who's not a hundred
miles from here.

STUFF [*going off at the left*]: I got to set my chairs.
[STUFF *re-enters at once carrying two chairs. Sets them at
tables while* MISS LUCY *talks.*]

MISS LUCY: I open the jewel box an' start to remove the
great big diamond clip in it. I just got my fingers on it, and
start to remove it and the old son of a bitch slams the lid of
the box on my fingers. One fingernail is still blue. And the
boss says to me, "Now go downstairs to the cocktail lounge
and go in the ladies' room and describe this diamond clip
with lipstick on the ladies' room mirror down there. Hanh?—
and he put the jewel box in his pocket and slammed the
door so hard goin' out of my suite that a picture fell off the
wall.

STUFF [*setting the chairs at the table*]: Miss Lucy, you
are the one that said, "I wish you would see what's written
with lipstick on the ladies' room mirror" las' Saturday night.

MISS LUCY: To you! Because I thought I could trust you.

STUFF: Other people were here an' all of them heard it.

MISS LUCY: Nobody but you at the bar belonged to the Youth for Boss Finley Club.

[*Both stop short. They've noticed a tall man who has entered the cocktail lounge. He has the length and leanness and luminous pallor of a face that El Greco gave to his saints. He has a small bandage near the hairline. His clothes are country.*]

Hey, you.

HECKLER: Evenin', ma'am.

MISS LUCY: You with the Hillbilly Ramblers? You with the band?

HECKLER: I'm a hillbilly, but I'm not with no band.

[*He notices* MISS LUCY'S *steady, interested stare.* STUFF *leaves with a tray of drinks.*]

MISS LUCY: What do you want here?

HECKLER: I come to hear Boss Finley talk. [*His voice is clear but strained. He rubs his large Adam's apple as he speaks.*]

MISS LUCY: You can't get in the ballroom without a jacket and a tie on. . . . I know who you are. You're the heckler, aren't you?

HECKLER: I don't heckle. I just ask questions, one question or two or three questions, depending on how much time it takes them to grab me and throw me out of the hall.

404

MISS LUCY: Those questions are loaded questions. You gonna repeat them tonight?

HECKLER: Yes, ma'am, if I can get in the ballroom, and make myself heard.

MISS LUCY: What's wrong with your voice?

HECKLER: When I shouted my questions in New Bethesda last week I got hit in the Adam's apple with the butt of a pistol, and that affected my voice. It still ain't good, but it's better. [*Starts to go.*]

MISS LUCY [*goes to back of bar, where she gets jacket, the kind kept in places with dress regulations, and throws it to* HECKLER]: Wait. Here, put this on. The Boss's talking on a national TV hookup tonight. There's a tie in the pocket. You sit perfectly still at the bar till the Boss starts speaking. Keep your face back of this *Evening Banner.* O.K.?

HECKLER [*opening the paper in front of his face*]: I thank you.

MISS LUCY: I thank you, too, and I wish you more luck than you're likely to have.

[STUFF *re-enters and goes to back of the bar.*]

FLY [*entering on the gallery*]: Paging Chance Wayne. [*auto horn offstage*] Mr. Chance Wayne, please. Paging Chance Wayne. [*He leaves.*]

MISS LUCY [*to* STUFF *who has re-entered*]: Is Chance Wayne back in St. Cloud?

STUFF: You remember Alexandra Del Lago?

MISS LUCY: I guess I do. I was president of her local fan club. Why?

405

CHANCE [*offstage*]: Hey, Boy, park that car up front and don't wrinkle them fenders.

STUFF: She and Chance Wayne checked in here last night.

MISS LUCY: Well I'll be a dawg's mother. I'm going to look into that. [LUCY *exits.*]

CHANCE [*entering and crossing to the bar*]: Hey, Stuff! [*He takes a cocktail off the bar and sips it.*]

STUFF: Put that down. This ain't no cocktail party.

CHANCE: Man, don't you know . . . phew . . . nobody drinks gin martinis with olives. Everybody drinks vodka martinis with lemon twist nowadays, except the squares in St. Cloud. When I had your job, when I was the barman here at the Royal Palms, I created that uniform you've got on. . . . I copied it from an outfit Vic Mature wore in a Foreign Legion picture, and I looked better in it than he did, and almost as good in it as you do, ha, ha. . . .

AUNT NONNIE [*who has entered at the right*]: Chance. Chance . . .

CHANCE: Aunt Nonnie! [*to* STUFF] Hey, I want a table-cloth on that table, and a bucket of champagne . . . Mumm's Cordon Rouge. . . .

AUNT NONNIE: You come out here.

CHANCE: But, I just ordered champagne in here. [*Suddenly his effusive manner collapses, as she stares at him gravely.*]

AUNT NONNIE: I can't be seen talking to you. . . .

[*She leads him to one side of the stage. A light change has occurred which has made it a royal palm grove with a bench. They cross to it solemnly.* STUFF *busies himself at*

406

*the bar, which is barely lit. After a moment he exits with
a few drinks to main body of the cocktail lounge off left.
Bar music. Quiereme Mucho.]*

CHANCE [*following her*]: Why?

AUNT NONNIE: I've got just one thing to tell you, Chance,
get out of St. Cloud.

CHANCE: Why does everybody treat me like a low criminal
in the town I was born in?

AUNT NONNIE: Ask yourself that question, ask your con-
science that question.

CHANCE: What question?

AUNT NONNIE: You know, and I know you know . . .

CHANCE: Know what?

AUNT NONNIE: I'm not going to talk about it. I just can't
talk about it. Your head and your tongue run wild. You
can't be trusted. We have to live in St. Cloud. . . . Oh, Chance,
why have you changed like you've changed? Why do you
live on nothing but wild dreams now, and have no address
where anybody can reach you in time to—reach you?

CHANCE: Wild dreams! Yes. Isn't life a wild dream? I
never heard a better description of it. . . . [*He takes a pill
and a swallow from a flask.*]

AUNT NONNIE: What did you just take, Chance? You
took something out of your pocket and washed it down with
liquor.

CHANCE: Yes, I took a wild dream and—washed it down
with another wild dream, Aunt Nonnie, that's my life now. . . .

AUNT NONNIE: Why, son?

407

CHANCE: Oh, Aunt Nonnie, for God's sake, have you forgotten what was expected of me?

AUNT NONNIE: People that loved you expected just one thing of you—sweetness and honesty and . . .

[STUFF *leaves with tray.*]

CHANCE [*kneeling at her side*]: No, not after the brilliant beginning I made. Why, at seventeen, I put on, directed, and played the leading role in "The Valiant," that one-act play that won the state drama contest. Heavenly played in it with me, and have you forgotten? You went with us as the girls' chaperone to the national contest held in . . .

AUNT NONNIE: Son, of course I remember.

CHANCE: In the parlor car? How we sang together?

AUNT NONNIE: You were in love even then.

CHANCE: God, yes, we were in love!

[*He sings softly*]

"If you like-a me, like I like-a you,
And we like-a both the same"

TOGETHER:
"I'd like-a say, this very day,
I'd like-a change your name."

[CHANCE *laughs softly, wildly, in the cool light of the palm grove.* AUNT NONNIE *rises abruptly.* CHANCE *catches her hands.*]

AUNT NONNIE: You—*Do*—Take unfair advantage. . . .

CHANCE: Aunt Nonnie, we didn't win that lousy national contest, we just placed second.

AUNT NONNIE: Chance, you didn't place second. You got honorable mention. Fourth place, except it was just called honorable mention.

CHANCE: Just honorable mention. But in a national contest, honorable mention means something. . . . We would have won it, but I blew my lines. Yes, I that put on and produced the damn thing, couldn't even hear the damn lines being hissed at me by that fat girl with the book in the wings. [*He buries his face in his hands.*]

AUNT NONNIE: I loved you for that, son, and so did Heavenly, too.

CHANCE: It was on the way home in the train that she and I—

AUNT NONNIE [*with a flurry of feeling*]: I know, I— I—

CHANCE [*rising*]: I bribed the Pullman Conductor to let us use for an hour a vacant compartment on that sad, home-going train—

AUNT NONNIE: I know, I— I—

CHANCE: Gave him five dollars, but that wasn't enough, and so I gave him my wrist watch, and my collar pin and tie clip and signet ring and my suit, that I'd bought on credit to go to the contest. First suit I'd ever put on that cost more than thirty dollars.

AUNT NONNIE: Don't go back over that.

CHANCE: —To buy the first hour of love that we had together. When she undressed, I saw that her body was just then, barely, beginning to be a woman's and . . .

AUNT NONNIE: Stop, Chance.

409

CHANCE: I said, oh, Heavenly, no, but she said yes, and I cried in her arms that night, and didn't know that what I was crying for was—youth, that would go.

AUNT NONNIE: It was from that time on, you've changed.

CHANCE: I swore in my heart that I'd never again come in second in any contest, especially not now that Heavenly was my—Aunt Nonnie, look at this contract. [*He snatches out papers and lights lighter.*]

AUNT NONNIE: I don't want to see false papers.

CHANCE: These are genuine papers. Look at the notary's seal and the signatures of the three witnesses on them. Aunt Nonnie, do you know who I'm with? I'm with Alexandra Del Lago, the Princess Kosmonopolis is my—

AUNT NONNIE: Is your what?

CHANCE: Patroness! Agent! Producer! She hasn't been seen much lately, but still has influence, power, and money— money that can open all doors. That I've knocked at all these years till my knuckles are bloody.

AUNT NONNIE: Chance, even now, if you came back here simply saying, "I couldn't remember the lines, I lost the contest, I—failed," but you've come back here again with—

CHANCE: Will you just listen one minute more? Aunt Nonnie, here is the plan. A local-contest-of-Beauty.

AUNT NONNIE: Oh, Chance.

CHANCE: A local contest of talent that she will win.

AUNT NONNIE: Who?

CHANCE: Heavenly.

AUNT NONNIE: No, Chance. She's not young now, she's faded, she's . . .

CHANCE: Nothing goes that quick, not even youth.

AUNT NONNIE: Yes, it does.

CHANCE: It will come back like magic. Soon as I . . .

AUNT NONNIE: For what? For a fake contest?

CHANCE: For love. The moment I hold her.

AUNT NONNIE: Chance.

CHANCE: It's not going to be a local thing, Aunt Nonnie. It's going to get national coverage. The Princess Kosmonopolis's best friend is that sob sister, Sally Powers. Even you know Sally Powers. Most powerful movie columnist in the world. Whose name is law in the motion . . .

AUNT NONNIE: Chance, lower your voice.

CHANCE: I want people to hear me.

AUNT NONNIE: No, you don't, no you don't. Because if your voice gets to Boss Finley, you'll be in great danger, Chance.

CHANCE: I go back to Heavenly, or I don't. I live or die. There's nothing in between for me.

AUNT NONNIE: What you want to go back to is your clean, unashamed youth. And you can't.

CHANCE: You still don't believe me, Aunt Nonnie?

AUNT NONNIE: No, I don't. Please go. Go away from here, Chance.

CHANCE: Please.

AUNT NONNIE: No, no, go away!

CHANCE: Where to? Where can I go? This is the home of my heart. Don't make me homeless.

AUNT NONNIE: Oh, Chance.

CHANCE: Aunt Nonnie. Please.

AUNT NONNIE [*rises and starts to go*]: I'll write to you. Send me an address. I'll write to you.

[*She exits through bar.* STUFF *enters and moves to bar.*]

CHANCE: Aunt Nonnie . . .

[*She's gone.*]

[CHANCE *removes a pint bottle of vodka from his pocket and something else which he washes down with the vodka. He stands back as two couples come up the steps and cross the gallery into the bar: they sit at a table.* CHANCE *takes a deep breath.* FLY *enters lighted area inside, singing out "Paging* MR. CHANCE WAYNE, MR. CHANCE WAYNE, *pagin'* MR. CHANCE WAYNE."—*Turns about smartly and goes back out through lobby. The name has stirred a commotion at the bar and table visible inside.*]

EDNA: Did you hear *that?* Is *Chance Wayne* back in St. Cloud?

[CHANCE *draws a deep breath. Then, he stalks back into the main part of the cocktail lounge like a matador entering a bull ring.*]

VIOLET: My God, yes—there he is.

[CHANCE *reads* FLY'S *message.*]

CHANCE [*to* FLY]: Not now, later, later.

[*The entertainer off left begins to play a piano . . . The "evening" in the cocktail lounge is just beginning.*]

[FLY *leaves through the gallery.*]

Well! Same old place, same old gang. Time doesn't pass in St. Cloud. [*To* BUD *and* SCOTTY] Hi!

BUD: How are you . . .

CHANCE [*shouting offstage*]: [FLY *enters and stands on terrace*] Hey, Jackie . . . [*Piano stops.* CHANCE *crosses over to the table that holds the foursome.*] . . . remember my song? Do you—remember my song? . . . You see, he remembers my song. [*The entertainer swings into "It's a Big Wide Wonderful World."*] Now I feel at home. In my home town . . . Come on, everybody—sing!

[*This token of apparent acceptance reassures him. The foursome at the table on stage studiously ignore him. He sings:*]

"When you're in love you're a master
Of all you survey, you're a gay Santa Claus.
There's a great big star-spangled sky up above you,
When you're in love you're a hero . . ."

Come on! Sing, ev'rybody!

[*In the old days they did; now they don't. He goes on, singing a bit; then his voice dies out on a note of embarrassment. Somebody at the bar whispers something and another laughs.* CHANCE *chuckles uneasily and says:*]

What's wrong here? The place is dead.

STUFF: You been away too long, Chance.

CHANCE: Is that the trouble?

413

STUFF: That's all. . . .

[JACKIE, *off, finishes with an arpeggio. The piano lid slams. There is a curious hush in the bar.* CHANCE *looks at the table.* VIOLET *whispers something to* BUD. *Both girls rise abruptly and cross out of the bar.*]

BUD [*yelling at* STUFF]: Check, Stuff.

CHANCE [*with exaggerated surprise*]: Well, *Bud and Scotty.* I didn't see you at all. Wasn't that Violet and Edna at your table? [*He sits at the table between* BUD *and* SCOTTY.]

SCOTTY: I guess they didn't recognize you, Chance.

BUD: Violet did.

SCOTTY: Did Violet?

BUD: She said, "My God, Chance Wayne."

SCOTTY: That's recognition and profanity, too.

CHANCE: I don't mind. I've been snubbed by experts, and I've done some snubbing myself. . . . Hey! [MISS LUCY *has entered at left.* CHANCE *sees her and goes toward her.*] —Is that Miss Lucy or is that Scarlett O'Hara?

MISS LUCY: Hello there, Chance Wayne. Somebody said that you were back in St. Cloud, but I didn't believe them. I said I'd have to see it with my own eyes before . . . Usually there's an item in the paper, in Gwen Phillips's column saying "St. Cloud youth home on visit is slated to play featured role in important new picture," and me being a movie fan I'm always thrilled by it. . . . [*She ruffles his hair.*]

CHANCE: Never do that to a man with thinning hair. [CHANCE's *smile is unflinching; it gets harder and brighter.*]

MISS LUCY: Is your hair thinning, baby? Maybe that's the difference I noticed in your appearance. Don't go 'way till I get back with my drink. . . .

[*She goes to back of bar to mix herself a drink. Meanwhile,* CHANCE *combs his hair.*]

SCOTTY [*to* CHANCE]: Don't throw away those golden hairs you combed out, Chance. Save 'em and send 'em each in letters to your fan clubs.

BUD: Does Chance Wayne have a fan club?

SCOTTY: The most patient one in the world. They've been waiting years for him to show up on the screen for more than five seconds in a crowd scene.

MISS LUCY [*returning to the table*]: Y'know this boy Chance Wayne used to be so attractive I couldn't stand it. But now I can, almost stand it. Every Sunday in summer I used to drive out to the municipal beach and watch him dive off the high tower. I'd take binoculars with me when he put on those free divin' exhibitions. You still dive, Chance? Or have you given that up?

CHANCE [*uneasily*]: I did some diving last Sunday.

MISS LUCY: Good, as ever?

CHANCE: I was a little off form, but the crowd didn't notice. I can still get away with a double back somersault and a—

MISS LUCY: Where was this, in Palm Beach, Florida, Chance?

[HATCHER *enters.*]

CHANCE [*stiffening*]: Why Palm Beach? Why there?

415

MISS LUCY: Who was it said they seen you last month in Palm Beach? Oh yes, Hatcher—that you had a job as a beach-boy at some big hotel there?

HATCHER [*stops at steps of the terrace, then leaves across the gallery*]: Yeah, that's what I heard.

CHANCE: Had a job—as a beach-boy?

STUFF: Rubbing oil into big fat millionaires.

CHANCE: What joker thought up that one? [*His laugh is a little too loud.*]

SCOTTY: You ought to get their names and sue them for slander.

CHANCE: I long ago gave up tracking down sources of rumors about me. Of course, it's flattering, it's gratifying to know that you're still being talked about in your old home town, even if what they say is completely fantastic. Hahaha.

[*Entertainer returns, sweeps into "Quiereme Mucho."*]

MISS LUCY: Baby, you've changed in some way, but I can't put my finger on it. You all see a change in him, or has he just gotten older? [*She sits down next to* CHANCE.]

CHANCE [*quickly*]: To change is to live, Miss Lucy, to live is to change, and not to change is to die. You know that, don't you? It used to scare me sometimes. I'm not scared of it now. Are you scared of it, Miss Lucy? Does it scare you?

[*Behind* CHANCE'S *back one of the girls has appeared and signaled the boys to join them outside.* SCOTTY *nods and holds up two fingers to mean they'll come in a couple of minutes. The girl goes back out with an angry head-toss.*]

416

SCOTTY: Chance, did you know Boss Finley was holding a Youth for Tom Finley rally upstairs tonight?

CHANCE: I saw the announcements of it all over town.

BUD: He's going to state his position on that emasculation business that's stirred up such a mess in the state. Had you heard about that?

CHANCE: No.

SCOTTY: He must have been up in some earth satellite if he hasn't heard about that.

CHANCE: No, just out of St. Cloud.

SCOTTY: Well, they picked out a nigger at random and castrated the bastard to show they mean business about white women's protection in this state.

BUD: Some people think they went too far about it. There's been a whole lot of Northern agitation all over the country.

SCOTTY: The Boss is going to state his own position about that thing before the Youth for Boss Finley Rally upstairs in the Crystal Ballroom.

CHANCE: Aw. Tonight?

STUFF: Yeah, t'night.

BUD: They say that Heavenly Finley and Tom Junior are going to be standing on the platform with him.

PAGEBOY [*entering*]: Paging Chance Wayne. Paging . . .

[*He is stopped short by* EDNA.]

CHANCE: I *doubt* that story, somehow I *doubt* that story.

SCOTTY: You doubt they cut that nigger?

CHANCE: Oh, no, that I don't doubt. You know what that is, don't you? Sex-envy is what that is, and the revenge for sex-envy which is a widespread disease that I have run into personally too often for me to doubt its existence or any manifestation. [*The group push back their chairs, snubbing him.* CHANCE *takes the message from the* PAGEBOY, *reads it and throws it on the floor.*] Hey, Stuff—What d'ya have to do, stand on your head to get a drink around here?—Later, tell her.—Miss Lucy, can you get that Walgreen's soda jerk to give me a shot of vodka on the rocks? [*She snaps her fingers at* STUFF. *He shrugs and sloshes some vodka onto ice.*]

MISS LUCY: Chance? You're too loud, baby.

CHANCE: Not loud enough, Miss Lucy. No. What I meant that I doubt is that Heavenly Finley, that only I know in St. Cloud, would stoop to stand on a platform next to her father while he explains and excuses on TV this random emasculation of a young Nigra caught on a street after midnight. [CHANCE *is speaking with an almost incoherent excitement, one knee resting on the seat of his chair, swaying the chair back and forth. The* HECKLER *lowers his newspaper from his face; a slow fierce smile spreads over his face as he leans forward with tensed throat muscles to catch* CHANCE'S *burst of oratory.*] No! That's what I do not believe. If I believed it, oh, I'd give you a diving exhibition. I'd dive off municipal pier and swim straight out to Diamond Key and past it, and keep on swimming till sharks and barracuda took me for live bait, brother. [*His chair topples over backward, and he sprawls to the floor. The* HECKLER *springs up to catch him.* MISS LUCY *springs up too, and sweeps between* CHANCE *and the* HECKLER, *pushing the* HECKLER *back with a quick, warning look or gesture. Nobody notices the* HECKLER. CHANCE *scrambles back to his feet, flushed, laughing.* BUD *and* SCOTTY *outlaugh him.* CHANCE *picks up his chair and continues. The laughter stops.*] Because I have come back to St. Cloud to take her out of St. Cloud. Where I'll take her is not to a place anywhere except to her place in my heart. [*He has removed a pink capsule from his pocket, quickly and furtively, and drunk it down with his vodka.*]

BUD: Chance, what did you swallow just now?

CHANCE: Some hundred-proof vodka.

BUD: You washed something down with it that you took out of your pocket.

SCOTTY: It looked like a little pink pill.

CHANCE: Oh, ha ha. Yes, I washed down a goof-ball. You want one? I got a bunch of them. I always carry them with me. When you're not having fun, it makes you have it. When you're having fun, it makes you have more of it. Have one and see.

SCOTTY: Don't that damage the brain?

CHANCE: No, the contrary. It stimulates the brain cells.

SCOTTY: Don't it make your eyes look different, Chance?

MISS LUCY: Maybe that's what I noticed. [*as if wishing to change the subject*] Chance, I wish you'd settle an argument for me.

CHANCE: What argument, Miss Lucy?

MISS LUCY: About who you're traveling with. I heard you checked in here with a famous old movie star.

[*They all stare at him. . . . In a way he now has what he wants. He's the center of attraction: everybody is looking*

419

at him, even though with hostility, suspicion and a cruel sense of sport.]

CHANCE: Miss Lucy I'm traveling with the vice-president and major stockholder of the film studio which just signed me.

MISS LUCY: Wasn't she once in the movies and very well known?

CHANCE: She was and still is and never will cease to be an important, a legendary figure in the picture industry, here and all over the world, and I am now under personal contract to her.

MISS LUCY: What's her name, Chance?

CHANCE: She doesn't want her name known. Like all great figures, world-known, she doesn't want or need and refuses to have the wrong type of attention. Privacy is a luxury to great stars. Don't ask me her name. I respect her too much to speak her name at this table. I'm obligated to her because she has shown faith in me. It took a long hard time to find that sort of faith in my talent that this woman has shown me. And I refuse to betray it at this table. [*His voice rises; he is already "high."*]

MISS LUCY: Baby, why are you sweating and your hands shaking so? You're not sick, are you?

CHANCE: Sick? Who's sick? I'm the least sick one you know.

MISS LUCY: Well, baby, you know you oughtn't to stay in St. Cloud. Y'know that, don't you? I couldn't believe my ears when I heard you were back here. [*to the two boys*] Could you all believe he was back here?

SCOTTY: What did you come back for?

CHANCE: I wish you would give me one reason why I shouldn't come back to visit the grave of my mother and pick out a monument for her, and share my happiness with a girl that I've loved many years. It's her, Heavenly Finley, that I've fought my way up for, and now that I've made it, the glory will be hers, too. And I've just about persuaded the powers to be to let her appear with me in a picture I'm signed for. Because I . . .

BUD: What is the name of this picture?

CHANCE: . . . Name of it? "Youth!"

BUD: Just "Youth?"

CHANCE: Isn't that a great title for a picture introducing young talent? You all look doubtful. If you don't believe me, well, look. Look at this contract. [*Removes it from his pocket.*]

SCOTTY: You carry the contract with you?

CHANCE: I happen to have it in this jacket pocket.

MISS LUCY: Leaving, Scotty? [SCOTTY *has risen from the table.*]

SCOTTY: It's getting too deep at this table.

BUD: The girls are waiting.

CHANCE [*quickly*]: Gee, Bud, that's a clean set of rags you're wearing, but let me give you a tip for your tailor. A guy of medium stature looks better with natural shoulders, the padding cuts down your height, it broadens your figure and gives you a sort of squat look.

BUD: Thanks, Chance.

SCOTTY: You got any helpful hints for my tailor, Chance?

CHANCE: Scotty, there's no tailor on earth that can disguise a sedentary occupation.

MISS LUCY: Chance, baby . . .

CHANCE: You still work down at the bank? You sit on your can all day countin' century notes and once every week they let you slip one in your pockets? That's a fine set-up, Scotty, if you're satisfied with it but it's starting to give you a little pot and a can.

VIOLET [*appears in the door, angry*]: Bud! Scotty! Come on.

SCOTTY: I don't get by on my looks, but I drive my own car. It isn't a Caddy, but it's my own car. And if my own mother died, I'd bury her myself; I wouldn't let a church take up a collection to do it.

VIOLET [*impatiently*]: Scotty, if you all don't come now I'm going home in a taxi.

[*The two boys follow her into the Palm Garden. There they can be seen giving their wives cab money, and indicating they are staying.*]

CHANCE: The squares have left us, Miss Lucy.

MISS LUCY: Yeah.

CHANCE: Well . . . I didn't come back here to fight with old friends of mine. . . . Well, it's quarter past seven.

MISS LUCY: Is it?

[*There are a number of men, now, sitting around in the darker corners of the bar, looking at him. They are not ominous in their attitudes. They are simply waiting for something, for the meeting to start upstairs, for some-*

thing. . . . MISS LUCY *stares at* CHANCE *and the men, then again at* CHANCE, *nearsightedly, her head cocked like a puzzled terrier's.* CHANCE *is discomfited.*]

CHANCE: Yep . . . How is that Hickory Hollow for steaks? Is it still the best place in town for a steak?

STUFF [*answering the phone at the bar*]: Yeah, it's him. He's here. [*Looks at* CHANCE *ever so briefly, hangs up.*]

MISS LUCY: Baby, I'll go to the checkroom and pick up my wrap and call for my car and I'll drive you out to the airport. They've got an air-taxi out there, a whirly-bird taxi, a helicopter, you know, that'll hop you to New Orleans in fifteen minutes.

CHANCE: I'm not leaving St. Cloud. What did I say to make you think I was?

MISS LUCY: I thought you had sense enough to know that you'd better.

CHANCE: Miss Lucy, you've been drinking, it's gone to your sweet little head.

MISS LUCY: Think it over while I'm getting my wrap. You still got a friend in St. Cloud.

CHANCE: I still have a girl in St. Cloud, and I'm not leaving without her.

PAGEBOY [*offstage*]: Paging Chance Wayne, Mr. Chance Wayne, please.

PRINCESS [*entering with* PAGEBOY]: Louder, young man, louder . . . Oh, never mind, here he is!

[*But* CHANCE *has already rushed out onto the gallery. The* PRINCESS *looks as if she had thrown on her clothes to*

423

*escape a building on fire. Her blue-sequined gown is un-
zipped, or partially zipped, her hair is disheveled, her eyes
have a dazed, drugged brightness; she is holding up the
eyeglasses with the broken lens, shakily, hanging onto her
mink stole with the other hand; her movements are un-
steady.*]

MISS LUCY: I know who you are. Alexandra Del Lago.

[*Loud whispering. A pause.*]

PRINCESS [*on the step to the gallery*]: What? Chance!

MISS LUCY: Honey, let me fix that zipper for you. Hold
still just a second. Honey, let me take you upstairs. You
mustn't be seen down here in this condition. . . .

[CHANCE *suddenly rushes in from the gallery: he conducts
the* PRINCESS *outside: she is on the verge of panic. The*
PRINCESS *rushes half down the steps to the palm garden:
leans panting on the stone balustrade under the ornamental
light standard with its five great pearls of light. The interior is dimmed as* CHANCE *comes out behind her.*]

PRINCESS: Chance! Chance! Chance! Chance!

CHANCE [*softly*]: If you'd stayed upstairs that wouldn't
have happened to you.

PRINCESS: I did, I stayed.

CHANCE: I told you to wait.

PRINCESS: I waited.

CHANCE: Didn't I tell you to wait till I got back?

PRINCESS: I did, I waited forever, I waited forever for you.
Then finally I heard those long sad silver trumpets blowing
through the palm garden and then—Chance, the most won-

derful thing has happened to me. Will you listen to me? Will you let me tell you?

MISS LUCY [*to the group at the bar*]: Shhh!

PRINCESS: Chance, when I saw you driving under the window with your head held high, with that terrible stiff-necked pride of the defeated which I know so well; I knew that your come-back had been a failure like mine. And I felt something in my heart for you. That's a miracle, Chance. That's the wonderful thing that happened to me. I felt something for someone besides myself. That means my heart's still alive, at least some part of it is, not all of my heart is dead yet. Part's alive still. . . . Chance, please listen to me. I'm ashamed of this morning. I'll never degrade you again, I'll never degrade myself, you and me, again by—I wasn't always this monster. Once I wasn't this monster. And what I felt in my heart when I saw you returning, defeated, to this palm garden, Chance, gave me hope that I could stop being a monster. Chance, you've got to help me stop being the monster that I was this morning, and you can do it, can help me. I won't be ungrateful for it. I almost died this morning, suffocated in a panic. But even through my panic, I saw your kindness. I saw a true kindness in you that you have almost destroyed, but that's still there, a little. . . .

CHANCE: What kind thing did I do?

PRINCESS: You gave my oxygen to me.

CHANCE: Anyone would do that.

PRINCESS: It could have taken you longer to give it to me.

CHANCE: I'm not that kind of monster.

PRINCESS: You're no kind of monster. You're just—

425

CHANCE: What?

PRINCESS: Lost in the beanstalk country, the ogre's country at the top of the beanstalk, the country of the flesh-hungry, blood-thirsty ogre—

[*Suddenly a voice is heard from off.*]

VOICE: Wayne?

[*The call is distinct but not loud.* CHANCE *hears it, but doesn't turn toward it; he freezes momentarily, like a stag scenting hunters. Among the people gathered inside in the cocktail lounge we see the speaker,* DAN HATCHER. *In appearance, dress and manner he is the apotheosis of the assistant hotel manager, about* CHANCE'S *age, thin, blond-haired, trim blond mustache, suave, boyish, betraying an instinct for murder only by the ruby-glass studs in his matching cuff links and tie clip.*]

HATCHER: Wayne!

[*He steps forward a little and at the same instant* TOM JUNIOR *and* SCOTTY *appear behind him, just in view.* SCOTTY *strikes a match for* TOM JUNIOR'S *cigarette as they wait there.* CHANCE *suddenly gives the* PRINCESS *his complete and tender attention, putting an arm around her and turning her toward the Moorish arch to the bar entrance.*]

CHANCE [*loudly*]: I'll get you a drink, and then I'll take you upstairs. You're not well enough to stay down here.

HATCHER [*crossing quickly to the foot of the stairs*]: Wayne!

[*The call is too loud to ignore:* CHANCE *half turns and calls back.*]

426

CHANCE: Who's that?

HATCHER: Step down here a minute!

CHANCE: Oh, *Hatcher!* I'll be right with you.

PRINCESS: Chance, don't leave me alone.

[At this moment the arrival of BOSS FINLEY *is heralded by the sirens of several squad cars. The forestage is suddenly brightened from off Left, presumably the floodlights of the cars arriving at the entrance to the hotel. This is the signal the men at the bar have been waiting for. Everybody rushes off Left. In the hot light all alone on stage is* CHANCE; *behind him, is the* PRINCESS. *And the* HECKLER *is at the bar. The entertainer plays a feverish tango. Now, off Left,* BOSS FINLEY *can be heard, his public personality very much "on." Amid the flash of flash bulbs we hear off:]*

BOSS *[off]*: Hahaha! Little Bit, smile! Go on, smile for the birdie! Ain't she Heavenly, ain't that the right name for her!

HEAVENLY *[off]*: Papa, I want to go in!

[At this instant she runs in—to face CHANCE. . . . *The* HECKLER *rises. For a long instant,* CHANCE *and* HEAVENLY *stand there: he on the steps leading to the Palm Garden and gallery; she in the cocktail lounge. They simply look at each other . . . the* HECKLER *between them. Then the* BOSS *comes in and seizes her by the arm. . . . And there he is facing the* HECKLER *and* CHANCE *both. . . . For a split second he faces them, half lifts his cane to strike at them, but doesn't strike . . . then pulls* HEAVENLY *back off Left stage . . . where the photographing and interviews proceed during what follows.* CHANCE *has seen that* HEAVENLY *is going to go on the platform with her father. . . . He stands there stunned. . . .]*

PRINCESS: Chance! Chance? [*He turns to her blindly.*] Call the car and let's go. Everything's packed, even the . . . tape recorder with my shameless voice on it. . . .

[*The* HECKLER *has returned to his position at the bar. Now* HATCHER *and* SCOTTY *and a couple of other of the boys have come out. . . . The* PRINCESS *sees them and is silent. . . . She's never been in anything like this before. . . .*]

HATCHER: Wayne, step down here, will you.

CHANCE: What for, what do you want?

HATCHER: Come down here, I'll tell you.

CHANCE: You come up here and tell me.

TOM JUNIOR: Come on, you chicken-gut bastard.

CHANCE: Why, hello, Tom Junior. Why are you hiding down there?

TOM JUNIOR: You're hiding, not me, chicken-gut.

CHANCE: You're in the dark, not me.

HATCHER: Tom Junior wants to talk to you privately down here.

CHANCE: He can talk to me privately up here.

TOM JUNIOR: Hatcher, tell him I'll talk to him in the washroom on the mezzanine floor.

CHANCE: I don't hold conversations with people in washrooms. . . .

[TOM JUNIOR *infuriated, starts to rush forward. Men restrain him.*]

What is all this anyhow? It's fantastic. You all having a little conference there? I used to leave places when I was

428

told to. Not now. That time's over. Now I leave when I'm ready. Hear that, Tom Junior? Give your father that message. This is my town. I was born in St. Cloud, not him. He was just called here. He was just called down from the hills to preach hate. I was born here to make love. Tell him about that difference between him and me, and ask him which he thinks has more right to stay here. . . . [*He gets no answer from the huddled little group which is restraining* TOM JUNIOR *from perpetrating murder right there in the cocktail lounge. After all, that would be a bad incident to precede the* BOSS'S *all-South-wide TV appearance . . . and they all know it.* CHANCE, *at the same time, continues to taunt them.*] Tom, Tom Junior! What do you want me for? To pay me back for the ball game and picture show money I gave you when you were cutting your father's yard grass for a dollar on Saturday? Thank me for the times I gave you my motorcycle and got you a girl to ride the buddy seat with you? Come here! I'll give you the keys to my Caddy. I'll give you the price of any whore in St. Cloud. You still got credit with me because you're Heavenly's brother.

TOM JUNIOR [*almost bursting free*]: Don't say the name of my sister!

CHANCE: I said the name of my girl!

TOM JUNIOR [*breaking away from the group*]: I'm all right, I'm all right. Leave us alone, will you. I don't want Chance to feel that he's outnumbered. [*He herds them out.*] O.K.? Come on down here.

PRINCESS [*trying to restrain* CHANCE]: No, Chance, don't.

TOM JUNIOR: Excuse yourself from the lady and come on down here. Don't be scared to. I just want to talk to you quietly. Just talk. Quiet talk.

429

CHANCE: Tom Junior, I know that since the last time I was here something has happened to Heavenly and I—

TOM JUNIOR: Don't—speak the name of my sister. Just leave her name off your tongue—

CHANCE: Just tell me what happened to her.

TOM JUNIOR: Keep your ruttin' voice down.

CHANCE: I know I've done many wrong things in my life, many more than I can name or number, but I swear I never hurt Heavenly in my life.

TOM JUNIOR: You mean to say my sister was had by somebody else—diseased by somebody else the last time you were in St. Cloud? . . . I know, it's possible, it's barely possible that you didn't know what you done to my little sister the last time you come to St. Cloud. You remember that time when you came home broke? My sister had to pick up your tabs in restaurants and bars, and had to cover bad checks you wrote on banks where you had no accounts. Until you met this rich bitch, Minnie, the Texas one with the yacht, and started spending week ends on her yacht, and coming back Mondays with money from Minnie to go on with my sister. I mean, you'd sleep with Minnie, that slept with any goddam gigolo bastard she could pick up on Bourbon Street or the docks, and then you would go on sleeping again with my sister. And sometime, during that time, you got something besides your gigolo fee from Minnie and passed it onto my sister, my little sister that had hardly even heard of a thing like that, and didn't know what it was till it had gone on too long and—

CHANCE: I left town before I found out I—

[*The lamentation music is heard.*]

TOM JUNIOR: You found out! Did you tell my little sister?

CHANCE: I thought if something was wrong she'd write me or call me—

TOM JUNIOR: How could she write you or call you, there're no addresses, no phone numbers in gutters. I'm itching to kill you—here, on this spot! . . . My little sister, Heavenly, didn't know about the diseases and operations of whores, till she had to be cleaned and cured—I mean spayed like a dawg by Dr. George Scudder's knife. That's right— by the knife! . . . And tonight—if you stay here tonight, if you're here after this rally, you're gonna get the knife, too. You know? The knife? That's all. Now go on back to the lady, I'm going back to my father. [TOM JUNIOR *exits*.]

PRINCESS [*as* CHANCE *returns to her*]: Chance, for God's sake, let's go now . . .

[*The Lament is in the air. It blends with the wind-blown sound of the palms.*]

All day I've kept hearing a sort of lament that drifts through the air of this place. It says, "Lost, lost, never to be found again." Palm gardens by the sea and olive groves on Mediterranean islands all have that lament drifting through them. "Lost, lost". . . . The isle of Cyprus, Monte Carlo, San Remo, Torremolenas, Tangiers. They're all places of exile from whatever we loved. Dark glasses, wide-brimmed hats and whispers, "Is that her?" Shocked whispers. . . . Oh, Chance, believe me, after failure comes flight. Nothing ever comes after failure but flight. Face it. Call the car, have them bring down the luggage and let's go on along the Old Spanish Trail. [*She tries to hold him.*]

CHANCE: Keep your grabbing hands off me.

[Marchers offstage start to sing "Bonnie Blue Flag."]

PRINCESS: There's no one but me to hold you back from destruction in this place.

CHANCE: I don't want to be held.

PRINCESS: Don't leave me. If you do I'll turn into the monster again. I'll be the first lady of the Beanstalk Country.

CHANCE: Go back to the room.

PRINCESS: I'm going nowhere alone. I can't.

CHANCE *[in desperation]*: Wheel chair! *[Marchers enter from the left,* TOM JUNIOR *and* BOSS *with them.]* Wheel chair! Stuff, get the lady a wheel chair! She's having another attack!

*[*STUFF *and a* BELLBOY *catch at her . . . but she pushes* CHANCE *away and stares at him reproachfully. . . . The* BELLBOY *takes her by the arm. She accepts this anonymous arm and exits.* CHANCE *and the* HECKLER *are alone on stage.]*

CHANCE *[as if reassuring, comforting somebody besides himself]*: It's all right, I'm alone now, nobody's hanging onto me.

[He is panting. Loosens his tie and collar. Band in the Crystal Ballroom, muted, strikes up a lively but lyrically distorted variation of some such popular tune as the Liechtensteiner Polka. CHANCE *turns toward the sound. Then, from Left stage, comes a drum majorette, bearing a gold and purple silk banner inscribed, "Youth For Tom Finley," prancing and followed by* BOSS FINLEY, HEAVENLY *and* TOM JUNIOR, *with a tight grip on her arm, as if he were conducting her to a death chamber.]*

432

TOM JUNIOR: Papa? Papa! Will you tell Sister to march?

BOSS FINLEY: Little Bit, you hold your haid up *high* when we march into that ballroom. [*Music up high . . . They march up the steps and onto the gallery in the rear . . . then start across it. The* BOSS *calling out:*] Now march! [*And they disappear up the stairs.*]

VOICE [*offstage*]: Now let us pray. [*There is a prayer mumbled by many voices.*]

MISS LUCY [*who has remained behind*]: You still want to try it?

HECKLER: I'm going to take a shot at it. How's my voice?

MISS LUCY: Better.

HECKLER: I better wait here till he starts talkin', huh?

MISS LUCY: Wait till they turn down the chandeliers in the ballroom. . . . Why don't you switch to a question that won't hurt his daughter?

HECKLER: I don't want to hurt his daughter. But he's going to hold her up as the fair white virgin exposed to black lust in the South, and that's his build-up, his lead into his Voice of God speech.

MISS LUCY: He honestly believes it.

HECKLER: I don't believe it. I believe that the silence of God, the absolute speechlessness of Him is a long, long and awful thing that the whole world is lost because of. I think it's yet to be broken to any man, living or any yet lived on earth,—no exceptions, and least of all Boss Finley.

[STUFF *enters, goes to table, starts to wipe it. The chandelier lights go down.*]

MISS LUCY [*with admiration*]: It takes a hillbilly to cut down a hillbilly. . . . [*to* STUFF] Turn on the television, baby.

VOICE [*offstage*]: I give you the beloved Thomas J. Finley.

[STUFF *makes a gesture as if to turn on the TV, which we play in the fourth wall. A wavering beam of light, flickering, narrow, intense, comes from the balcony rail.* STUFF *moves his head so that he's in it, looking into it. . . .* CHANCE *walks slowly downstage, his head also in the narrow flickering beam of light. As he walks downstage, there suddenly appears on the big TV screen, which is the whole back wall of the stage, the image of* BOSS FINLEY. *His arm is around* HEAVENLY *and he is speaking. . . . When* CHANCE *sees the* BOSS'S *arm around* HEAVENLY, *he makes a noise in his throat like a hard fist hit him low. . . . Now the sound, which always follows the picture by an instant, comes on . . . loud.*]

BOSS [*on TV screen*]: Thank you, my friends, neighbors, kinfolk, fellow Americans. . . . I have told you before, but I will tell you again. I got a mission that I hold sacred to perform in the Southland. . . . When I was fifteen I came down barefooted out of the red clay hills. . . . Why? Because the Voice of God called me to execute this mission.

MISS LUCY [*to* STUFF]: He's too loud.

HECKLER: Listen!

BOSS: And what is this mission? I have told you before but I will tell you again. To shield from pollution a blood that I think is not only sacred to me, but sacred to Him.

[*Upstage we see the* HECKLER *step up the last steps and make a gesture as if he were throwing doors open. . . . He advances into the hall, out of our sight.*]

MISS LUCY: Turn it down, Stuff.

434

STUFF [*motioning to her*]: Shh!

BOSS: Who is the colored man's best friend in the South? That's right . . .

MISS LUCY: Stuff, turn down the volume.

BOSS: It's me, Tom Finley. So recognized by both races.

STUFF [*shouting*]: He's speaking the word. Pour it on!

BOSS: However—I can't and will not accept, tolerate, condone this threat of a blood pollution.

[MISS LUCY *turns down the volume of the TV set.*]

BOSS: As you all know I had no part in a certain operation on a young black gentleman. I call that incident a deplorable thing. That is the one thing about which I am in total agreement with the Northern radical press. It was a deplorable thing. However . . . I understand the emotions that lay behind it. The passion to protect by this violent emotion something that we hold sacred: our purity of our own blood! But I had no part in, and I did not condone the operation performed on the unfortunate colored gentleman caught prowling the midnight streets of our Capitol City....

CHANCE: Christ! What lies. What a liar!

MISS LUCY: Wait! . . . Chance, you can still go. I can still help you, baby.

CHANCE [*putting hands on* MISS LUCY'S *shoulders*]: Thanks, but no thank you, Miss Lucy. Tonight, God help me, somehow, I don't know how, but somehow I'll take her out of St. Cloud. I'll wake her up in my arms, and I'll give her life back to her. Yes, somehow, God help me, somehow!

[STUFF *turns up volume of TV set.*]

435

HECKLER [*as voice on the TV*]: Hey, Boss Finley! [*The TV camera swings to show him at the back of the hall.*] How about your daughter's operation? How about that operation your daughter had done on her at the Thomas J. Finley hospital here in St. Cloud? Did she put on black in mourning for her appendix? . . .

[*We hear a gasp, as if the* HECKLER *had been hit.*]

[*Picture:* HEAVENLY *horrified. Sounds of a disturbance. Then the doors at the top of stairs up Left burst open and the* HECKLER *tumbles down. . . . The picture changes to* BOSS FINLEY. *He is trying to dominate the disturbance in the hall.*]

BOSS: Will you repeat that question. Have that man step forward. I will answer his question. Where is he? Have that man step forward, I will answer his question. . . . Last Friday . . . Last Friday, Good Friday. I said last Friday, Good Friday . . . Quiet, may I have your attention please. . . . Last Friday, Good Friday, I seen a horrible thing on the campus of our great State University, which I built for the State. A hideous straw-stuffed effigy of myself, Tom Finley, was hung and set fire to in the main quadrangle of the college. This outrage was inspired . . . inspired by the Northern radical press. However, that was Good Friday. Today is Easter. I saw that was Good Friday. Today is Easter Sunday and I am in St. Cloud.

[*During this a gruesome, not-lighted, silent struggle has been going on. The* HECKLER *defended himself, but finally has been overwhelmed and rather systematically beaten. . . . The tight intense follow spot beam stayed on* CHANCE. *If he had any impulse to go to the* HECKLER'S *aid, he'd be discouraged by* STUFF *and another man who stand behind*

436

him, watching him. . . . At the height of the beating, there are bursts of great applause. . . . At a point during it, HEAVENLY *is suddenly escorted down the stairs, sobbing, and collapses. . . .*]

CURTAIN

A while later that night: the hotel bedroom. The shutters in the Moorish Corner are thrown open on the Palm Garden: scattered sounds of disturbance are still heard: something burns in the Palm Garden: an effigy, an emblem? Flickering light from it falls on the PRINCESS. *Over the interior scene, the constant serene projection of royal palms, branched among stars.*

PRINCESS [*pacing with the phone*]: Operator! What's happened to my driver?

[CHANCE *enters on the gallery, sees someone approaching on other side—quickly pulls back and stands in shadows on the gallery.*]

You told me you'd get me a driver. . . . Why can't you get me a driver when you said that you would? Somebody in this hotel can surely get me somebody to drive me at any price asked!—out of this infernal . . .

[*She turns suddenly as* DAN HATCHER *knocks at the corridor door. Behind him appear* TOM JUNIOR, BUD *and* SCOTTY, *sweaty, disheveled from the riot in the Palm Garden.*]

Who's that?

SCOTTY: She ain't gonna open, break it in.

PRINCESS [*dropping phone*]: What do you want?

HATCHER: Miss Del Lago . . .

BUD: Don't answer till she opens.

PRINCESS: Who's out there! What do you want?

SCOTTY [*to shaky* HATCHER]: Tell her you want her out of the goddamn room.

HATCHER [*with forced note of authority*]: Shut up. Let me handle this . . . Miss Del Lago, your check-out time was three-thirty P.M., and it's now after midnight. . . . I'm sorry but you can't hold this room any longer.

PRINCESS [*throwing open the door*]: What did you say? Will you repeat what you said! [*Her imperious voice, jewels, furs and commanding presence abash them for a moment.*]

HATCHER: Miss Del Lago . . .

TOM JUNIOR [*recovering quickest*]: This is Mr. Hatcher, assistant manager here. You checked in last night with a character not wanted here, and we been informed he's stayin' in your room with you. We brought Mr. Hatcher up here to remind you that the check-out time is long past and—

PRINCESS [*powerfully*]: My check-out time at any hotel in the world is *when I want to check out.* . . .

TOM JUNIOR: This ain't any hotel in the world.

PRINCESS [*making no room for entrance*]: Also, I don't talk to assistant managers of hotels when I have complaints to make about discourtesies to me, which I do most certainly have to make about my experiences here. I don't even talk to managers of hotels, I talk to owners of them. Directly to hotel owners about discourtesies to me. [*Picks up satin sheets on bed.*] These sheets are mine, they go with me. And I have never suffered such dreadful discourtesies to me at any hotel at any time or place anywhere in the world. Now I have found out the name of this hotel owner. This is a chain hotel under the ownership of a personal friend of mine whose guest I have been in foreign capitals such as . . . [TOM

JUNIOR *has pushed past her into the room.*] What in hell is he doing in my room?

TOM JUNIOR: Where is Chance Wayne?

PRINCESS: Is that what you've come here for? You can go away then. He hasn't been in this room since he left this morning.

TOM JUNIOR: Scotty, check the bathroom. . . . [*He checks a closet, stoops to peer under the bed.* SCOTTY *goes off at right.*] Like I told you before, we know you're Alexandra Del Lago traveling with a degenerate that I'm sure you don't know. That's why you can't stay in St. Cloud, especially after this ruckus that we— [SCOTTY *re-enters from the bathroom and indicates to* TOM JUNIOR *that* CHANCE *is not there.*] —Now if you need any help in getting out of St. Cloud, I'll be—

PRINCESS [*cutting in*]: Yes. I want a driver. Someone to drive my car. I want to leave here. I'm desperate to leave here. I'm not able to drive. I have to be driven away!

TOM JUNIOR: Scotty, you and Hatcher wait outside while I explain something to her. . . . [*They go and wait outside the door, on the left end of the gallery.*] I'm gonna git you a driver, Miss Del Lago. I'll git you a state trooper, half a dozen state troopers if I can't get you no driver. O.K.? Some time come back to our town n' see us, hear? We'll lay out a red carpet for you. O.K.? G'night, Miss Del Lago.

[*They disappear down the hall, which is then dimmed out.* CHANCE *now turns from where he's been waiting at the other end of the corridor and slowly, cautiously, approaches the entrance to the room. Wind sweeps the Palm Garden; it seems to dissolve the walks; the rest of the play is acted against the night sky. The shuttered doors on the veranda open and* CHANCE *enters the room. He has gone a good deal further across the border of reason since we last saw him. The* PRINCESS *isn't aware of his entrance until he slams the shuttered doors. She turns, startled, to face him.*]

PRINCESS: Chance!

CHANCE: You had some company here.

PRINCESS: Some men were here looking for you. They told me I wasn't welcome in this hotel and this town because I had come here with "a criminal degenerate." I asked them to get me a driver so I can go.

CHANCE: I'm your driver. I'm still your driver, Princess.

PRINCESS: You couldn't drive through the palm garden.

CHANCE: I'll be all right in a minute.

PRINCESS: It takes more than a minute, Chance, will you listen to me? Can you listen to me? I listened to you this morning, with understanding and pity, I did, I listened with pity to your story this morning. I felt something in my heart for you which I thought I couldn't feel. I remembered young men who were what you are or what you're hoping to be. I saw them all clearly, all clearly, eyes, voices, smiles, bodies clearly. But their names wouldn't come back to me. I couldn't get their names back without digging into old programs of plays that I starred in at twenty in which they said, "Madam, the Count's waiting for you," or—Chance? They almost made it. Oh, oh, Franz! Yes, Franz . . . what? Albertzart. Franz Albertzart, oh God, God, Franz Albertzart . . . I had to fire him. He held me too tight in the waltz scene, his anxious fingers left bruises once so violent, they, they dislocated a disc in my spine, and—

CHANCE: I'm waiting for you to shut up.

441

PRINCESS: I saw him in Monte Carlo not too long ago. He was with a woman of seventy, and his eyes looked older than hers. She held him, she led him by an invisible chain through Grand Hotel . . . lobbies and casinos and bars like a blind, dying lap dog; he wasn't much older than you are now. Not long after that he drove his Alfa-Romeo or Ferrari off the Grand Corniche—accidentally?—Broke his skull like an eggshell. I wonder what they found in it? Old, despaired-of ambitions, little treacheries, possibly even little attempts at blackmail that didn't quite come off, and whatever traces are left of really great charm and sweetness. Chance, Franz Albertzart is Chance Wayne. Will you please try to face it so we can go on together?

CHANCE [*pulls away from her*]: Are you through? Have you finished?

PRINCESS: You didn't listen, did you?

CHANCE [*picking up the phone*]: I didn't have to. I told you that story this morning—I'm not going to drive off nothing and crack my head like an eggshell.

PRINCESS: No, because you can't drive.

CHANCE: Operator? Long distance.

PRINCESS: You would drive into a palm tree. Franz Albertzart . . .

CHANCE: Where's your address book, your book of telephone numbers?

PRINCESS: I don't know what you think that you are up to, but it's no good. The only hope for you now is to let me lead you by that invisible loving steel chain through Carltons and Ritzes and Grand Hotels and—

CHANCE: Don't you know, I'd die first? I would rather die first . . . [*into phone*] Operator? This is an urgent person-to-person call from Miss Alexandra Del Lago to Miss Sally Powers in Beverly Hills, California. . . .

PRINCESS: Oh, no! . . . Chance!

CHANCE: Miss Sally Powers, the Hollywood columnist, yes, Sally Powers. Yes, well get information. I'll wait, I'll wait. . . .

PRINCESS: Her number is Coldwater five-nine thousand. . . . [*Her hand goes to her mouth—but too late.*]

CHANCE: In Beverly Hills, California, Coldwater five-nine thousand.

[*The* PRINCESS *moves out onto forestage; surrounding areas dim till nothing is clear behind her but the palm garden.*]

PRINCESS: Why did I give him the number? Well, why not, after all, I'd have to know sooner or later . . . I started to call several times, picked up the phone, put it down again. Well, let him do it for me. Something's happened. I'm breathing freely and deeply as if the panic was over. Maybe it's over. He's doing the dreadful thing for me, asking the answer for me. He doesn't exist for me now except as somebody making this awful call for me, asking the answer for me. The light's on me. He's almost invisible now. What does that mean? Does it mean that I still wasn't ready to be washed up, counted out?

CHANCE: All right, call Chasen's. Try to reach her at Chasen's.

PRINCESS: Well, one thing's sure. It's only this call I care for. I seem to be standing in light with everything else

443

dimmed out. He's in the dimmed out background as if he'd never left the obscurity he was born in. I've taken the light again as a crown on my head to which I am suited by something in the cells of my blood and body from the time of my birth. It's mine, I was born to own it, as he was born to make this phone call for me to Sally Powers, dear faithful custodian of my outlived legend. [*Phone rings in distance.*] The legend that I've out-lived. . . . Monsters don't die early; they hang on long. Awfully long. Their vanity's infinite, almost as infinite as their disgust with themselves. . . . [*Phone rings louder: it brings the stage light back up on the hotel bedroom. She turns to* CHANCE *and the play returns to a more realistic level.*] The phone's still ringing.

CHANCE: They gave me another number. . . .

PRINCESS: If she isn't there, give my name and ask them where I can reach her.

CHANCE: Princess?

PRINCESS: What?

CHANCE: I have a personal reason for making this phone call.

PRINCESS: I'm quite certain of that.

CHANCE [*into phone*]: I'm calling for Alexandra Del Lago. She wants to speak to Miss Sally Powers— Oh, is there any number where the Princess could reach her?

PRINCESS: It will be a good sign if they give you a number.

CHANCE: Oh?—Good, I'll call that number . . . Operator? Try another number for Miss Sally Powers. It's Canyon seven-five thousand . . . Say it's urgent, it's Princess Kosmonopolis . . .

PRINCESS: Alexandra Del Lago.

CHANCE: Alexandra Del Lago is calling Miss Powers.

PRINCESS [*to herself*]: Oxygen, please, a little. . . .

CHANCE: Is that you, Miss Powers? This is Chance Wayne talking . . . I'm calling for the Princess Kosmonopolis, she wants to speak to you. She'll come to the phone in a minute. . . .

PRINCESS: I can't. . . . Say I've . . .

CHANCE [*stretching phone cord*]: This is as far as I can stretch the cord, Princess, you've got to meet it halfway.

[PRINCESS *hesitates; then advances to the extended phone.*]

PRINCESS [*in a low, strident whisper*]: Sally? Sally? Is it really you, Sally? Yes, it's me, Alexandra. It's what's left of me, Sally. Oh, yes, I was there, but I only stayed a few minutes. Soon as they started laughing in the wrong places, I fled up the aisle and into the street screaming Taxi—and never stopped running till now. No, I've talked to nobody, heard nothing, read nothing . . . just wanted—dark . . . What? You're just being kind.

CHANCE [*as if to himself*]: Tell her that you've discovered a pair of new stars. Two of them.

PRINCESS: One moment, Sally, I'm—breathless!

CHANCE [*gripping her arm*]: And lay it on thick. Tell her to break it tomorrow in her column, in all of her columns, and in her radio talks . . . that you've discovered a pair of young people who are the stars of tomorrow!

PRINCESS [*to* CHANCE]: Go into the bathroom. Stick your head under cold water. . . . Sally . . . Do you really think

445

so? You're not just being nice, Sally, because of old times— Grown, did you say? My talent? In what way, Sally? More depth? More what, did you say? More power!—well, Sally, God bless you, dear Sally.

CHANCE: Cut the chatter. Talk about me and *HEAVENLY!*

PRINCESS: No, of course I didn't read the reviews. I told you I flew, I flew. I flew as fast and fast as I could. Oh. Oh? Oh . . . How very sweet of you, Sally. I don't even care if you're not altogether sincere in that statement, Sally. I think you know what the past fifteen years have been like, because I do have the—"out-crying heart of an—artist." Excuse me, Sally, I'm crying, and I don't have any Kleenex. Excuse me, Sally, I'm crying. . . .

CHANCE [*hissing behind her*]: Hey. Talk about me! [*She kicks* CHANCE'S *leg.*]

PRINCESS: What's that, Sally? Do you really believe so? Who? For what part? Oh, my God! . . . Oxygen, oxygen, quick!

CHANCE [*seizing her by the hair and hissing*]: Me! Me!— You bitch!

PRINCESS: Sally? I'm too overwhelmed. Can I call you back later? Sally, I'll call back later. . . . [*She drops phone in a daze of rapture.*] My picture has broken box-office records. In New York and L. A.!

CHANCE: Call her back, get her on the phone.

PRINCESS: Broken box-office records. The greatest comeback in the history of the industry, that's what she calls it. . . .

CHANCE: You didn't mention me to her.

446

PRINCESS [*to herself*]: I can't appear, not yet. I'll need a week in a clinic, then a week or ten days at the Morning Star Ranch at Vegas. I'd better get Ackermann down there for a series of shots before I go on to the Coast. . . .

CHANCE [*at phone*]: Come back here, call her again.

PRINCESS: I'll leave the car in New Orleans and go on by plane to, to, to—Tucson. I'd better get Strauss working on publicity for me. I'd better be sure my tracks are covered up well these last few weeks in—hell!—

CHANCE: Here. Here, get her back on this phone.

PRINCESS: Do what?

CHANCE: Talk about me and talk about Heavenly to her.

PRINCESS: Talk about a beach-boy I picked up for pleasure, distraction from panic? Now? When the nightmare is over? Involve my name, which is Alexandra Del Lago with the record of a— You've just been using me. Using me. When I needed you downstairs you shouted, "Get her a wheel chair!" Well, I didn't need a wheel chair, I came up alone, as always. I climbed back alone up the beanstalk to the ogre's country where I live, now, alone. Chance, you've gone past something you couldn't afford to go past; your time, your youth, you've passed it. It's all you had, and you've had it.

CHANCE: Who in hell's talking! Look. [*He turns her forcibly to the mirror.*] Look in that mirror. What do you see in that mirror?

PRINCESS: I see—Alexandra Del Lago, artist and star! Now it's your turn, you look and what do you see?

CHANCE: I see—Chance Wayne. . . .

447

PRINCESS: The face of a Franz Albertzart, a face that tomorrow's sun will touch without mercy. Of course, you were crowned with laurel in the beginning, your gold hair was wreathed with laurel, but the gold is thinning and the laurel has withered. Face it—pitiful monster. [*She touches the crown of his head.*] . . . Of course, I know I'm one too. But one with a difference. Do you know what that difference is? No, you don't know. I'll tell you. We are two monsters, but with this difference between us. Out of the passion and torment of my existence I have created a thing that I can unveil, a sculpture, almost heroic, that I can unveil, which is true. But you? You've come back to the town you were born in, to a girl that won't see you because you put such rot in her body she had to be gutted and hung on a butcher's hook, like a chicken dressed for Sunday. . . . [*He wheels about to strike at her but his raised fist changes its course and strikes down at his own belly and he bends double with a sick cry. Palm Garden wind: whisper of The Lament.*] Yes, and her brother who was one of my callers, threatens the same thing for you: castration, if you stay here.

CHANCE: That can't be done to me twice. You did that to me this morning, here on this bed, where I had the honor, where I had the great honor . . .

[*Windy sound rises: They move away from each other, he to the bed, she close to her portable dressing table.*]

PRINCESS: Age does the same thing to a woman. . . . [*Scrapes pearls and pillboxes off table top into handbag.*] Well . . .

[*All at once her power is exhausted, her fury gone. Something uncertain appears in her face and voice betraying the fact which she probably suddenly knows, that her*

448

*future course is not a progression of triumphs. She still
maintains a grand air as she snatches up her platinum
mink stole and tosses it about her: it slides immediately
off her shoulders; she doesn't seem to notice. He picks the
stole up for her, puts it about her shoulders. She grunts
disdainfully, her back to him; then resolution falters; she
turns to face him with great, dark eyes that are fearful,
lonely, and tender.]*

PRINCESS: I am going, now, on my way. [He nods slightly,
loosening the Windsor-knot of his knitted black silk tie. Her
eyes stay on him.] Well, are you leaving or staying?

CHANCE: Staying.

PRINCESS: You can't stay here. I'll take you to the next
town.

CHANCE: Thanks but no thank you, Princess.

PRINCESS [*seizing his arm*]: Come on, you've got to leave
with me. My name is connected with you, we checked in
here together. Whatever happens to you, my name will be
dragged in with it.

CHANCE: Whatever happens to me's already happened.

PRINCESS: What are you trying to prove?

CHANCE: Something's got to mean something, don't it,
Princess? I mean like your life means nothing, except that
you never could make it, always almost, never quite? Well,
something's still got to mean something.

PRINCESS: I'll send a boy up for my luggage. You'd better
come down with my luggage.

CHANCE: I'm not part of your luggage.

PRINCESS: What else can you be?

CHANCE: Nothing . . . but not part of your luggage.

[NOTE: *in this area it is very important that* CHANCE'S *attitude should be self-recognition but* not *self-pity—a sort of deathbed dignity and honesty apparent in it. In both* CHANCE *and the* PRINCESS, *we should return to the huddling-together of the lost, but not with sentiment, which is false, but with whatever is truthful in the moments when people share doom, face firing squads together. Because the* PRINCESS *is really equally doomed. She can't turn back the clock any more than can* CHANCE, *and the clock is equally relentless to them both. For the* PRINCESS: *a little, very temporary, return to, recapture of, the spurious glory. The report from* SALLY POWERS *may be and probably is a factually accurate report: but to indicate she is going on to further triumph would be to falsify her future. She makes this instinctive admission to herself when she sits down by* CHANCE *on the bed, facing the audience. Both are faced with castration, and in her heart she knows it. They sit side by side on the bed like two passengers on a train sharing a bench.*]

PRINCESS: Chance, we've got to go on.

CHANCE: Go on to where? I couldn't go past my youth, but I've gone past it.

[*The Lament fades in, continues through the scene to the last curtain.*]

PRINCESS: You're still young, Chance.

CHANCE: Princess, the age of some people can only be calculated by the level of—level of—rot in them. And by that measure I'm ancient.

PRINCESS: What am I?—I know, I'm dead, as old Egypt
. . . Isn't it funny? We're still sitting here together, side by
side in this room, like we were occupying the same bench on
a train—going on together . . . Look. That little donkey's
marching around and around to draw water out of a well. . . .
[*She points off at something as if outside a train window.*]
Look, a shepherd boy's leading a flock.—What an old country, timeless.—Look—

[*The sound of a clock ticking is heard, louder and louder.*]

CHANCE: No, listen. I didn't know there was a clock in
this room.

PRINCESS: I guess there's a clock in every room people live
in. . . .

CHANCE: It goes tick-tick, it's quieter than your heart-beat,
but it's slow dynamite, a gradual explosion, blasting the
world we lived in to burnt-out pieces. . . . Time—who could
beat it, who could defeat it ever? Maybe some saints and
heroes, but not Chance Wayne. I lived on something, that—
time?

PRINCESS: Yes, time.

CHANCE: . . . Gnaws away, like a rat gnaws off its own
foot caught in a trap, and then, with its foot gnawed off and
the rat set free, couldn't run, couldn't go, bled and died. . . .

[*The clock ticking fades away.*]

TOM JUNIOR [*offstage left*]: Miss Del Lago . . .

PRINCESS: I think they're calling our—station. . . .

TOM JUNIOR [*still offstage*]: Miss Del Lago, I have got a
driver for you.

451

[*A trooper enters and waits on gallery.*]

[*With a sort of tired grace, she rises from the bed, one hand lingering on her seat-companion's shoulder as she moves a little unsteadily to the door. When she opens it, she is confronted by* TOM JUNIOR.]

PRINCESS: Come on, Chance, we're going to change trains at this station. . . . So, come on, we've got to go on. . . . Chance, please. . . .

[CHANCE *shakes his head and the* PRINCESS *gives up. She weaves out of sight with the trooper down the corridor.*]

[TOM JUNIOR *enters from steps, pauses and then gives a low whistle to* SCOTTY, BUD, *and third man who enter and stand waiting.* TOM JUNIOR *comes down bedroom steps and stands on bottom step.*]

CHANCE [*rising and advancing to the forestage*]: I don't ask for your pity, but just for your understanding—not even that—no. Just for your recognition of me in you, and the enemy, time, in us all.

[*The curtain closes.*]

THE END